Special thanks to
Therese Kelly, project coordinator,
and Caroline Green, Clare Jacobson,
Mark Lamster, and Annie Nitschke
of Princeton Architectural Press.
— Kevin Lippert, publisher

PUBLISHED BY PRINCETON ARCHITECTURAL PRESS 37 EAST 7th Street NY NY 10003 212-995-9620
©1996 PRINCETON UNIVERSITY SCHOOL OF ARCHITECTURE, ALL RIGHTS RESERVED
Book Design by BUREAU (NEW YORK), copy edited by CLAUDIA SWAN, printed and bound in the United States
Cover Design by BUREAU with MICHAEL PERELMAN; photographer LORING McALPIN; model JEFFREY CAYLE
Flyleaves: front JOHN LINDELL back ROBERT GOBER

ISBN: 1-56898-076-0
First Edition
99 98 97 96 4 3 2 1

Library of Congress Cataloging-in-Publication Data
Stud: architectures of masculinity / [Joel Sanders, editor].
p. cm. --
ISBN 1-56898-076-0 (paper : alk. paper)
1. Architecture--Human Factors, 2. Masculinity (Psychology)
I. Sanders, Joel, 1958-
NA25542.4.S78 1996
720'. 108--dc20
96-14859
CIP

For a free catalog of other books
published by Princeton Architectural Press,
call toll free (800) 722-6657

ARCHITECTURES *of* MASCULINITY

EDITED
by
JOEL
SANDERS

Home

Homework

Bathroom

Gym

Outings

ACKNOWLEDGMENTS

Producing STUD was made possible by the help and support of numerous friends and colleagues—architects, artists, and critics who represent the different disciplines this book address-es and attempts to bridge. The initial idea for a book about masculinity and architecture arose during meetings held in 1994 by Princeton's junior architectural faculty (Beatriz Colomina, Elizabeth Diller, Thomas Leeser, Alessandra Ponte, and Mark Wigley) to discuss a departmental book series. Subsequently, numerous people helped me formulate and clarify the book's concept. In particular, I am grateful to Russell Ferguson, Sarah Bayliss, Loring McAlpin, Tom Keenan, Peggy Deamer, Mark Robbins, Terence Riley, and Marc Tsurumaki for their valuable insights and advice.

I am also grateful for the institutional support of the students, faculty, and staff of Princeton University. My studio and seminar students posed some of the provocative questions about men and architecture explored in this book. The experience of working closely with Rocco Giannetti and Calvert Wright, two graduate students who pursued queer thesis topics, encouraged me to think seriously about gay men's relationships to space. My research assistant Henry Urbach offered valuable editorial insights while attending to the often frustrating task of tracking down authors and images. I thank Claudia Swan for carefully and intelligently copy editing manuscripts and Jamie Oliveri for his help in writing captions.

Because STUD depends as much on visual images as on texts, I especially appreciate the contributions of those who have helped make this book stimulating to the eye as well as to the mind. The Andrea Rosen, Pat Hearn, Barbara Gladstone, Morris Healy and Paula Cooper galleries all generously provided images of works by the artists they represent. Richard C. Wandel, the archivist at the National Museum and Archive of Lesbian and Gay History, helped me to locate and permitted me to reproduce rare historical images of queer public spaces in New York. The assistance of Marcia Terrones at *Playboy* Magazine was vital to including images of vintage Bachelor Pads originally published in 1956. Command architect Duane Boyle and Chief of Special Collections Duane Reed provided photographs of the U.S. Airforce Academy at Colorado Springs. I have been especially fortunate to work with Marlene McCarty, Donald Moffett, and Claudia Brandenburg of Bureau, who saw the commission to design STUD as an opportunity to rethink the relationship between masculinity and graphic design.

Two people, both contributors to STUD, deserve extra special thanks. From beginning to end, John Lindell was instrumental in helping me to conceptualize this volume and to identify relevant visual projects. His keen intelligence and sophisticated eye was matched only by his patience—especially when I informed him on the airplane *en route* to the U.S. Airforce Academy at Colorado Springs that my driver's license had lapsed. An accomplished theorist who I suspect harbors secret desires to be an architect, Diana Fuss helped me to shape the theoretical underpinnings of this volume while also giving generously of her time, tirelessly reading and editing first versions of manuscripts. Most important, a valued friend and colleague, she gave me the intellectual and emotional encouragement that sustained me throughout this project. —*J.S.*

This book is

dedicated

to the

memory of

John Pozzi.

The love,

strength, and

compassion

he showed

during his life

exemplify

for me

the best

aspects of

masculinity.

— *J.S.*

Introduction
JOEL
SANDERS

In the opening passage of
Ayn Rand's novel, *The Fountainhead*, its architect hero Howard Roark stands
naked at the edge of a granite cliff surveying a panoramic view of a wooded valley below. *The Fountainhead* achieves its author's stated goal—"the
presentation of an ideal man"[1]—by portraying its male protagonist as an
architect, capitalizing on the popular cultural perception that authors of
buildings, like the structures they design, embody the very essence of manhood. Conflating the male architect's body with the landscape that elevates
him, Rand's hard-edged prose lodges both masculinity and architecture in a
transcendental natural world: "His face was like a law of nature—a thing one
could not question, alter or implore" (15). Roark's robust physique, composed of "long, straight lines and angles, each curve broken into planes,"
seen silhouetted against the sky, reads like a description of Frank Lloyd
Wright's famous house "Fallingwater," also a composition of hard geometric
forms set against a rugged forest setting. An unfettered and independent
creator singlemindedly concerned with "the conquest of nature," the professional architect mines his intrinsic "manly" faculties; possessing both
physical and mental prowess, Roark shapes and masters the natural forces
that sustain him (679). "These rocks,
he thought, are here for me: waiting
for the drill, the dynamite and my
voice; waiting to be split, ripped,
pounded, reborn; waiting for the
shape my hands will give them"(16).
Rand's portrait of the architect as ele-
mental man vividly dramatizes how
culture relies upon architecture as a
foundation for the construction of
masculinity, a theme this volume seeks both to explore and to challenge.

1 Quoted from Ayn Rand's 1969 preface to *The Fountainhead* (New York: Penguin Books, 1971), p. vii. Originally published in 1952. Hereafter, all page numbers cited in the text.

2 For a discussion of how Renaissance architectural theo-rists (Alberti, Filarete, Di Giorgio) privilege the male body while excluding the female figure in their discussions of the human form as architectural prototype, see Diana Agrest, "Architecture from Without: Body, Logic, and Sex," in her *Architecture from Without: Theoretical Framings for a Critical Practice* (Cambridge: MIT Press, 1991), pp 173-195.

Architecture and masculinity, two appar-
ently unrelated discursive practices, are seen to operate reciprocally in this
remarkable opening scene from *The Fountainhead*. Rand exploits building
metaphors to articulate the theme of "manworship," while the portrait of Howard
Roark as creator sanctifies architectural doctrine. In the novel's central dramatic scene, the courtroom scene in which Roark is tried for dynamiting one of his
own buildings "disfigured" during construction, Rand's uncompromising male
idealist defends the principles of modern architecture with arguments comparing
built structures to masculine virtue, claiming buildings have integrity, just like
men. Roark's narcissistic proclamation echoes the words of Western architects
and theorists from Vitruvius to Le Corbusier who, in their attempt to locate and
to fix architecture's underlying principles in a vision of transhistorical nature,
recruit masculinity to justify practice. Rand's architecture of masculinity offers
one of the most dramatic, although certainly not the earliest, renditions of the
notion that buildings derive from the human form itself—specifically from the
unity, scale, and proportions of the male body.[2] *The Fountainhead*'s portrayal of
the architect as virile stud ultimately reveals architecture and masculinity to be

mutually reinforcing ideologies, each invoking the other to naturalize and to uphold its particular claims and intentions.[3]

In one of modern intellectual history's stranger alliances, contemporary cultural theorists have recently borrowed from architectural discourse the language of "construction" to *denaturalize* sexual identity. Arguing that identity is "constructed" rather than natural, "mapped" rather than given, these theorists draw on the popular perception of architecture as manmade precisely in order to de-essentialize gender. But in the process of erecting an argument about gender, cultural theory draws on a view of architecture—architecture as human artifice—that the discipline itself has, throughout its long history, sought either implicitly to camouflage or emphatically to deny.

Taking as its touchstone the complex interdependency of gender and architecture as cultural productions, *Stud* brings together, in one volume, two historically allied discourses rarely afforded the opportunity to address one another directly. *Stud* invites both theorists and architects, writers and artists, to expand the notion of cultural construction by investigating the active role that architectural constructions play in the making of gender. Through its mobilization of architectural metaphors to describe the "built" male body, Ayn Rand's *The Fountainhead* illustrates one crucial way that culture enlists architecture to construct gender. The contributions to this volume broach the same question from the opposite direction, investigating how architecture, as a concrete material practice, works to institute sexual identities by delimiting and demarcating the interaction of human subjects in *actual* space. While previous studies have tended to concentrate on architecture's role in the formation of feminine identities,[4] *Stud* interrogates how, through the precise organization and distribution of materials, objects, and bodies in space, physical structures assist in the fabrication of masculine identities at specific sites and at precise moments in history.

Although engineering masculinity is a herculean task, architecture never lets you see it sweat. Unless a building stands out as a monument with inscriptions literally incised in stone on its surface, we tend to think of architecture as unencumbered by politics and ideology. Normally, we regard edifices as empty or neutral containers, facilitating the free interaction of sovereign subjects in space. But as the essays in this volume will suggest, the ostensibly innocent conventions of architecture work in covert fashion to transmit social values in unexpected places—the everyday and often banal places where our daily lives unfold. For this reason, *Stud* investigates a series of

[3] Pursuing his ongoing interest in the reciprocity of architecture and philosophy, Mark Wigley traces "the relationships between the role of gender in the discourse of space and the role of space in the discourse of gender" in his essay "Untitled: The Housing of Gender," in *Sexuality and Space*, ed. Beatriz Colomina (New York: Princeton Architectural Press, 1992), pp. 327-389, esp. p. 329.

[4] A partial list of significant works that examine architecture's impact on women from a feminist perspective includes Dolores Hayden, *The Grand Domestic Revolution: A History of Feminist Designs for American Homes, Neighborhoods, and Cities* (Cambridge: MIT Press, 1981); Gwendolyn Wright, *Moralism and the Modern Home: Domestic Architecture and Cultural Conflict in Chicago, 1873-1913* (Chicago: University of Chicago Press, 1980); Susana Torre, *Women in Architecture, an Historic and Contemporary Perspective* (New York: Whitney Library of Design, 1977); Leslie Kanes Weisman, *Discrimination By Design, a Feminist Critique of the Man-made Environment* (Chicago: University of Illinois Press, 1994); and Ellen Lupton and J. Abbott Miller, *The Bathroom, The Kitchen, and the Aesthetics of Waste: A Process of Elimination* (New York: Princeton Architectural Press, 1992).

commonplace but ideologically overdetermined spaces—houses, bathrooms, gyms, offices, streets, parks—environments that we habitually take for granted but that quietly and decisively participate in the manufacture of male subjectivity.

But how, exactly, does architecture work to construct gender identity through the distribution of bodies and objects in space? Recent critical theory offers us the suggestive notion of sexual identity as performance—as the compulsory repetition of culturally prescribed codes and utterances.[5] This book proceeds from the premise that architecture behaves as one of the subjectivating norms that constitute gender performativity. Programmatic functions in architecture are commonly associated with specific, although culturally contingent, spatial configurations, often referred to as building "types." For example, dwelling locates itself within the house, research within the library, working within the office—all formulaic structures made up of recurring formal elements offering relatively few variations. Working within the spatial limits dictated by custom, and by a building industry driven by economic forces that encourage standardization, the architect or builder modifies a type in response to the particular pressures of a unique site or program.

Those moments in a design that do allow for the possibility of inflection and variation represent potential sites in architecture where norms and their attending ideologies can be reviewed, resisted, and revised. Although purportedly outside the domain of politics, the way buildings distribute our activities within standard spatial configurations has a profound ideological impact on social interaction—regulating, constraining, and (on occasion) liberating the human subject. Architecture, through the establishment and alteration of reiterated types and conventions, creates the space—the stage—where human subjectivity is enacted and performed.

[5] Drawing on the spatial metaphor of the theater, critics like Eve Kosofsky Sedgwick, Marjorie Garber, and Judith Butler all theorize gender as performance, a notion useful for thinking about architecture as the space that supports and frames identity. Cautioning against thinking of gender as a choice made by a sovereign subject who freely fashions a self by performing a role, Judith Butler writes that "performativity is a matter of reiterating or repeating the norms by which one is constituted: it is not a radical fabrication of a gendered self. It is a compulsory repetition of prior and subjectivating norms, ones which cannot be thrown off at will, but which work, animate, and constrain the gendered subject, and which are also the resources from which resistance, subversion, displacement are to be forged." See Butler's "Critically Queer," *GLQ* 1:1 (1993), p. 22.

What, then, are the formal codes and conventions that architecture deploys to erect masculinity, and where do they occur? Considering the problem at different scales—from the design of furniture and wall coverings to the layout of public parks—*Stud*'s contributors collectively identify four architectural strategies that enhance male performance: dressing wall surfaces, demarcating boundaries, distributing objects, and organizing gazes.

DRESSING WALL SURFACES

The suggestion that architecture stages masculine performance through the treatment of interior and exterior wall surfaces contradicts one of the central tenets of architectural doctrine. By identifying manliness as "genuine" and womanliness as "artifice," architects since Vitruvius have associated the ornamented surface with femininity, not masculinity. Discussing the origins of Doric and Ionic columns, Vitruvius writes: "in the invention of the two types of columns, they borrowed manly beauty, naked and unadorned for the one, and for the other the delicacy, adornment, and proportions characteristic of women."[6] Because of its long-standing associations with the feminine, ornament has come under sustained attack in this century from architectural modernists invested in upholding the notion of a building's pared-down inner truth.[7] Searching for an authentic, rational, and timeless architecture, Le Corbusier and others have found their archetypal model in the image of the male nude ("naked and unadorned," like Ayn Rand's architect hero) rather than in the picture of the female masquerader, embellished with clothes and makeup. But while the image of the male nude was seen to embody masculine ideals of rationality and strength, the functional imperative that requires buildings to wear a protective outer skin implicitly challenged modernism's devaluation of ornamentation. As Mark Wigley notes, Le Corbusier's "Law of Ripolin"—the thin coat of white wash painted on the pristine walls of modern buildings and associated with such "masculine" traits as logic, hygiene, and truth—functions, despite its apparent invisibility, as an applied layer, a form of clothing added to the surface of buildings.[8] Recognizing the practical indispensability of this second skin for dressing the building surface, Adolf Loos recommends that designers emulate the timeless simplicity of the Englishman's austere, standardized wardrobe. Both examples suggest that masculinity, no less than femininity, is constructed through the use of supplemental surfaces.

6 Vitruvius, *The Ten Books on Architecture*, trans. Morris Hicky Morgan (New York: Dover, 1960), pp. 103-4.

7 See Mary McCleod, "Undressing Architecture: Fashion, Gender, and Modernity," and Mark Wigley, "White Out: Fashioning the Modern," both in *Architecture: In Fashion* (New York: Princeton Architectural Press, 1994), pp. 38-123 and pp. 148-268, respectively.

8 Wigley, "White Out."

Even the materials employed to construct buildings are implicated in a process of architectural engendering. Coded as ruggedly masculine, wood paneling is conventionally used for sheathing recreational and professional interiors (men's clubs, bars, law courts, corporate board rooms). Because of their hard, cold, crystalline surfaces, building materials such as glass, steel, and stone are similarly attributed masculine properties. Often these materials evoke the "manly" environments that produced them: wood conjures up a vision of a preindustrialized, predomesticated masculine wilderness, while steel invokes a picture of virile laborers shaping molten metals in foundries. Le Corbusier derived his lexicon of materials from building types mainly inhabited by men (factories and monasteries) as well as from the traditionally male domain of transportation (cars, ships, airplanes). But while these materials directly recall male environments, they also more subtly convey the social values associated with them. A building's architectural integrity derives from the masculinization of its materials, made to bear the weight of all the cultural values masculinity purportedly connotes, above all austerity, authenticity, and permanence. Ironically, architects value the supplemental skins used to register masculinity precisely because of their innate, hence "manly," characteristics. Electing to forego the use of applied ornament, architects like Mies van der Rohe (at the Barcelona Pavilion) and Adolf Loos (at the American Bar, Vienna) favor wood and marble, materials prized for their inherent natural patterns of wood graining and marble veins.

*p.*54Two projects in this volume invite us to see through the masculine garb of modern architecture. *Playboy's* *Penthouse Apartment for a Bachelor* by an unidentified designer (1956) and *Air Force Academy at Colorado Springs* by **Skidmore, Owings & Merrill** (1958) each reveal, in their respective attempts to *p.*68showcase masculine austerity, an almost obsessive concern with style.[9] Eschewing the upholstered furniture and applied fabrics and wallpapers that conventionally define a feminine interior, the designs for both the *Playboy* bachelor apartment and the Air Force Academy show single-sex environments tacitly organized for the performance and display of masculine power. *Playboy's* "handsome haven" places stylish pieces of designer furniture made of steel, leather, and wood— a Florence Knoll desk, an Eames lounge chair, a Noguchi coffee table—within spaces defined by wood and glass partitions.[*] The Air Force Academy interiors and furnishings, created by Walter Dorwin Teague Associates use similar materials (dark wood paneling and aluminum framed furniture) to create orderly and highly regimented living quarters where cadets train to become men. The exhibitionist overtones of even the most spartan masculine spaces is particularly striking in the Air Force Academy design, where built-in wood closets, opened daily for inspections, reveal military uniforms custom-designed by Hollywood director and designer Cecil B. DeMille. When seen framed within the closets and hung in a series prescribed by military protocol, these uniforms reinforce the image of masculine regimentation, hierarchy, and control symbolized by the outfits themselves.

[9] For a detailed historical discussion of the design and construction of Skidmore, Owings & Merrill's military complex, see *Modernism at Mid-Century: The Architecture of the Air Force Academy*, ed. Robert Bruegmann (Chicago: University of Chicago Press, 1994).

[*] **Millhouse, Lambertsville, N.J.**
KEENEN/RILEY ARCHITECTS
Updating the modernist vocabulary that characterized the 1950's bachelor pad, Keenen/Riley's *Millhouse* in Lambertsville, N.J. demonstrates that the notion of the male domestic precinct persists even today. An independent "casino" removed from the main residence and built on the stone foundations of the former mill, this structure was expressly commissioned as a private space where its owner can smoke cigars and play pool (on a custom-designed pool table) undisturbed by the rest of the family.

The Air Force Academy closets demonstrate how the wall dressings that adorn a building work analogously to the clothes that outfit a body. But more often than not, architecture fabricates a masculine environment by undressing rather than dressing its surfaces: less is more *masculine*. Thus the campus plan of the Air Force Academy illustrates how "masculine" space is created by reducing architecture to its bare essentials. Each academy building, whose design is generated from a seven-foot grid derived from the module of a cadet's bed, is set on a vast, barren horizontal podium that levels the rugged topography to afford an uninterrupted view of the horizon. These empty plazas create an atmosphere as spare and forbidding as the bare Rocky Mountain range that serves as their imposing backdrop. The building interiors are also conspicuously lacking in detail, conveying the same virtues of cleanliness, order, and restraint connoted by the academy's spartan exteriors.

Artists **Andrea Zittel** and **John Lindell** also fabricate austere manly environments, employing the severe aesthetic associated with the rational languages of modern architecture and minimalist art. Zittel's "A to Z" lexicon of domestic prototypes consists of reductive geometric objects that accommodate and contain household functions—eating, sleeping, bathing—within a minimum, often collapsible space. While Zittel's proposals for contemporary spartan living would seem to situate her within the masculinist tradition of the heroic modern architect, confident in his abilities to forge a rational world through the creation of standardized artifacts that obey universal human needs, her status as a contemporary female artist makes it ambiguous whether Zittel intends her interpretation of modernist austerity to be read as prescription, parody, or critique. In his installations, John Lindell both celebrates and subverts the masculine visual codes he appropriates. In *Untitled*, Lindell uses his signature template of abstract symbols denoting male erogenous zones to overturn the logic of the "flow chart," diagrams commonly used by natural and social scientists to represent the steps of rational processes and procedures. Conflating the language of science and geometric abstraction, the crisp black lines and abstract shapes that Lindell draws on the pristine white gallery walls map activities that fall outside the binary logic of heterosexuality—representing instead the ecstatic, even delirious geometries of gay male pleasure. Both Zittel's and Lindell's projects underscore how the articulation of masculine space often obeys a logic of absence—a logic implicitly predicated on the eradication of "feminine" excess or ornamentation.

p. 140

p. 78

A third project in this volume, **Renée Green's** *Commemorative Toile Fabric*, calls into question the traditional association of ornamentation with femininity by demonstrating how the ostensibly feminine surfaces of toile fabric historically embody masculine civic virtue. A commodity traded by French merchants in exchange for slaves, 18th-century toile fabric featured idyllic pastoral scenes representing an Enlightenment idealization of untamed nature. Exposing the violence of the sexual and racial economies that supported the trade in toile fabric, Green's contemporary designs for this material seamlessly splice together engraved scenes of rape, abduction, lynching, and slavery. By showing, through her visual alterations, how a material as supposedly neutral as toile fabric can encode dominant cultural ideologies, Green reminds us that the female domestic interior is not opposed to but is wholly complicit with the politics of the male public sphere.

p. 98

This opposition of public and private, upon which sexual binaries like male/female and heterosexual/homosexual crucially depend, is itself grounded on the prior spatial dualism, inside/out-side.[10] Through the erection of partitions that divide space, architecture colludes in creating and upholding prevailing social hierarchies and distinctions. Working on vastly different scales—from developer house plans that sequester the housewife in the kitchen from the husband in the family room, to large-scale urban masterplans that isolate the feminine world of the suburb from the masculine world of the city—architecture's bounding surfaces reconsolidate cultural gender differences by monitoring the flow of people and the distribution of objects in space.

The spatial differentiation of the sexes may find its most culturally visible form in the construction of the sexually segregated public bathroom. It is not by accident that Jacques Lacan chooses, as his privileged example of the institutionalization of sexual difference, adjoining public bathrooms in a railway station. Seated opposite one another by the window of a train pulling into a station, a boy and a girl misrecognize their socially prescribed destinations: "'Look,' says the brother, 'We're at Ladies!' 'Idiot!' replies his sister, 'Can't you see we're at Gentlemen?'"[11] In this parable of what he calls the "laws of urinary segregation," Lacan attributes the division of the sexes to the powerful signifying effects of language. But sexual difference is also a function here of *spatial* division. Lacan's reduction of the problem of sexual difference to the two-dimensional surface of a pair of bathroom doors, one labelled "Ladies" and the other "Gentlemen," conceals the more complex ways that the actual three-dimensional space of the public bathroom assigns sex and gender identity. The architecture of the public bathroom, where physical walls literally segregate the sexes, naturalizes gender by separating "men" and "women" according to the biology of bodily functions.

10 For more on the spatial metaphorics of sexual identity, see Diana Fuss's introduction to *Inside/Out: Lesbian Theories, Gay Theories*, ed. Diana Fuss (New York and London: Routledge, 1991), pp. 1-10.

11 Jacques Lacan, *Écrits: A Selection*, trans. Alan Sheridan (New York: W.W. Norton, 1977), p. 153.

While Lacan shows us two bathroom doors identical in every respect except for their labels, we never see beyond the doors to the interiors themselves, which in fact are quite different. The common assumption that purely functional requirements specified by anatomical difference dictate the spatial layout and fixture design of restroom architecture reinforces the reigning essentialist notion of sexual identity as an effect of biology. Just one look inside the typical domestic bathroom shared by both sexes discloses the ways in which segregated public restroom facilities answer to the requirements of culture, not nature.

Two public bathroom renovations in this volume, one by *Interim Office of Architecture* and the other by Sheila Kennedy and Frano Violich, emphasize the contingent status of a cultural site generally considered functionally fixed and

p. *162*

inevitable. In their renovations of the public bathrooms at two urban arts centers, these design teams attempt to make visible the architectural codes of the bathroom that shape and regulate sexual identity. In their modernization of the Boston Arts Center, a 19th-century exhibition hall, **Kennedy and Violich** invert conventional gender assignments by placing the building's new women's room where the men's room used to be and the men's room

p. **162**

in the space formerly occupied by the women's room. Bruce Tomb and John Randolph of IOOA reconfigure the laws of urinary segregation by converting the bathroom at the Headlands in San Francisco, once a single-sex military latrine, into a coed public lavatory. Each design team exposes architectural remains normally concealed in a bathroom renovation. A row of freestanding "dysfunctional" urinals at the Headlands and a row of urinal floor drains left beneath the newly installed sinks in the women's room at the Boston Arts Center are intrusive reminders of the culturally encoded urinary postures enforced by the architectural practices that govern sexual difference.

The men's room appears to function as a cultural space that consolidates masculine authority around the centrality of phallic power. But as the lead-in essay to *Stud*'s section on the bathroom suggests, this particular hygenic site also operates as a theater of heterosexual anxiety. **Lee Edelman** argues that the anus, an orifice open to penetration, must be

p. **152**

closeted in a stall to protect against the "homophobically abjectified desires" provoked by the "loosening of the sphincter." The internal spatial boundary within the men's room that separates the urinals from the enclosed toilets, together with the cultural prohibition against looking at one's neighbor while urinating, actually initiate what the structure of the men's room was designed to ward off: fear of the abject and homosexual desire. Edelman's discussion of a chic New York restaurant's men's room, where televisions are installed over the urinals to fix wandering glances, reflects on the capacity of architecture to participate in the formation of heterosexual identity by giving cultural play to the forbidden and threatening desires its spatialized boundaries purportedly labor to conceal. In the overdetermined site of the public men's room, the door apparently swings both ways.

Philippe Starck's designs for public bathrooms effectively challenge the conventions of men's room architecture, highlighting and encouraging those activities and

p. **180**

desires that standard ones elicit and suppress. While facilities for urinating and defecating are normally discretely placed opposite one another, at the Royalton Hotel in Manhattan they share a common wall: the urinal, which takes the form of a vertical steel plane, is situated between flanking cubicle doors. Registering the movements of both the eye and the body, the urinal's metallic surface reflects wandering glances while a motion detector, activated by unzipping flies, initiates the flow of a sheet of water down its face. Further rejecting the norm of the isolated bathroom fixture separated by partitions that insures an individual's sense of hygiene and propriety, at both the Royalton and the Teatriz in Madrid, Starck creates communal sinks that make washing a truly public activity as well.

A number of the visual projects in *Stud* highlight the ideological instability of the partition ordinarily found in toilets, gyms, peep shows, and sex clubs. Translucent partitions counteract the visual privacy afforded by Kennedy and Violich's restroom stalls, while flexible plumbing hoses shake when flushed in IOOA bathroom restoration, immediately undermining the authority of the undulating 1/4-inch steel priva-

*p.*293

cy screen rendered tough as military armor. Looking at this con- tentious membrane from an explicitly queer perspective, media critic **Bill Horrigan's** essay, which frames architect **Mark Robbins's** project, *Framing American Cities (New York),* shows how the cubicle refers not only to toilet stalls but to peep shows and

*p.*292

confessionals. Robbins's installation demonstrates how this vulnerable, pen- etratable boundary, originally designed as a spatial bulwark against the threat of homosexual predation, actually serves as an eroticized site of gay male sexual coupling. Taking as its point of departure an analysis of the peep show booths located in the gay video arcade next door, **Matthew Bannister's** design for a gym at the foot of Christopher Street in

*p.*210

Manhattan also rethinks the architecture of the vanity screen. In Bannister's project this com- monplace architectural element under- goes extraordinary permutations, from literal toilet partitions in the locker rooms to the collosal rock-climbing wall inter- sected by diving tanks that rises out of the center of the facility. Bannister manipu- lates and transforms the codes of conduct engendered by the complex boundary demarcated by partitions, facilitating new kinds of physical and scopic exchanges between recreating bodies at the gym.

12 For historical explanations of the modern crisis in mas- culinity, see Michael S. Kimmel, "Consuming Manhood: The Feminization of American Culture and the Recreation of the Male Body, 1832-1920," in *The Male Body: Features, Destinies, Exposures,* ed. Lawrence Goldstein (Ann Arbor: University of Michigan Press, 1994), pp. 12-41, and Anthony Rotundo, *American Manhood: Transformations in Masculinity from the Revolution to the Modern Era* (New York: Basic Books, 1993). For a psychoanalytic reading of masculinity as masquerade, see Kaja Silverman, *Male Subjectivity at the Margins* (New York and London: Routledge, 1992).

DISTRIBUTING OBJECTS

Within the spaces articulated by the enclosing boundaries of architecture, any performance of masculinity requires its props. A number of the contributions to this volume consider the obsessive, even hysterical ways that men relate to the objects that surround and define them. Men's overestimation of certain fetish objects points to the vulnerability at the very heart of masculine identity. Historians attribute the crisis in masculinity to specific historical events—the industrial revolution, World War II—that transformed tradi- tional roles both in the workplace and in the home. Psychoanalysts attribute the rents in male subjectivity to the formation of sexual identity itself, where the bio- logical penis can never live up to the mystique of the cultural phallus.[12] In both readings, objects are seen to locate and to reconfigure masculine identity in histori- cally specific and psychologically powerful ways.

The urinal itself is just such a culturally weighted sign, a brace for the erection and support of male subjectivity. By facil- itating the manly posture of upright urination, the urinal illustrates the capacity of objects to function as foils against which a performing body assumes its gender. But objects not only supplement the body, they also metaphorically stand in for it. In the famous cabaret scene of the film *Blue Angel*, Marlene Dietrich's long legs and lithe torso pose seductively against the contours of a Thonet chair, theatricalizing a feminine identity in contradistinction to her masculine attire. In itself a gender-neutral object, the Thonet chair behaves almost like a human partner, providing a prop for the interactive articulation of sexual identity. In much the same way as Dietrich's chair, **Robert Gober's** urinals emphasize the anthropomorphic qualities of architectural objects. *p.* **174** Acting like surrogate males, their protruding profiles suggest a cross section through the male body. But unlike the polished, mass-produced, machine-made urinals whose dimensions are derived from the standard of an ideal male, Gober's hand-made plaster urinals impersonate masculine vulnerability. Eroding the show of masculine invincibility represented by the traditional porcelain urinal, Gober's urinals present emblems of an ideal but unrealizable masculinity, vacillating uneasily between power and privilege on the one hand and failure and insufficiency on the other.

"Boy-toys," electronic gadgets and appliances that compensate for an imperiled masculinity, figure prominently in two essays in this collection that take the postwar American male as their subject. *p.* **28** **Steven Cohan** attributes Rock Hudson's success as a playboy in the 1959 film *Pillow Talk* to his impressive equipment; his modern telephone, hi-fi, and electronically operated sofa-bed all function as technological sex aids that compensate for, while nonethe-*p.* **42** less accentuating, Hudson's fragile virility. And **Ellen Lupton** describes how another post-war domestic gadget, the electric carving knife, was designed to bolster the insecure ego of America's new suburban husband. The electric carving knife, a household appliance originally marketed for women, was eventually adopted by men as a device that allowed them to perform the traditional male ritual of meat carving with greater prowess and confidence. However, in rendering simple a task that once required artistry, strength, and skill, this mechanical prosthesis also functioned as a powerful reminder of the social castration of the American male. Thus, in both authors' accounts, mechanical objects designed to proclaim phallic mastery disguise a deeper anxiety, as American men struggled to shore up a stable masculine identity against the emasculating effects of post-war consumer culture and the corporate workplace.

While domestic prosthetics compensate *p.* **104** for the suburban male's imagined sense of his lost virility, at **Rem Koolhaas's** Villa in Floriac a mechanical device enables its owner—a man recently confined to a wheelchair—to overcome his actual loss of physical mobility. Ironically, it is now the husband rather than the housewife who needs to be "liberated" from the "prison" of the traditional home. But while buildings for the physically challenged typically avoid level changes, this design welcomes the challenge posed by its mountainside setting. The project consists of three stacked "houses" intersected by a hydraulic lift—a moving room that allows the husband to circulate freely between floors. Its status literally elevated by the lift, the wheelchair, once an index of its owner's vulnerability, now confers power. Located adjacent to the lift, a storage wall vertically penetrates the house, providing the husband easy access to his possessions—books, artworks, wine—which allow him to cultivate his worldly pursuits. From the vantage point of his moving perch, floor to ceiling windows on the second level afford the husband unobstructed panoramic views. The prosthetic architecture of Koolhaas's Villa restores to its owner visual and physical freedom, attributes necessary for the successful performance of masculinity.

Artist **Matthew Barney** takes this consideration of masculine performativity as the overcoming of _p._**216** physical obstacles even further, unveiling masculinity as an overt challenge—a trial performed under constant pressure and anxiety. Barney's OTTOshaft, an installation mounted in the concrete parking garage at Documenta IX (Kassel), investigates how the mainstays of masculinity present literal obstacles to the achievement of gender identity. This installation's meticulously crafted objects (exercise mats covered in tapioca, blocking sleds used in football training lathered in petroleum jelley, and collapsed gym lockers made of pink plastic typically used for prosthetic devices) define masculinity in its relation to sports, sex, and metabolic functions. Using these objects as performance props, Barney enacts a variety of masculine roles for the videos that he both shoots and displays within the installation space itself. The videos show us Barney, wearing only a harness, subjecting his naked flesh to an excruciating and bizarre set of physical endurance tests. Scaling an elevator shaft, dropping from the ceiling, and even submitting to anal probes, Barney's contemporary rite of heroic self-fashioning parodies what it seeks to impersonate, intentionally implicating himself, in his role as male performance artist, in the very rituals of masculine display he aims to unmask.

Like Matthew Barney, **George Stoll** also seeks to disturb traditional notions of artistic male performance, but in contrast to Barney's hypermasculine objects, Stoll's _p._**92** artistry recuperates a domestic object usually associated with the female homemaker. Stoll's Tupperware series alludes to minimalist sculpture; the bright colors and malleable wax surfaces of these stacked serial forms subvert the macho connotations of an American art movement notable for its excessive masculine posturing. Manhandling another commonplace object belonging to women, _p._**86** **Vito Acconci** invokes the erotic and maternal aspects of femininity embodied by that quintessential male fetish—the bra. Recognizing the overlap of clothing and architecture, Acconci's installation exploits the tectonic affinities of wall and bra, both artifacts composed of white surfaces concealing their inner structures. Acconci borrows from the language of fashion to rethink architecture: like walls, his overscaled bras not only partition space, but, like undergarments, they also literally envelop and support the body. Intended to be strapped in various configurations to the surfaces of domestic spaces, Acconci's Wall Bras promote different modes of social engagement. When installed upright at a 90-degree angle, the bra serves as the ultimate male retreat; doubling as stereo speaker and enclosure, the cups shape a womb-like, self-sufficient environment reminiscent of a bachelor pad. However, when assembled freestanding and at right angles to each other, the cups encourage intimate conversation between two occupants. By interfering with the traditional oppositions between feminine and masculine, domestic and artistic realms, both Stoll's and Acconci's work suggests alternative ways for men to engage with the everyday objects around them.

ORGANIZING GAZES

Architecture regulates subjectivity not only through the arrangement of objects in particular spatial structures but also through the organization of spectatorship within those same spaces. From panoptic prisons to pornographic theaters, numerous building types endow men with visual authority while relegating disempowered subjects—especially women—to the position of scopophilic objects. But while visual control remains a recurrent theme in the architectural construction of masculinity, in many circumstances the spatial distribution of the gaze undermines men's culturally privileged access to vision. Several of the pieces in this volume demonstrate how specific architectural spaces work to destabilize the active/passive, subject/object, male/female binaries upon which conventional theories of spectatorship depend. This disturbance of the gaze works in at least two ways: masculine subjects endowed with visual authority can be dispossessed of the gaze through changing configurations of spatial boundaries, while even the most traditional masculine environments are capable of encouraging a transvestite logic of viewing, inviting men to be both subjects and objects of the gaze. [13]

13 A significant body of work in contemporary film theory examines the notion of male spectacle and its potentially destabilizing effects for regimes of spectatorship. See, for example, Richard Dyer's "Don't Look Now: The Male Pin-up," and Steve Neale's "Masculinity as Spectacle," both in *The Sexual Subject: A Screen Reader in Sexuality* (New York and London: Routledge, 1992), pp. 265-276 and pp. 277-287. The classic analysis of the gender politics of spectatorship can be found in Laura Mulvey's "Visual Pleasure and Narrative Cinema," in her *Visual and Other Pleasures* (Bloomington: Indiana University Press, 1989), pp. 14-26.

The essay by **Diana Fuss and Joel Sanders** takes up the first of these possibilities, mapping the visual organization of Sigmund Freud's Vienna office to explore the complicated play of power and transference at work within the spatial and historical scene of psychoanalysis. This essay calls into question the traditional view of Freud's professional office as a space of male dominion, in which patients are rendered powerless in the face of the analyst's absolute scopic authority. The actual architectural configuration of Freud's office and the arrangement of furniture and objects within it suggest a far more complicated dynamic between patient and doctor, a scenario in which Freud more often than not adopts a passive position while his patient is permitted to occupy the room's center of activity. In the highly mediated settings of both his study and his consulting room, Freud assumes a spatially marginalized position, one that leaves him perpetually vulnerable to the risk of feminization.

p. *112*

Focussing on a very different kind of cultural arena, one perhaps more obviously overdetermined as a site of masculine performance, **Marcia Ian** analyzes the gym as a socially sanctioned space where men become the object of the gaze. The success of the male bodybuilder who pumps iron to "substitute the rock hard for the soft, the monumental for the human, and the masculine for the feminine" is registered through the visual admiration of his fellow bodybuilders. Within the con-

p. *188*

fines of the gym, whose mirrored surfaces disperse the gaze in many directions, men willingly submit to a process of scopophilic objectification, readily assuming a receptive position so that they might ultimately attain physical supremacy.

The homoerotic possibilities of the gym return us once more to one of this volume's most important subtexts: the role of architecture in the formation of the modern sexual subject. *Stud*'s final section, "Outings," focuses specifically on the architectonics of gay male sexuality, mapping the spaces of male desire across an urban landscape of streets and parks, sex clubs and theaters, bathrooms and bars. Throughout this volume, numerous contributors draw on queer theory to interrogate the ideological production of normative architectural spaces, a process that often involves shoring up a vulnerable straight masculinity by disavowing the specter of gay sexuality. *Stud*'s concluding essays consider instances of queer appropriation of space: gay men annexing, inhabiting, and recoding public space. Arguing against any essentialist notion of "queer space," these projects demonstrate instead the many inventive and resourceful ways men have appropriated everyday public domains in the formation of a gay social identity.

Overturning the assumption that urban queer visibility commences with Stonewall, **George Chauncey** investigates the many ways that the public spaces of the *p.*__224__

city have been claimed in the past by the gay community. His historical research on New York City's homosexual underground from 1890 to 1940 demonstrates that gay men have in fact

14   David Miller, "Anal Rope," in *Inside/Out*, p.131.

appropriated as venues for social interaction and sexual desire a wide variety of urban spaces, including bars, streets, beaches, and *p.*__268__

parks. Even the piano bar, which figures so centrally in **D.A. Miller's** essay, has the capacity to be reclaimed as a public space that allows men to ritually assemble to sing Broadway show tunes. Only within this exclusive social space—a safe haven out of earshot of the "legitimate" theater—can the queer subtexts of Broadway lyrics finally be heard, if not performed.

The diverse physical characteristics of queer spaces resist categorization. Although gays stereotypically congregate in dark deserted sites like abandoned piers and overgrown parks situated at the fringes of the city, they just as often make contact in busy open streets and squares. Yet a common feature possessing significant spatial implications belongs to all of these divergent spaces—the central importance of the gaze. Elsewhere, D.A. Miller has written: "Perhaps the most salient index to male homosexuality, socially speaking, consists precisely in how a man looks at other men."[14] Constantly subject to the threat of public (and even private) surveillance, gay men have invented strategies for remaining invisible to the public at large while at the same time, and in the same spaces, becoming visible or readily identifiable to one another. For this reason queers have had to depend not only on legible signs—clothing, grooming, mannerisms—but on the visibility of the look itself to identify other queers.[15] In his important study *Tearoom Trade: Impersonal Sex in Public Spaces*, sociologist Laud Humphreys has shown how communication through eye contact governs the carefully staged choreography of cruising.[16] His study documents how the precise layout of restroom architecture—the location and number of urinals in relation to the placement of stalls—shapes the relay of desiring gazes that signals each player's shifting but precisely defined role in sexual encounters. Humphreys emphasizes that the carnal pleasures initiated by visual exchanges presuppose spaces capable of monitoring and surveillance; open or broken windows and squeaking doors permit the vigilant "lookout" to detect hostile intruders.

Tom Burr's physical reconstruction of the Platzspitz Park in Zurich clarifies not only that the space of desire is also the space of surveillance, but that spaces *p.*278 appropriated by socially dispossessed groups can also be reappropriated through public renovation. Burr reconstructs the Platzspitz Park as it appeared in the 1970s, when its secluded enclaves and dimly lit paths provided fertile terrain for the emergence of a gay urban space. His account describes how gays actively altered the spaces they annexed, introducing hidden paths and sheltered areas made readable to the initiated by deposits of litter and forgotten clothing. Burr's full-scale mock-up of the Platzspitz's design, displayed in the Landesmuseum overlooking the park itself, stands in stark contrast to the park's current landscape, which features well-lighted sweeping vistas and open spaces. These dramatic renovations, introduced to maximize visibility, are designed to eradicate the presence of the very community that had previously so successfully carved out in the park its own private sanctuary.

Queer appropriations of the gaze undermine normative codes of spectatorship by creating a reversible look that allows men to be at once both subject and object of the gaze, both spectator and spectacle. The architecture of queer visibility troubles the heterosexist assumptions behind the look by overturning the social interdictions forbidding male spectacle.[17] **Steven Barker's** hidden camera eye documents a recently closed sex club that occupied a former movie theater. Previously, the building's proscenium arch focused the uni-directional gaze of the audience on a discretely framed moving image. Now the gay men who occupy the theatre and engage in openly visible sex acts consent to see

*p.*284

15 Ironically, at the same time that gay men have had to rely on visual codes in the formation of countercultural space, they have had to evade the punitive gaze of mainstream culture that has endeavored to render the always ambiguous face of the gay male as visibly discernible. Lee Edelman describes how in its frustrated efforts to police the homosexual whose threatening presence risks exposing the unstable foundations of heterosexuality itself, the dominant order has attempted to denaturalize the gay male body and to scrutinize it for signs of its difference from "authentic" heterosexual maleness. See his "Imagining the Homosexual: *Laura* and the Other Face of Gender," in his *Homographesis: Essays in Gay Literary and Cultural Theory* (New York and London: Routledge, 1994), pp. 192-241.

16 Laud Humphreys, *Tearoom Trade: Impersonal Sex in Public Spaces* (New York: Aldine De Gruyter, 1970).

17 Patriarchal spectatorship is predicated on the strict division between identification and desire. Conventionally, men, as bearers of the active look, are prohibited from identifying with women, the passive objects of their desire, because to be seen is to be emasculated, castrated by a sadistic male gaze. Jacques Lacan describes the castrating power of the exteriorized gaze in *The Four Fundamental Concepts of Psychoanalysis*, trans. Alan Sheridan (New York: Norton, 1978).

and be seen, thereby blurring the boundary between spectator and
spectacle, voyeur and exhibitionist. Similarly, **Thanhauser and** *p.*206
Esterson's back-lit translucent dressing room doors at a fitness
center register the ephemeral shadows cast by nude bodies displayed
before the eyes of fellow gym members.*

      All human inhabitants of space, regard-
less of their gender identity, assume, to varying degrees, reversible and fluctu-
ating scopic positions; gay men merely exploit a visual condition that patriarchal
heterosexuality considers threatening. These essays and projects that collectively reveal the structure of a homoerotic look already inscribed within public space
call our attention to the always unstable and fluid nature of all kinds of visual
relays transacted through space.

*p.*304   The final entry in
this volume, **Felix Gonzalez-
Torres's** billboards, takes us
back full circle to *Stud*'s initial
treatment of masculinity and domesticity. Gonzalez-Torres presents, in different
urban settings, the same ambiguous
image: bathed in ethereal light, a rum-
pled bed and two pillows bear the traces
of two recently departed occupants. This
open-ended tableau serves as a timeless elegy to all lovers (both gay and
straight) as well as a more timely work of
mourning, evoking the memory of those
lost to AIDS. An eloquent commentary
on how the contemporary domestic
scene is inevitably shaped by a global
medical crisis, Gonzalez-Torres's billboards sum up *Stud*'s two major related
themes: the permeable boundaries
between public and private, heterosexual and homosexual space.

      This book invites its
community of authors, operating from
various critical assumptions and disciplinary vantage points, to unmask masculinity—to refute, dismantle, or re-envision the diverse spatial field of male
performance. The essays by cultural theorists that open each of this book's
five sections explore the multifarious ways that a generic architectural site collaborates in the social production of masculinity. The visual projects by artists
and architects that follow these opening essays propose new opportunities for
reshaping sexual identities by reconfiguring the spaces that house them.
Together, these theoretical and visual projects make visible the ideologies of
gendered space: architectures of masculinity.

*
Root Guest House, Ormond Beach, Florida
STEVEN HARRIS & ASSOCIATES, ARCHITECTS
Architect Steven Harris explores the reversible nature of the
gaze in domestic space in the *Root Guest House*. Playing on
the reciprocity between window and mirror, an operable
round mirror either covers or reveals an interior ocular window linking the bedroom with the living room—a spatial condition that continually reminds the occupant that he/she is
always subjected to an externalized gaze. With the mirror in
the closed position, the guest voyeuristically observes his/her
own reflection aligned with the bed. With the mirror slid open,
the guest is presented with a magnificent ocean view visible
through windows in the living room beyond. Yet this aperture
that frames the landscape also frames the spectator: conventional notions of domestic privacy and propriety are relin-
quished to the degree that possessing the view requires the
guest to consent to become spectacle as well as spectator.

end

ESSAYS BY

STEVEN COHAN

ELLEN LUPTON

WORKS BY

PLAYBOY

SKIDMORE, OWINGS & MERRILL

ANDREA ZITTEL

VITO ACCONCI

GEORGE STOLL

RENÉE GREEN

REM KOOLHAAS

me

So Functional for its Purposes: Rock Hudson's Bachelor Apartment in Pillow Talk
STEVEN COHAN

Perhaps the most memorable feature of *Pillow Talk* (1959; dir. Michael Gordon) is the way the film situates the sexuality of its male lead, bachelor songwriter Brad Allen (Rock Hudson), against the theatrical backdrop of his apartment, a fantasy playpen where domestic technology serves a single purpose—seduction. Flip a switch and the front door locks, the light goes out, and a record player starts to play mood music. Flip a second switch and the sleeper sofa opens out into a double bed made with baby blue sheets. When career girl Jan Morrow (Doris Day), the unmarried interior decorator whom Brad ultimately marries, reluctantly agrees to accept the job of redecorating his bachelor pad, she asks, "Why redecorate? It's so functional for your purposes." While Jan's sarcastic remark equates the bachelor pad unequivocally with a den of seduction, the bachelor pad, an architectural type prominently featured in the popular media during the 1950s and 1960s, functions as more than just the spider web (as Jan refers to it) where male traps unsuspecting female. In the following reading of the bachelor pad as it was represented on the pages of *Playboy* magazine and in the film *Pillow Talk*, I will demonstrate how this multi-coded space represented the culture's deepest anxieties about the stability, coherence, and normality of American maleness, underscoring the homophobia that structured the cultural meaning of "masculinity" as the opposite of "femininity."[1]

Jan's stinging comment about the functionality of Brad's playboy residence makes one wonder just what his purposes are, and the answer is not the obvious one. The bachelor pad operated as a site of consumerism; it marked the single man's marginal position in relation to the domestic ideology of the period, while at the same time allowing for his recuperation as a consumer whose masculinity could be redeemed—even glamorized—by the things he bought to accessorize his virility. More importantly, the elaborate technology of Brad's apartment does more than simply lure women into his bed; it reinforces the film's grounding of the playboy's sexuality in masquerade by providing an arena for his self-conscious performance of heterosexual masculinity.

The plot of *Pillow Talk* theatricalizes the characteristics of straight masculinity most effectively through Brad's impersonation of Rex Stetson, a wealthy Texan whose identity Brad assumes to prevent Jan from discovering his real identity as the playboy with whom she shares a party line. Brad and Jan repeatedly clash on the telephone over his dominance of their party line; he uses the telephone morning and night to serenade women, preventing her from making or receiving business calls. But the two antagonists are connected by more than the telephone company's failure to upgrade its technology. Jan, it turns out, is being relentlessly but unsuccessfully wooed by Brad's best friend and client, Jonathan Forbes (Tony Randall). Eventually, Brad meets the woman at the other end of his party line and instantly decides to make a play for her, masquerading as Rex Stetson to prevent Jan from discovering his real identity as her nemesis on the telephone.

1 See Barbara Ehrenreich, *The Hearts of Men: American Dreams and the Flight from Commitment* (New York: Doubleday, 1983), p. 20. Ehrenreich's account emphasizes the role that homosexuality played in designating gender disorder: the male who did not conform to the breadwinner ethic "was either not fully adult or not fully masculine"—and hence, the logic went, immature, mother-fixated, and homosexual.

This career girl had everything but love.

This bachelor had nothing else but.

They had absolutely nothing in common except a party line.

They believed passionately in the motto, "hate thy neighbor."

Then he met the body that went with the voice he hated.

What would you do?

That's what he did . . . Pretend he was two other guys.

And then the wooing got frantic. [2]

The opening voiceover narration of the theatrical trailer for *Pillow Talk* unwittingly discloses the film's subtext; it is imprecise as a summary of its plot because it refers to two masquerades on the part of the bachelor ("That's what he did . . . Pretend he was two other guys."). This slip (the correct phrasing should be, "two different guys") suggests, however unintentionally, that both Brad and Rex are pretenses, thereby underscoring the notion that straight masculinity has no origin outside gender masquerade, no reference outside of its multiple representations. The trailer also alludes to the carefully cultivated heterosexuality of Rock Hudson's star persona, acknowledging, if only accidentally, that Hudson, the homosexual star pretending to be two "straight" guys in this film, also depends upon an elaborate and doubled pretense of his heterosexuality in order to project masculinity on screen. As my analysis of *Pillow Talk* will show, an architectural setting collaborates to sustain the riven masculinity anchored by Hudson's star persona. Brad Allen's bachelor pad serves, in short, as a space in which the playboy performs his heterosexual masculinity.

[2] All quotations from the trailer and the film itself in this essay are transcriptions of the soundtrack of the MCA laser disc recording of *Pillow Talk*.

PLAYBOY'S BACHELOR APARTMENT

Epitomized on screen by stars like Dick Powell (*Susan Slept Here*, 1954), Frank Sinatra (*The Tender Trap*, 1955*)*, Gary Cooper (*Love in the Afternoon*, 1957), Cary Grant (*Indiscreet* and *An Affair to Remember*, both 1958), Tony Curtis (*Some Like it Hot*, 1959), and, of course, Rock Hudson (*Pillow Talk* and its follow-up*, Lover Come Back*, 1961), the bachelor playboy was more than just a romantic male role in movie comedies of the fifties. Interpreted with suspicion on account of his refusal to embrace the package of privileges and responsibilities that marriage was supposed to offer the male in compensation for his reigned-in sexuality, the bachelor cut an ambiguous figure: he was at once a lady killer and a woman hater, a party animal and a lonely guy. His single status signified a fundamental "immaturity," "irresponsibility," "insecurity," and "latent homosexuality" that simultaneously needed correction (to preserve the family breadwinner ethos) and expression (to confirm his heterosexuality). The bachelor was a reversible figure, located on the margins of domestic ideology and central to its perpetuation. Consequently, while the figure of the bachelor was seen to embody arrested development, it was just as easily inverted to critique the breadwinner ethic and to offer an alternative style of masculinity: the bachelor, in the words of Hugh Hefner's *Playboy* magazine, was "sophisticated, intelligent, urban—a young man-about-town, who enjoys good, gracious living."[3]

Launched in December 1953, *Playboy* magazine represented bachelorhood as a form of male liberation from domestic ideology from the outset. In articles with titles such as "Open Season on Bachelors," "Virginity: An Important Treatise on a Very Important Subject," "A Vote for Polygamy," "Will She or Won't She? A New Way to Answer the Age-Old Question," and "The Dream House and How to Avoid it,"[4] the magazine packaged the single life as an alternative representation of masculinity—social historian Barbara Ehrenreich goes so far as to call its agenda a "male rebellion"[5]—with the aim of resisting the stifling ethic of the breadwinner by asserting that "responsibility" was *not* inherent to male nature. On the contrary, *Playboy* took as its motto the axiom that "woman wants to be a wife long before man wants to be a husband."[6] The centerfold in every issue, which gave *Playboy* its instant notoriety, was the cornerstone of the magazine's own ideological agenda; female nudity offered visible confirmation of its male readers' heterosexuality, guarding against any suspicions as to why a bachelor might want to remain single.

3 "The Playboy Reader," *Playboy* (September 1955), p. 36. Ehrenreich elaborates upon the way marriage was psychologized as the index to a male's maturity and she shows how *Playboy* was designed as a critique of the conformity demanded of domestic ideology; see Ehrenreich, *The Hearts of Men*, chapters 2 and 4. My own reading of *Playboy*—indeed, of bachelorhood in general in fifties culture—was inspired by Ehrenreich's commentary.

4 Burt Zollo, "Open Season on Bachelors," *Playboy* (June 1954), pp. 37-38; Frankenstein Smith, "Virginity: An Important Treatise on a Very Important Subject," *Playboy* (September 1954), pp. 9, 40, 50; Jay Smith, "A Vote for Polygamy," *Playboy* (July 1955), pp. 15-16; Jules Archer, "Will She or Won't She? A New Way to Answer the Age-Old Question," *Playboy* (January 1956), pp. 13, 64; and Shepherd Mead, "The Dream House and How to Avoid It," *Playboy* (July 1956), pp. 53-54, 60.

5 Ehrenreich, *The Hearts of* Men, p. 50.

6 Zollo, "Open Season," p. 37.

7 "Volume I, Number I," *Playboy* (December 1953), p. 3.

Imagined as the site for liberating masculinity from the constraints of domestic ideology, the bachelor apartment was fundamental to *Playboy*'s representation of bachelorhood as a viable alternative to married life. The bachelor apartment served as the primary setting for a playboy lifestyle in which the single man's supposedly undomesticated sexuality was absorbed into the more important activity of consumption. Hefner's lead editorial in the first issue of *Playboy* called attention to the magazine's difference from other male-oriented publications, "which spend all their time out-of-doors." By contrast, Hefner wrote, "We like our apartment. We enjoy mixing up cocktails and an *hors d'oeuvre* or two, putting a little mood music on the phonograph, and inviting in a female acquaintance for a quiet discussion on Picasso, Nietzsche, jazz, sex."[7] The bachelor apartment may have epitomized sexual freedom but it also served to regulate the bachelor, who was now expected to locate his sexuality in the consumption of a whole repertoire of new products and technologies promoting masculine glamour.

In 1956 *Playboy* ran a two-part article with a blueprint for the perfect bachelor digs, a penthouse apartment, "a high, handsome haven—pre-planned and furnished for the bachelor in town." [see **PAGES 54-67 IN THIS VOLUME**] From the opening paragraph, the article situates the reader, married or single, in the social and sexual position of the bachelor consumer.

> *A man yearns for quarters of his own. More than a place*
> *to hang his hat, a man dreams of his own domain, a*

place that is exclusively his. Playboy has designed,
planned and decorated, from the floor up, a penthouse
apartment for the urban bachelor—a man who enjoys
good living, a sophisticated connoisseur of the lively
arts, of food and drink, and congenial companions of
both sexes. A man very much, perhaps, like you. In such
a place, you might live in elegant comfort, in a man's
world which fits your mood and desires, which is a
tasteful, gracious setting for an urbane personality.[8]

The bachelor apartment is intended to
function as a setting for the performance of heterosexual masculinity, understood as a unified identity. In marked distinction to the typical suburban home
comprised of self-contained rooms, its architectural layout, characterized by
flowing interconnected spaces, reflects and supports the bachelor's holistic
subjectivity. "The apartment is not divided into cell-like rooms, but into function
areas well delineated for relaxation, dining, cooking, wooing and entertaining,
all interacting and yet inviting individual as well as simultaneous use." The
kitchen, for example, can be closed off from other rooms or "it may, more often,
be open onto the dining room, so the
host can perform for an admiring audience while sharing in conversation."
The kitchen effectively turns the playboy pad into an arena for performance.
The bachelor host can, when entertaining, integrate the cooking and dining
spaces in order to show off his culinary skills: "For this is a bachelor kitchen,
remember, and unless you're a very odd-ball bachelor indeed, you like to cook
and whomp up short-order specialities to exactly the same degree that you
actively dislike dishwashing, marketing and tidying up. All that's been taken
care of here," and in such a way as to associate the kitchen's modern appliances with masculine recreation ("the ultrasonic dishwasher uses inaudible hi-fi
sound to eliminate manual washing") while projecting virile associations for the
room (a "unique kitchen stool [is] constructed from a rugged, contoured tractor
seat"). And what does the bachelor perform? His masculinity *as* a bachelor: no
female competes with him for domination of his domestic space, and technology replaces the need for a female homemaker in this kitchen (though, as a
reminder of the bachelor's affiliation with the professional class, it still retains a
broom closet for "your once-a-week servant").

Ultimately, however, in spite of the uni-
fied arena implicit in its open plan, the bachelor pad accommodates a divided masculinity. While it may defy "the conventional plan of 'separated rooms
for various purposes'," it rearticulates an older division between public and
private space, a division drawn along gender lines.[9] In the Victorian era, Lynn
Spigel observes, "the doctrine of two spheres represented human activity in
spatial terms: the public world came to be conceived of as a place of pro-
ductive labor, while the home was seen as a site of rejuvenation and con-

8 This and the following quotations from "Playboy's
Penthouse Apartment," *Playboy* (September 1956), pp. 54,
60, 58.

9 "Playboy's Penthouse Apartment. Part II," *Playboy* (October
1956), p. 65.

sumption."[10] The polarization of public/private spaces within American culture had long posited the workplace as a masculine province governed by men, and the home as a feminine one dominated by women. As Spigel shows, though, that gender binary and the sexual politics informing it came to be repositioned, during the 1950s, entirely within the private sphere. *Playboy*'s bachelor apartment, in its turn, further interiorizes this division between public and private, making it a condition of unmarried masculinity: "there are two basic areas, an active zone for fun and partying and a quiet zone for relaxation, sleep and such."[11] As described in the article, the "active zone" of the apartment (kitchen, dining, and living rooms) is an arena for performance, while the "quiet zone" (bedroom, bath, and study), on the other hand, is a private space of withdrawal and escape.

In a tellingly redundant manner, then, the "quiet zone" recreates the "active zone" as a more private, more singularly male version of bachelor heaven. Actual references to the "active zone" recur in the bedroom, among them the mate to a "Saarinen chair" from the living room, for example, and even a second eating and drinking area "cannily concealed in a bar and small refrigerator, just large enough for ice cubes, mixers and midnight snacks—a boon to the barefoot bachelor in PJs who's reluctant to trek to the kitchen for his good-night potation, or perhaps unwilling to interrupt the dulcet dialogue he's been sharing." In the bedroom, "multiple controls" on the bed's headboard "control every light in the place," as well as fastening the locks on doors and windows and drawing the drapes. The control panel also operates the appliances in the kitchen: if the bachelor plans wisely before retiring, he can start his breakfast from his bed the next morning. The bed, in fact, is so laden with technology—built-in speakers for the remote controlled hi-fi system located in the living room, storage cupboards that convert to bedside tables, a telephone, "and miscellaneous bed-time items"—that it seems to reduplicate the bachelor apartment itself, and exceeds the ostensible purpose of a bed in this context, which is to host sex.[12] Likewise, by means of a sliding translucent glass screen, "the outsize bathroom" is easily converted into its own "active" and "quiet zones"; a master bath "ensur[es] total privacy" for the host, who can dress while guests on the other side of the wall freshen themselves up. Special amenities in the private lavatory ("a bidet, magazine rack, ash tray, and telephone") help to guarantee a long stay, in recognition, the article confides, of the bachelor's inclination "to spend quite a lot of time in the throne room—maybe as a hangover from younger days of living at home, when it was the only place to get away from it all," and to do you know what.

Of all the areas, the study is the most private, self-contained room of all, and is described as "the sanctum sanctorum, where women are seldom invited, where we can work or read or just sit and think while gaz-

10 Lynn Spigel, *Make Room for TV: Television and the Family Ideal in Postwar America* (Chicago: University of Chicago Press, 1992), p. 73. On the separation of sexual spheres in Victorian America, its establishment in the early nineteenth century and its collapse starting in the 1920s, see John D'Emilio and Estelle B. Freedman, *Intimate Matters: A History of Sexuality in America* (New York: Harper and Row, 1988). For an analysis of the impact of the doctrine of separate spheres on Victorian masculinity, see E. Anthony Rotundo, *American Manhood: Transformations in Masculinity from the Revolution to the Modern Era* (New York: Basic Books, 1993).

11 "Playboy's Penthouse Apartment. Part II," pp. 65, 67.

12 "Playboy's Penthouse Apartment. Part II," pp. 67-68, 70. A later article in the magazine confirms this impression. "The Playboy Bed," *Playboy* (November 1959), The elaborate Rube Goldberg-type of sleeping contraption featured in "The Playboy Bed," *Playboy* (November 1959) condenses everything from the well-appointed bachelor apartment into the single piece of furniture, so that built into the frame of the bed are remote controls for lights and air-conditioning, a television set, hi-fi, a speakerphone, a dictaphone, a timed coffee maker, lamps, book cases, two bars, a refrigerator, pantry, table, and so on. Truly, this bed "will shame all other beds, those naively constructed for sleep alone" (p. 104).

ing into the fireplace." Here, the bachelor is nested in a haven of floor to ceiling bookcases, comfortable furniture, a fireplace, and, of course, the requisite "binaural hi-fi speakers." "With a study like this, even the most dedicated pub crawler or theater and nightclub buff will be tempted to stay at home of an evening, content within his own surroundings and savoring the city's glamour via the enchanted view from the window wall." Significantly, the centerpiece of the study is "an enormously comfortable upholstered, contoured Herman Miller armchair with footstool, a lord-of-the domain chair reserved for you alone, which holds all of you evenly supported in the right places and fits in with your relaxed posture so that you and the chair are like twin spoons nested together."[13] The spoon metaphor used to describe the bachelor's physical pleasure in that chair, with its erotic implications of necking or "spooning," suggests the possibility of the bachelor's having sex with his own double when he sits languidly in his study and idly daydreams. Even more than the bachelor bedroom or bathroom, the bachelor's study enables the occupant to return to an imaginary state of complete and perfect self-unity, overcoming the division of male subjectivity inscribed in the actual design of the apartment.

The fact that the "quiet zone" offered the bachelor the experience of a hermetically-sealed psychic unity is crucial. If the "active" sphere of the apartment, which is oriented towards entertaining and exhibitionism, can be said to theatricalize bachelorhood as a public spectacle, then the "quiet" sphere, which connotes shelter and security, can as easily be seen to enclose bachelorhood in a closet. The closet, as Eve Kosofsky Sedgwick has observed, occupies a boundary that effects only to obscure the seemingly clear-cut difference between hetero- and homosexual signs.[14] As the mainstay of heterosexual regulation of masculinity, the homosexual closet needs to be understood as constructing much more than a stable place of refuge: the closet maintains a sliding signifying relation— rather like the sliding walls in *Playboy*'s ideal bachelor apartment, which establish the borders between the active and quiet zones. *Playboy*'s ideal bachelor apartment, while obviously committed wholeheartedly to a heterosexual masculinity, ends up evoking the specter of the homosexual closet because of the way the layout simultaneously seeks to theatricalize (in the "active zone") and contain (in the "quiet zone") male sexuality within a single domestic space. When *Pillow Talk* sets Brad Allen's masculinity against the backdrop of his bachelor apartment, with its own "active" and "quiet zones," the locale implies something similar about the ambiguously divided sexuality of its playboy hero, whose masculinity the film represents as an ongoing and multiple masquerade that positions him even more uneasily between secrecy and spectacle.

TOO MANY BEDROOMS

When, in the course of *Pillow Talk*, Jan discovers Brad's true identity, she taunts him, furiously, with the promiscuous implications of his insincerity: "Bedroom problems! At least mine can be solved in one bedroom. You couldn't solve yours in a thousand." Actually, Brad appears to be solving his nicely enough in *two* bedrooms, or at least in two beds: his electronically operated sofa-bed downstairs in the spacious living room, which functions as the "active

13 "Playboy's Penthouse Apartment. Part II," p. 70.

14 See Eve Kosofsky Sedgwick, *Epistemology of the Closet* (Berkeley: University of California Press, 1990), esp. Chapter 1.

The Bachelor Apartment in Pillow Talk
[1959]
Universal Pictures
Film Still

zone" of his bachelor apartment, and his double bed in his bedroom upstairs, which functions as the "quiet zone," where all we see him doing is talking on the phone to Jan as both Brad and Rex. Brad's quarters downstairs comprise a perfectly self-contained living space with a bathroom (which we see) as well as a place to sleep (the sofa-bed). So if Brad also has a perfectly good double bed upstairs—and the spiral staircase leading there is almost always present in the *mise en scène* of his living room—why does he need to use the sofa-bed downstairs to have sex? Let me put the question more broadly: why does the representation of the bachelor apartment in *Pillow Talk* insist on the inclusion of Brad's upstairs bedroom, and distinguish his own bed from the one where he (presumably) has sex?

In considering Brad's bachelor apartment as a representation of gendered sexuality, it is also necessary to examine the difference between it and Jan's apartment. While both Jan's and Brad's apartments contain many of the same types of furnishings and betray a similar overall style, Brad's apartment differs from Jan's in its usage. The career woman's apartment is the more functional for its occupant's purposes (to sleep, to dress, to have breakfast). Whereas Jan maintains a strict distinction between her professional and personal lives within her domestic space (even when she wants to make business calls from home Brad's monopolization of their party line prevents her from doing so), Brad does just the opposite, working at the piano and also playing it as a tool of seduction. His automated sofa-bed epitomizes the blending of public (the sofa) and private (the bed); on the whole, the "active zone" of Brad's apartment serves to visualize the ease with which this playboy combines work and play.

The film further differentiates Brad's apartment from Jan's, engendering it as masculine by way of the various instruments that allow his apartment to function so well for his purposes. Brad's success as a playboy depends upon the technology of seduction installed in his apartment to the point where his virility is signified primarily by his impressive equipment—the piano, the telephone, the hi-fi, the fireplace, the control panel behind the sofa-bed. This instrumentation is what turns Brad's living room into a theater where he can perform his masculinity for an audience, particularly when he talks on the telephone. Designed as a setting that theatricalizes his virility as the quintessential bachelor playboy, Brad's living room functions to bring out the performative basis of his heterosexuality. The telephone, his primary mode of seduction, also figures prominently in the *mise en scène* of his apartment because, even more than the piano, it is the prop most central to his playboy performance. Not a traditional male symbol, the telephone is the phallus that guarantees Brad's virility; much to Jan's chagrin in the opening scenes, it is the prosthesis that lets him keep going and going morning and night. And since the automated sofa-bed suggests that Brad has sex downstairs rather than in his bedroom, it is reasonable to assume that when in that piece of furniture with one of his mistresses, he really *is* expected to perform.

Brad's bedroom upstairs, which the film takes pain to show at several points once he begins impersonating Rex, visually marks the spatial division of his apartment, expressive of the divided masculinity that Brad himself comes to represent on account of his masquerading. Given the rakish characterization of this playboy, the quiet use to which this upstairs room is put is surprising—until one recalls how the bedroom similarly establishes the "quiet zone" of *Playboy*'s ideal bachelor apartment. The resemblance is not quite exact, however. While Brad's bachelor apartment shares the two-part layout of *Playboy*'s, it inverts the purposes of the latter's division into "active" and "quiet zones." The differentiation of public and private areas of *Playboy*'s apartment posits, in the spatial terms of the "quiet zone," a unified male subjectivity. The bachelor apartment in *Pillow Talk* repeats the spatial dualism of "active" and "quiet zones" but produces the opposite effect; its multi-level layout amounts to a spatial recognition of a divided subjectivity. Work and leisure coexist in the "active zone" of Brad's apartment, suggesting an illusory unity. But the "quiet zone" of his bedroom exposes this apparent unity as a false front, a masquerade enabled by the excessive theatricality of the "active zone" downstairs. Insofar as it produces a more jarring sense of the bachelor's sexual contradiction, the bachelor apartment in *Pillow Talk* is a much more transgressive site than the apartment featured in *Playboy*.

Pillow Talk does not imagine Brad's bedroom as a place where he has sex with women; confining his romantic liaisons to the apartment's "active zone" prevents his heterosexuality from ever transcending theatricality. And Brad's upstairs bedroom openly recognizes the divided masculinity that the downstairs disguises in its theatricality. Consequently, the bedroom has to keep appearing in the film as Brad becomes more and more embroiled in his masquerade. Ultimately, the bachelor's bedroom is the site from which *Pillow Talk* queries the singularity, stability, and authenticity of the playboy's heterosexual masculinity; the view from that private world upstairs is the critical vantage point of the closet.

15 Judith Butler, *Gender Trouble: Feminism and the Subversion of Identity* (New York and London: Routledge, 1990), p. 25.

PRETENDING TO BE TWO OTHER GUYS

Following the conventions of romantic comedy, *Pillow Talk* implies in its closure that when Jan marries Brad he somehow integrates the two opposing sides of his personality. But to what extent can Brad and Rex be satisfactorily combined into a unified and whole male identity? The film fails to provide a straightforward answer. Rex's gentle persona works effectively to critique Brad's wolfish playboy bachelor, offering an alternative figuration of unmarried masculinity (which is why Jan thinks she hits "the jackpot" with Rex). Furthermore, *Pillow Talk* does not differentiate between the contrasting male personae of Brad Allen and Rex Stetson simply on the basis of one being a truthful identity and the other a disguise. On the contrary, through the persona of Rex, whose attractive masculinity consists of a series of gender performances, *Pillow Talk* implies that every expression of masculinity is theatrical.

The success of Brad's performance as Rex is ample evidence of the playboy's own gender trouble. The persona of Rex points to the fact, as Judith Butler puts it in a similar (though non-cinematic) context, that "there is no gender identity behind the expressions of gender; that identity is performatively constituted by the very 'expressions' that are said to be its results."[15] The specter of Rex's being queer, of his not being "like all the others," hangs over his persona from the moment he fails to kiss Jan good night for the first time. Moreover, Brad's masquerading as Rex evokes a sense of the ongoing gender performance that was expected of closeted gay men in the fifties, when a bachelor like Rex often had to pretend he was another guy, someone virile and outwardly heterosexual—in short, someone like Brad.

What *Pillow Talk* does, then, is to invert the masquerade required of the closet, so that the virile male made in the image of all the others (the confirmed bachelor) is the one who poses in public as the different kind of male, the one not like the others (the queer man). Brad, in this regard, comes out of his bedroom-closet as Rex, the man Jan falls in love with for his very *un*phallic masculine characteristics. Originally, Brad's intention in posing as Rex is extremely aggressive: to get back at Jan for her behavior on the phone, add another notch onto the headboard of his sofa-bed, and steal her from his best friend, all in one crafty maneuver. "I don't know how long I can get away with this act," he thinks in voiceover as he sits next to Jan in the taxi after they first meet. "But she's sure worth a try." After seeing her to her apartment, he sizes up the situation: "I'd say five or six dates ought to do it." The film shows that Jan *is* worth the effort to get to know; but more to the point, the effort, not to say expense, that Brad undertakes in wooing her indicates that he has more of an investment in his masquerade (the inspiration for which he finds in the Southern accent of a woman, his flavor of the moment Marie) than he ever realizes. If Rex's interest in the minute details of Jan's work as an interior decorator implies his gayness (as Brad himself states), what are we to make of

16 Louella Parsons, "Rock Hudson: 'Marriage is not for me'," *Los Angeles Examiner* (October 25, 1959); Rock Hudson file, Margaret Herrick Library of the Academy of Motion Pictures Arts and Sciences.

Brad's own interest in the fine points of *his* masquerade, right down to going to the trouble of renting a room at the Plaza Hotel simply for the dramatic effect of not putting the moves on Jan? Or what about the pleasure he evinces in the details of Rex's fictional biography, as when he tries to get Jan to visualize his mountain in Texas, using the objects on the restaurant table as props? The masquerade acquires an importance for Brad that exceeds his original rakish intentions and is in that sense liberating for him, not only because he doesn't have to play the wolf with Jan, but because his sheep's clothing allows him to come out of his bachelor apartment with the truth about his heterosexuality, which is that it is neither whole nor natural but an ongoing and discontinuous cultural performance.

ROCK HUDSON'S BACHELORHOOD

> *Rock Hudson is more of a romantic figure today than at any time in his life. His divorce from Phyllis Gates became final in August, and he joined the ranks of the eligible Hollywood males.* [16]

Louella Parsons's observation about the timing of Rock Hudson's huge popularity at the time of *Pillow Talk*'s release in 1959 evokes the essential paradox of his star persona. If, as most of Hudson's fans now know, his 1955 marriage to Phyllis Gates was arranged by his agent (and her employer), Henry Willson, in order to preserve the actor's heterosexual persona, why was it that he became *more* of a romantic figure when his marriage publicly failed?

Richard Meyer believes that Hudson's popularity as a screen idol actually depended upon the recurring tension between the actor's representation of attractive heterosexuality in his films and his own active if closeted homosexuality in his private life. According to Meyer, the quiet, gentle, and unthreatening masculinity that Hudson personified for the fifties was a crucial effect of his homosexuality: "however disavowed by Hollywood, by the film viewer, or by Hudson himself, [it] registered in his star image, in the sexual immobility of his masculinity, in the way that women really *could* count on him to maintain his erotic distance." Meyer goes on to explain that what audiences perceived as attractive in Hudson's heterosexuality—on screen in the melodramas that made him a big star, intertextually in the beefcake imagery of fan magazines (which openly eroticized his body as his films rarely did), and off-screen in the short-lived marriage to Phyllis Gates—was actually the dividend of his living in the closet: the homosexual's expertise in passing as straight, the "knowledge of how to construct an ideal heterosexuality for, and in, representation."[17] The very success of Rock Hudson as a straight leading man thus confirms what *Pillow Talk* suggests through Brad's masquerade, namely, that *convincing* heterosexual masculinity is itself merely a question of "proper" representation.

In this regard it is important to appreciate that *Pillow Talk* did not, as Barbara Klinger maintains, simply reinvent the star persona of Rock Hudson for the sixties—by projecting a "heterosexually fixated" masculine bachelor image "at odds with his earlier, pristine image"[18]—so much as build into its plot a perceptive deconstructive reading of the pureboy star persona that had been so carefully cultivated in the melodramas made by Universal-International and through the combined efforts of his agent Henry Willson and the fan industry. It is still easily recognized, for instance, that when Brad masquerades as Rex, every woman's jackpot, he impersonates a Texas oilman much like the character Hudson himself played in *Giant* (1956), the performance that won him his only Oscar nomination. The masquerade that occurs in the plot of *Pillow Talk* thus cites Hudson's own persona to emphasize its basis in a gender performance as well. Like Rex, Hudson was supposed to be "gentle . . . by nature"; "basically shy, conservative and tolerant"; "a devoted son." As unlike playboy Brad as could be, Hudson, it was said, like Rex, "hates phonies and has learned to recognize them and keep them out of his life. He has also learned that he wants an uncomplicated girl who can adapt herself to his simple way of life."[19] At the same time that he knew what he wanted from the Hollywood rat race, the actor, again like Rex, was just the opposite of the womanizing playboy type: "shy, self-conscious and so utterly unsure of himself, his six-feet-three inches were actually a hindrance instead of a help."[20]

Whereas the allusions made by Rex's character to Hudson's persona invoke his previous film roles and the wholesome characteristics they conveyed, in Brad's case the allusions center upon the bachelor apartment. One of the central means through which the fan industry charac-

17   Richard Meyer, "Rock Hudson's Body," *Inside/Out: Lesbian Theories, Gay Theories*, ed. Diana Fuss (New York and London: Routledge, 1991), pp. 279-82, 272.

18   Barbara Klinger, *Melodrama and Meaning: History, Culture, and the Films of Douglas Sirk* (Bloomington: Indiana University Press, 1994), pp. 101, 115.

19   "Would You Marry One of These Men," *Movieland* (October 1954), p. 25.

20   "Rock, the New Giant," *Movieland* (April 1955), p. 39.

terized Hudson's persona was his own bachelor living arrangements since, when he became extremely popular before his marriage, he publicly maintained what was unthinkable according to domestic ideology: "a house without a wife!"[21] But then so did many unmarried male stars and without eliciting comment in the press. Highly indicative of the pressures that bachelorhood exerted upon Hudson's star persona is the fact that, as soon as he became a big star in 1954-55, following the success of *Magnificent Obsession*, articles describing his bachelor home appeared in an assortment of venues: *American Weekly,* a newspaper Sunday supplement, *Life*, and movie magazines such as *Photoplay.*[22]

These accounts of the star's bachelor digs help to illuminate just how carefully *Pillow Talk* incorporates Hudson's offscreen persona into the character of Brad Allen through the latter's high tech playboy apartment. Recurring details in these articles would go unnoticed now except for the fact that, when read alongside *Pillow Talk*, they acquire specific resonance as signs of "Rock Hudson." In the same vein, details about Brad presented in the film appear entirely self-contained until the fan discourse about Hudson's bachelor home reveals an added significance as a reference to his star persona surpassing the text. Thus, for instance, the articles appearing in *Life*, *American Weekly*, and *Photoplay* all take pains to mention how Hudson's piano, his one substantial piece of furniture, takes pride of place in his bachelor home; each article, moreover, features a photograph of him seated at a piano to reiterate the instrument's importance to his bachelor persona. Where *Pillow Talk* characterizes Brad as a wolfish playboy through his piano playing, this textual detail metonymically links the playboy with Hudson's off-screen persona in exactly the way that Rex's characterization as a "giant" Texas oilman does.

21 Pauline Swanson Townsend, "Bachelor Daze," *Photoplay* (May 1955), p. 53.

22 Liza Wilson, "How a Hollywood Bachelor Lives," *American Weekly* (May 23, 1954), Rock Hudson file, Margaret Herrick Library of the Academy of Motion Pictures Arts and Sciences; "The Simple Life of a Busy Bachelor," *Life* (October 3, 1955), pp. 128-30, 132; and Townsend, "Bachelor Daze," *passim.*

23 Wilson, "How a Hollywood Bachelor Lives," p. 13.

24 Townsend, "Bachelor Daze," p. 53.

The piano is not the only metonymical reference to Hudson's publicized bachelor persona that later appears in *Pillow Talk*. One of the mid-fifties articles includes a photo of him talking (bare-chested) on the phone, with a caption indicating that, as "a popular young bachelor" he phones a lot of women; the magazine then asks the reader to guess which popular young starlet he is calling. Moreover, and crucially, the same article announces that, like Brad's apartment, Hudson's house is wired! "Push a button in Rock's house and strange things happen—stoves cook, coffee perks, garbage dispenses, glass walls slide, garage doors open, hidden lights come on, and music floods all the rooms."[23] This description of Hudson's new house anticipates both the spatial fluidity of *Playboy*'s ideal bachelor apartment and the technology of Brad Allen's in *Pillow Talk*—which is also to say that the star's own bachelor pad is functional for his purposes in every possible way, as the *Photoplay* article also indirectly makes clear. The caption for a photograph of Hudson and "new date, Phyllis Gates" indicates how this bachelor's pad serves as a closet disavowing his homosexuality. "Usually voluble," *Photoplay* comments about Hudson, "he now clams up about dates, switches conversation to his new house!"[24]

On the one hand, the caption can be taken at face value: he no longer chats about his dates because he is really serious about Phyllis, as his marriage would prove. On the other hand, as his marriage did prove, Gates was instrumental in cloaking his homosexuality—as Meyer puts it, the "marriage was sufficient to secure and emit the sign 'heterosexuality' . . . [that] would remain publicly affixed to Rock Hudson's body for the following three decades"[25]—and the same can be said of the new house (which he apparently lost in the divorce). The bachelor home, that "house without a wife," was the public sign that displaced Hudson's homosexuality: it acknowledged what his bachelorhood potentially signified about his sexual life off-screen in the act of refuting any knowledge of it.

The mechanism of *Pillow Talk*'s subversion of Hudson's heterosexual pureboy bachelor persona may seem more obvious today than in the fifties because of the revelations about his private life following the actor's very public death from AIDS. In light of later knowledge about Hudson's homosexuality, there is, as Babington and Evans remark, "a particular irony about a great heterosexual icon of the cinema whose fabrication includes even the nature of his sexuality."[26] Such a revisionist account of Hudson is the point of Mark Rappaport's recent video collage, *Rock Hudson's Home Movies* (Couch Potato Films, 1992), which illustrates the queer undercurrent of Hudson's divided persona by taking scenes from his films out of their narrative contexts for a camp recoding. "It's not like it wasn't up there on the screen if you watched carefully," the actor impersonating Hudson informs the audience early on.

Rappaport doesn't have to camp up his clips of *Pillow Talk* very much, however, since this film already incorporates what would become the nineties revisionist view of Hudson's queer masculinity into its own fifties masquerade plot. As I have shown, through the masquerading bachelor (at once Brad *and* Rex) and his apartment (at once theater *and* closet), *Pillow Talk* articulates the sexual contradictions informing the movie industry's production of "Rock Hudson" as the ideal, eroticized bachelor of fifties American cinema. From an industrial standpoint, the many allusions to Hudson had the specific intent of reestablishing his star persona as an eligible straight "bachelor" following his divorce (which became final just weeks before the film's premiere); but the film, as I have demonstrated, does not make an effort to cover over the contradictions it locates in the star's masculine persona. The ongoing references to Hudson as a source for both Rex and Brad continually serve to divide the monolithic masculinity he represented in the fifties, and this splitting then subverts the star's male persona by heightening its performativity, its basis in masquerading. As *Pillow Talk* envelopes the playboy's heterosexuality so thoroughly in the masquerade, its comic plot then gives Brad's (and by implication Hudson's) bachelor apartment additional significance as the homosexual closet, a gloss reiterated in the film's use of that setting to evoke Rock Hudson's own persona and the fan discourse that mediated it.

25 Meyer, "Rock Hudson's Body," p. 274.

26 Bruce Babington and Peter William Evans, *Affairs to Remember: The Hollywood Comedy of the Sexes* (Manchester: Manchester University Press 1989), p. 205.

end

Power Tool for the DIning Room: The Electric Carving Knife
ELLEN LUPTON

The electric carving knife is a rare instance of a domestic appliance addressed to male users. A transitional object that mediates between the interior, service space of the kitchen and the public, ceremonial space of the dining room, the electric knife belongs to a population of machines that play an ancillary role in the larger architecture of the domestic environment, mechanizing the labors of modern life. The proliferation of domestic appliances since the 1920s has been fertile ground for feminist historians of design and technology, who have shown how the seemingly rational forms of "labor-saving" devices have fetishized hygiene and cleanliness and have romanticized an unrelenting series of chores.[1] Although considerable scholarly work has addressed the role of female consumers in design culture, few efforts have been made to position products engineered for male use within the gendered map of modern domesticity.

General Electric introduced the electric knife in January 1963. The engineering department created several experimental prototypes before arriving at a workable technical solution: the motor moves two parallel blades back and forth counter to one another, eliminating the need for sawing motions by the user. Competing knives that were fitted with a single blade cost less than half the price of GE's model, but proved ineffective.[2] "Reciprocating action" remains the mechanical principle for electric knives manufactured today.

Market surveys by GE's consumer panel suggested that the knife would be a welcome addition to the mechanically enhanced homes of the period. The perceived market included both men (who would use it for carving turkeys) and women (who would use it for general kitchen use). An in-house team led by industrial designers Olle Haggstrom and Ted Daher refined the details of the knife's handle, which houses the motor and the on/off switch and acts as a base for the knife when not in use. Daher enclosed the mechanism in a two-toned brown plastic shell, designed to "coordinate with the colors of food"— those of cooked meat, presumably.[3]

1 Feminist studies of design and technology include Ruth Schwartz Cowan, *More Work for Mother: The Ironies of Household Technology from Open Hearth to Microwave* (New York: Basic Books, 1983); Adrian Forty, *Objects of Desire* [New York: Pantheon, 1986]; and Penny Sparke, *Electrical Appliances: Twentieth-Century Design* (New York: E. P. Dutton, 1987).

2 On the differences between various electric knives on the market in 1964, see John H. Ingersoll, "Now... Carve with Power," *Popular Science* (December 1964), pp. 148-149.

3 Conversation with Olle Haggstrom, former GE Manager of Industrial Design, April 1994.

4 "Electric Housewares," *Industrial Design* 8 (December 1961), pp. 54-65.

5 In-house publication, General Electric, 1977.

The electric knife was born into a consumer culture of proliferating kitchen gadgetry. Sharing the small appliance market in 1961 were the Cory electric can opener, the Iona drink mixer, the GE toaster oven, and the Casco appliance center, which combined a mixer, blender, juicer, and knife sharpener into a single counter-top unit.[4] The electric knife quickly achieved success, reaching nearly $1 billion in annual sales by 1966. In 1977 more than 1.7 million units were sold.[5] In 1971 the British journal *Design* reported—in a tone of mild amusement—that one out of three American families owned an

New **Electric Carving Knife**
Model EK-1

CARVES AND SLICES FOOD PROFESSIONALLY! RIGHT IN YOUR OWN HOME

The New Electric Carving Knife
Advertisement for General Electric (1963)
The first electric knife was designed by Olle Haggstrom and Ted Daher for General Electric.

43

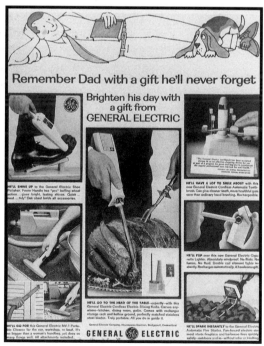

Advertisement for Sunbeam
[1967]
An electrified banquet of wedding gifts includes something for the groom: an electric knife.

Remember Dad with a Gift He'll Never Forget
Advertisement for General Electric [mid 1960s]
Competing as techno-gifts for Father's Day are the electric knife, the mechanical shoe polisher, and the automatic fire starter.

electric carving knife.[6] Since the mid-1980s sales of the electric knife have held steady at around 1.5 million units per year.[7]

Following GE's successful launch of the electric knife, other appliance manufacturers quickly produced competing models, marketing the new product as a gift item especially suited to men.[8] While electric skillets, coffee makers, and hair dryers were seen as appropriate for women, fire starters, shavers, and electric knives were packaged for Dad. A 1965 Ronson ad, published in time for Father's Day, presented its electric knife as a partner in a softly lit dinner for two: "Romps through a roast. Zips through a Porterhouse. And it looks terrific on the table, too. Makes any man a Michelangelo at mealtime."[9] Today, electric knives are rarely advertised and are sold primarily at Thanksgiving and Christmas—in most households, they are ceremonial objects rather than everyday necessities.[10]

GE introduced a cordless electric knife in January 1964. The rechargeable knife was abused by hunters and fishermen, an unanticipated market for the new appliance. Outdoorsmen exposed the knife to brutal natural elements—blood, guts, saltwater, etc.—that damaged the mechanism and led to numerous complaints from consumers: the electric knife, conceived as an indoor appliance—domestic and domesticated—failed to survive the rigors of the hunt.[11] Today, cordless knives for use inside the home are available at the high end of the market.[12]

Hamilton Beach redesigned the electric knife by inserting an open loop into the object's monolithic handle, leaving the motor enclosed in the structure below—this design typology was familiar from the popular electric mixer. The new model, introduced in 1966, was developed by in-house industrial designer Marlan Polhemuf and consultant designer Dave Chapman. The original "stick knife" had vibrated unpleasantly in the hand, an annoyance eliminated by the "hole-in-handle" model, whose slimmed-down grip also was considered more manageable for women.[13] The new electric knife received a Design in Housewares award in 1966 and was applauded by Industrial Design magazine for its "smooth, sculptured appearance."[14] Selling for $60 a unit, this deluxe appliance would be considered expensive even on today's market.

While Dave Chapman proposed visionary functional variations on the electric knife—such as a model

6 "US Gadget Gluttony and Power Politics," Design 268 (April 1971), p. 19.

7 Duke Ratliff, "Bread Machines Boost Sales of Electric Knives," Home Furnishings Daily (3 May 1993), p. 121.

8 According to Olle Haggstrom, GE originally conceived of the electric knife as a "new household necessity," but the product quickly became identified with the gift market.
  An invaluable source of advertising material on the electric knife and other appliances is the John W. Hartman Center for Sales, Advertising, and Marketing History, Special Collections Library, Duke University.

9 The New Yorker (5 June 1965).

10 Conversation with Pete Elshout, National Accounts Department, Black and Decker, April 1994.

11 Conversation with Robert Mazakane, former manager of product safety for GE's Housewares Division, May 1994.

12 Brian J. Hogan, "Custom-Made Motor Simplifies Rechargeable Electric Knife," Design News (21 October 1985), pp. 122-123.

13 Marlan Polhemuf was the primary product designer working on the electric knife at Hamilton Beach when the Chicago firm Dave Chapman, Goldsmith, and Yamasaki, Inc. was hired in the capacity of consultant. Polhemuf claims to have originated the "hole-in-handle" concept. Conversation with Marlan Polhemuf, April 1994.

14 "NHMA Award Winners," Industrial Design 13 (September 1966), pp. 82-86. The Design in Housewares prize is awarded by the National Housewares Manufacturers Association.

Brochure for Hamilton Beach
Hamilton Beach used a celebrity endorsement to dramatize its "hole-in-handle" electric knife, introduced in 1966 and designed by Marlan Polhemuf and Dave Chapman.

Designs, storage devices for Hamilton Beach electric knife [1965]
Dave Chapman proposed formal housing for the electric knife that would elevate its cultural status and make it at home with fine china and tableware. The Dave Chapman Papers, Department of Special Collections, Syracuse University Library.

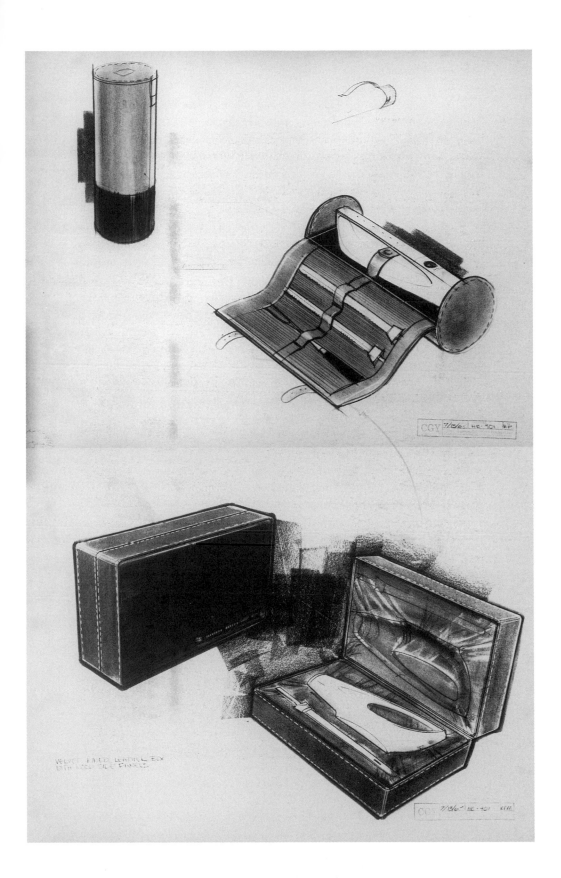

VELVET LINED LEATHER BOX
WITH LOOP TIE PANEL

CGY 7/2/21 HE-901 MP

CGY 7/2/21 HE-901 KM

powered by water from the kitchen faucet—he also presented packaging concepts to Hamilton Beach that concentrated on the object's cultural status.[15] One concept sketch shows the knife in a soft, dark wrapper modeled after the light-proof bags traditionally used for holding silverware; another sketch proposes a velvet-lined box with molded indentations for the handle unit and blades. These packaging ideas promoted the electric knife as a dignified object removed from the mundane world of the kitchen counter. In a similar spirit, Remington advertised a knife in 1965 whose brushed-chrome handle was designed "especially for the dining-room table"; photographed in a lady's gloved hand, this knife was "elegant enough to go with your best silver and china".[16]

It would take more than packaging or styling, however, to transform the electric slicer into an inconspicuous substitute for a skillfully deployed carving knife. As an appliance whose sheer physical presence—its size, weight, and sound—upstages the drama of the task at hand, the electric knife embraces a central aspect of modernist kitsch: the display of technological features exceeds the demands of the situation. In the words of Vittorio Gregotti, such "extravagant futility" typifies the realm of gadgets, as seen in the overly mechanized apartment of James Bond's arch-enemy Goldfinger, equipped with spectacular devices of surveillance, torture, and entrapment.[17]

Comments in contemporary trade articles and advertisements hinted at the absurdity of the electric knife, insinuating that the object signaled a lack on the part of the head of household. Heralding the electric knife in 1965 as one of the "hottest" items on the small appliance market, *Plastics World* proclaimed: "They've been given to men who pride themselves on their carving ability and to men whose friends and families felt they needed all the help that could be rendered to cut through the cheese."[18] A 1964 GE ad suggested the electric knife as a useful gift for the male carver, from skittish fumbler to skilled virtuoso: "Does a roast make him roar? Or is he deft with a blade? Carving is child's play with General Electric's new Electric Slicing Knife."[19] In 1967 Carvel Hall, a manufacturer of high-end conventional cutlery, condemned the electric knife as a travesty of male honor:

> You don't carve with an electric knife. You saw. Swiftly, yes. Effortlessly. Without difficulty. And without art. Which depresses us. Because we still believe there's something grand about carving. It takes a simple chore like divvying up a roast and turns it into a small but gala performance. It is, indeed, a man's only chance to shine during a meal.[20]

15 "Confidential Report to Hamilton Beach Company" by Dave Chapman, Goldsmith & Yamasaki Inc., with drawings dated 1965. The Dave Chapman Papers, Department of Special Collections, Syracuse University Library.

16 *Life* (3 December 1965).

17 Vittorio Gregotti, "Styling and Architecture," in *Kitsch: The World of Bad Taste*, ed. Gillo Dorfles (New York: Bell, 1968), p. 263.

18 Madeleine Crowell, "Merchandising Memo on Kitchens and Small Appliances," *Plastics World* 23 (December 1965), pp. 36-37.

19 *Brides* (March 1964).

20 *The New Yorker* (20 May 1967).

REMINGTON.®
The first electric knife elegant enough to go formal... and it's cordless!

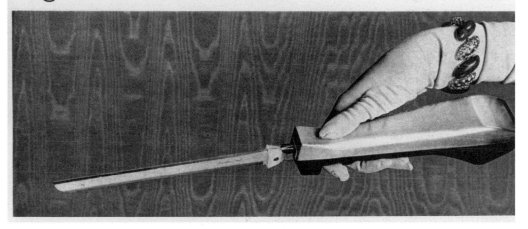

The first electric knife elegant enough to go formal...
Advertisement for Remington
Remington put a platinum finish on the electric knife to make it a suitable accessory for formal dining.

Carvel Hall's elegy to the art of carving mourned the decline of a traditional masculine skill in a world of burgeoning gadgetry.

The performance of many domestic chores was fundamentally changed by machines in the postwar period. The mechanization of laundry, for example, successfully lightened one of the house-wife's heaviest burdens. The washing machine also encouraged women to do laundry more often and to do nearly all of it at home. Thus, while such developments were heralded by many advertisers and commentators as a "revolution" that had liberated the modern woman from drudgery, the gendered assignment of chores remained unchanged. Likewise, the success of the electric knife was powered by traditional norms that defined carving as a masculine duty. Yet while the washing machine fundamentally altered a base and arduous task, the electric knife intervened in a ceremonial ritual, making it easier while rendering it somewhat ridiculous. The postwar man was no more "liberated" by his electric knife than his wife was set free by her blender. His new possession neither enhanced his status in the home nor freed him from a dreaded obligation.

From the primeval hunt to the royal feast, a long tradition of masculine performance surrounds the act of carving meat. In her anthropological study, *The Rituals of Dinner*, Margaret Visser examines the significance of cutting meat across a spectrum of cultural scenarios.[21] The perishable nature of animal flesh and the relative difficulty of procuring it, especially in hunting societies, makes meat a central focus of religious sacrifices and celebratory feasts:

> For thousands of years [meat] was placed before the family as a result of male enterprise and triumph; and men, with their knives, have insisted on carving it up, and even cooking it before the expectant crowd. Vegetables, on the other hand, were most often the result of steady, unexalted, cooperative, and often mainly female work.[22]

21 Margaret Visser, *The Rituals of Dinner: The Origins, Evolutions, Eccentricities, and Meaning of Table Manners* (New York: Penguin, 1991).

22 Ibid., p. 231.

23 Ibid.

24 Advertisers in the 1960s recognized the barbecue as a site for selling male cooking gadgets, including the electric knife and the automatic fire starter. GE promoted the mechanized cook-out in *Sunset* (June 1964).

According to Visser, the act of cutting meat in public dramatizes the difference in taste and texture between the diverse parts of an animal carcass, forcing the carver to decide who will receive the best pieces. In contrast to the hierarchical roast, an "egalitarian" pie or stew reduces all cuts of flesh to a common medium.[23] As Visser points out, the modern suburban barbecue—a festive, holiday event—rehearses this ancient pattern by putting men in control of the meat and women in charge of salads and desserts.[24]

In early modern Europe carving was a compelling spectacle at grand feasts; the task of cutting meat at the table was reserved for an important person of noble birth. A manual of carving written by

Outdoor entertaining with indoor ease:
5 ways from General Electric to have more fun with less fuss.

Vincenzo Cervio in 1581 describes the staggering levels of skill, strength, and confidence demanded by this art, and the burden of shame attached to failed performances. To serve a roasted bird the carver was expected to hold the entire carcass in the air on the end of a fork, while with the other hand slicing off perfect slivers of meat that would fall in a circular pattern on a platter waiting below.[25]

Mrs. Beeton's Book of Household Management, a famous British cooking guide first published in 1861, described with awe the feat of carving a bird in mid-air, witnessed at an exclusive London restaurant—by this time, such acrobatic serving techniques were no longer commonplace.[26] Painting a pathetic portrait of a man "entirely ignorant of carving," Mrs. Beeton bemoaned the state of the art in modern-day England:

> We have all seen him, offering in an emergency to
> assist his hostess, and trying with mere physical force
> to overcome his lack of skill; with red face and per-
> spiring forehead he hacks and tugs at the dish in front
> of him, and at every attempt the veins stand out more
> prominently in his head, while the face of his hostess
> grows graver each moment as she begins to realize the
> appalling fact that the dish will not go around.[27]

If skill is what the humiliated carver lacked, it would not be provided by the electric knife, which a hundred years later offered plenty of motorized muscle power but no knowledge of animal anatomy or guarantee of the appropriate distribution of flesh, fat, and gravy on diners' plates—both essential to the art of carving. The author of The Working Woman's Dream Kitchen, a late twentieth-century offspring of Mrs. Beeton's famous book, acknowledged the functional value of the electric knife, especially for carving large birds, but added this note of disapproval: "I am old fashioned and still like to see my husband manually carve the Thanksgiving turkey or the Christmas standing rib roast."[28]

25 See Visser, The Rituals of Dinner, pp. 235-237, and Masterpieces of Cutlery and the Art of Eating (London: Victoria and Albert Museum, 1979).

26 Mrs. Beeton's Book of Household Management, A Guide to Cookery in All Branches (London: Ward, Lock & Co., 1915), Chapter XXXIX, "The Art of Carving at the Table," pp. 1258-1274.

27 Ibid., p. 1259.

28 Hilde Gabriel Lee, The Working Woman's Dream Kitchen (White Hall, VA: Betterway Publications, 1990).

29 Life (3 December 1965).

The spectacle of the domestically incompetent male appears in various ads for the electric knife, flattering the female gift buyer and emphasizing the superiority of her own skills and duties. In 1965 Westinghouse imagined its electric knife provoking a Texas chainsaw-style massacre of the contents of the kitchen:

> After he's had a go at poultry, roasts, hams, there
> won't be any stopping him. He'll want to branch
> out . . . slice bread, vegetables, cheese, fruit, and cake
> for you. Let him go . . . . A Westinghouse Electric Knife
> is the one thing that can make him handy in the
> kitchen. And think what you can do with it when he
> isn't around.[29]

Recalling the ancient division between hunting and cultivating, various advertisements instruct men to employ the knife for meat, and women to use it for bread, cake, and vegetables—to carve is masculine and to slice is feminine, just as the traditional hunt was the work of men, while the cultivation of vegetables and the boiling of stews belonged in the domain of women. A 1965 Presto ad explained that the slim-handled electric knife "helps a man carve at dinnertime yet works just as well for everyday slicing of fruits, vegetables, even tender angel food.... Great for gals. But be generous... let Dad still carve at dinnertime, huh?"[30] Such comments reinforce the delineation between masculine and feminine duties in the home, and show that men were assigned ceremonial, occasional tasks while "everyday" routines were women's work.

Unlike shoe polishers or shop tools, the electric knife is linked to the female-identified world of cooking and serving; at the same time, however, it draws on a long history of masculine performance at the dinner table. Appearing on the market during a period of rapid expansion and dubious innovation in the field of small appliances, the electric knife was a masculine addition to a world of gadgets associated largely with female consumers. Plugging into a tradition of male duty that had come under question, the knife supplemented a disappearing domestic art with the brute strength—and short leash of electric power. Although it was designed for a ritual that signified male domestic leadership, the intrusive presence of the buzzing electric knife in the formal dining room signaled uncertainties in the hierarchy of the household.

30 *Ladies Home Journal* (December 1965).

RESEARCH:
SHERI SANDLER

***Playboy's Penthouse
Apartment,***
*a high handsome
haven for the bachelor
in town*

REFERENCE
INTRO. PAGE 15

PLAYBOY'S PENTHOUSE APARTMENT

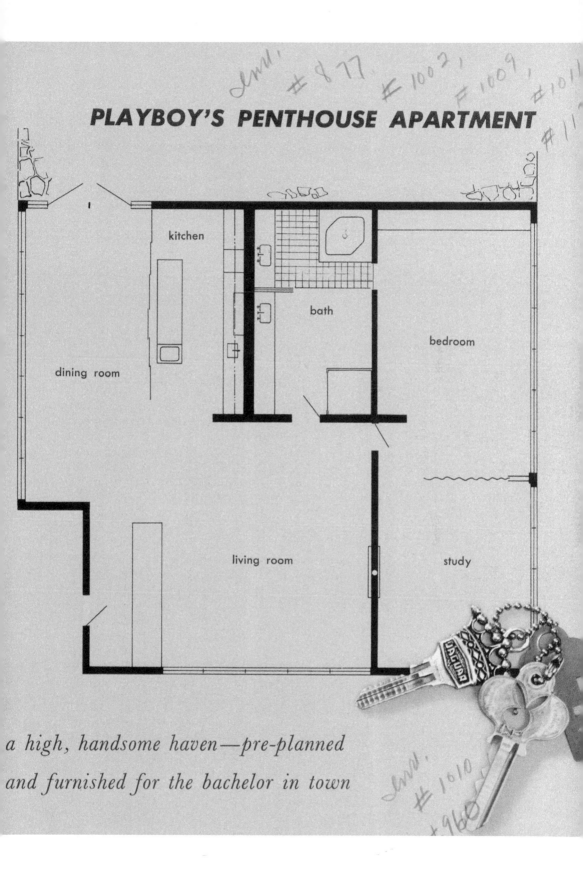

kitchen

bath

bedroom

dining room

living room

study

a high, handsome haven—pre-planned

and furnished for the bachelor in town

A MAN YEARNS for quarters of his own. More than a place to hang his hat, a man dreams of his own domain, a place that is exclusively his. PLAYBOY has designed, planned and decorated, from the floor up, a penthouse apartment for the urban bachelor — a man who enjoys good living, a sophisticated connoisseur of the lively arts, of food and drink and congenial companions of both sexes. A man very much, perhaps, like you. In such a place, you might live in

elegant comfort, in a man's world which fits your moods and desires, which is a tasteful, gracious setting for an urbane personality. Here is the key. Let's use it together and take a tour of discovery.

It is just after dark on an evening with a tang of autumn in the air. The front door (that's at the lower left) takes us into a hallway with a facing wall of primavera panels. One slides easily aside, a light goes on automatically within

and we hang our topcoats in a dust-proof closet. To our right is an illuminated aquarium and a wall-and-ceiling skylight, lending a romantic atmosphere to the entrance-way, and to our left, at the end of the hall, the apartment beckons warmly.

Coming down the hallway, we are able to view the entire width of the apartment and through the open casements, see the terrace and the winking towers of the city beyond. Then, quite suddenly, we are in the apartment proper — a modern kitchen adjoins the dining room and before us is the main living area.

The fire in the raised and recessed Swedish grate casts a magnetic glow on the

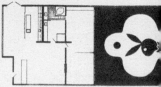

DINING ROOM

From left to right: Bruno Mathesson table ($220) comes in a variety of solid hardwoods (we've used elm in the apartment—it's shown here in teak), is an ingenious gateleg with four leaves; foyer to right of entry has illuminated aquarium, wall-and-ceiling skylight; one of the Miller cabinets in dining room which is equipped with sliding silver chest, adjustable shelves; one of eight Singer upholstered solid elm dining chairs, suitable elsewhere as needed.

Above: The unusual flip-flop couch by M. Singer & Sons (#194, $495), pictured in various stages of flip, including the flat, on which overnighters may flop. Below, Saarinen armchair by Knoll (#70, $285).

Below: rocking stools designed by Noguchi, built of hardwood and metal by Knoll (85T, 86T, $46.50, $48) offer casual living room seating in comfort.

Below: one of four Knoll tables (#305, $78), with foam cushions, may be used singly or together for seats or buffet.

LIVING ROOM

couch facing it, forming an intimately confined area, a romantic setting for a tête-à-tête. The floor beneath us is cork tile. The smooth plaster wall is in dramatic contrast to the stone hearth, which has a painting on its right and a raised planter with climbing vine on its left. The apartment's sense of masculine richness and excitement stems in part from such juxtapositions of textures — the smooth wall, the stone, the planter, the cork floor — and for visual impact the unadorned brick wall which closes off the bath and the kitchen area. Turn to the window wall. Here's drama and contrast again, a view of the city through casements richly hung with white dacron and slate gray silk shantung overdrapes. Below these are continous hanging storage cabinets.

The rest of the living room is best seen by utilizing a unique feature of the couch. It flips, literally: at the touch of a knob on its end, the back becomes seat and vice versa — and now we're facing the other way. Immediately before us are four low square tables, placed together. Each has a foam rubber cushion. Right now, two of the tables are being used as such and two for seating; with all four cushions in place, it becomes a large area for very casual lounging; with all cushions removed, it serves as a low table for drinks for up to eight guests sozzled enough to be sitting on the floor. A Saarinen couch and the classic Saarinen armchair with Versen floor lamp complete a charmed circle, a conversational grouping held together texturally and visually by the

Above: The kitchen's ultrasonic dishwasher uses inaudible hi-fi sound to eliminate manual washing. No soap, detergent or hot water are required in the three-minute washing and drying cycle. Left: unique kitchen stool constructed from rugged, contoured tractor seat.

The glass-domed oven in PLAYBOY'S kitchen is a rectangular modification of that by Frigidaire, shown above. The cooking "floor" of the unit is adjustable in height, can be lowered to accommodate the largest roasts, automatically rises to counter level when the dome is opened. It is radiantly heated, will roast, broil or barbecue with the luscious viands in tantalizing view. Joining it is the touch-cool induction heating stove, a solid surface on which cold foods may be prepared alongside bubbling pots. Because it's pots themselves that get hot, spilled foods can't stick to stove, which brings cold water to a boil in a matter of mere seconds.

deep-pile green nylon rug. And remember the foyer closet where we hung our things? We're now facing its living room side, a fourteen-foot wall faced with two-foot-square primavera panels, with flush-mounted color TV and built-in stereophonic speakers and hi-fi components behind them. This is our electronic entertainment installation. From it, lines go to individual speaker installations in every room, each with its own on-off and volume control. Here we can stack mood-music recordings on the automatic changer, or flood the apartment with music for dancing. Or, if the occasion calls for serious listening — to Bach or Baker — we switch to the manually-operated transcription turntable and pick up for the highest in fi. Here, too, are long- and short-wave tuners, FM tuner and tape recorder. Also, movie and stereo projectors that can throw pictures on a beaded screen which lines the back of the painting by the fireplace.

And speaking of entertainment, one of the hanging Knoll cabinets beneath the windows holds a built-in bar. This permits the canny bachelor to remain in the room while mixing a cool one for his intended quarry. No chance of missing the proper psychological moment — no chance of leaving her cozily curled up on the couch with her shoes off and returning to find her mind changed, purse in hand, and the young lady ready to go home, damn it. Here, conveniently at hand, too, is a self-timing rheostat which will gradually and subtly dim the lights to fit the mood — as opposed to the harsh click of a light switch that plunges all into sudden darkness and may send the fair game fleeing.

The same advance thinking prompted the placing of an on-off widget for the phone within the cabinet, too, so that the jangling bell
(continued on page 60)

KITCHEN

or, what's worse, a chatty call from the date of the night before, won't shatter the spell being woven. (Don't worry about missing out on any fun this way: there's a phone-message-taker hooked to the tape recorder.)

The PLAYBOY apartment brings back the dining room – done away with in many another modern apartment – but this is a dining room with multiple functions. For intimate dining *à deux* and in style, the four-leaf Mathesson gateleg table can have just one leaf raised. For less intimate occasions – say a midnight after-theater snack – the Shoji screens which close off the kitchen may be rolled back, and the kitchen's island counter becomes a cozy, handy spot to set up chafing dish and silver ice bucket in which nestles a bottle of Mumm's Gold Label.

For large formal dinners, the Mathesson table can be expanded to seat twelve, but for casual get-togethers or big informal parties it folds practically flat against a wall, where one leaf can be raised for cold or hot buffet.

It is when we wish to host a host of folks that the flexibility of the apartment's separate areas comes into full play. By moving aside the Saarinen chair, which acts as a psychological room divider between living and dining rooms, by rolling back the kitchen's Shoji screens and opening the terrace windows, all these areas become united and we can entertain half a hundred, if we're a mind. This is possible because the apartment is not divided into cell-like rooms, but into function areas well delineated for relaxation, dining, cooking, wooing and entertaining, all interacting and yet inviting individual as well as simultaneous use.

Consider again the dining room's multiple uses. Obviously, it's ideal for a full-production gala dinner, as no "dining alcove" is. Or, with its pull-down globe lighting, it's perfect for all-night poker games, stag or strip. Yet we've seen how simple it is to join it to the living room. Similarly, the kitchen may be closed off from the other rooms by pulling closed the sliding screens. But since the urban male prides himself on his culinary artistry it may, more often, be open onto the dining room, so the host can perform for an admiring audience while sharing in conversation.

Now let's review the areas we've seen, starting at the entry again. The hall is 4' x 14', closed off from the living room by the floor-to-ceiling storage wall. In addition to its clothes press, the hall side of this unit is partitioned to hold gear which no bachelor who takes pride in his home would want to lug through the house. Here are compartments with pegs and racks to hold skis, poles, waxing kit, rucksack. The floor of this space is linoleum tile. Adjoining is a ventilated, dehumidified cabinet for tennis rackets in presses, golf bag, bracket for trusty Evinrude, fishing gear. A vertical space has pegs for hanging the good things that come in leather cases: binoculars, stereo and reflex cameras, portable radio, guns. Other compartments hold wet weather and winter outer garments and footwear.

Starting from the end of the storage

wall and going around the dining room clockwise, we come first to the short 8-foot wall facing the terrace. This is walnut-panel veneer. Standing against it, on a low wrought-iron stand, is a garden-type parabolic planter with giant philodendron growing in it. The long adjacent wall – which measures roughly 20 feet – is smooth plaster, stark white, with high, 30-inch clerestory windows hung with blue drapes. Below them, serving as sideboard, are a grouping of Herman Miller storage cabinets in rosewood (No. 5520, $646). The window wall is approximately 14 feet long and consists of steel casements hung with translucent white dacron draw drapes, through which can be seen the weatherproof, metal, terrace furniture, all by Salterini.

Now we come to the kitchen wall. This consists of six Japanese-style Shoji screens, which can slide to completely close or completely open the kitchen. Frames are of elm, covering is translucent fiberglass. The Shojis are by Cal Craft of California.

Other dining room furniture is also elm: there are 8 dining chairs by Singer (No. 162, $122) upholstered in blue, and the Bruno Mathesson table already described. Two pull-down globular lighting fixtures provide even, ample light.

And now let's roll back those Shojis and enter the kitchen. Your first thought may be: where is everything? It's all there, as you shall see, but all is neatly stowed and designed for efficiency with the absolute mininum of fuss and hausfrau labor. For this is a bachelor kitchen, remember, and unless you're a very odd-ball bachelor indeed, you like to cook and whomp up short-order specialties to exactly the same degree that you actively dislike dishwashing, marketing and tidying up. All that's been taken care of here. Let's look it over.

Notice, first, that it's clean and functional, but doesn't have the antiseptic, medical look of so many modern kitchens. The walls are smooth gray, the floor of vinyl. Those hinged wood panels on the rear wall house a vertical freezer where you'll keep frozen fruits, vegetables, seafood, game, and plenty of meat. Even if your apartment's a haven for drop-in guests as well as planned pleasures, there's ample space here for weeks of good eating. Next to the freezer is a vertical wine bin, a honeycomb framework which holds the bottles horizontally. There's sufficient capacity here so you can exercise your canny skills in finding buys in, say, a special half case of rosé, a rich Burgundy that's on sale, or a few choice bottles of vintage Riesling – just right to go with your tossed-greens salad. Below the wine, which is stored hand height, are compartments for larger bottles, i.e., your stronger potations and *vin ordinaire*, which you order in bulk and pour as needed into decanters. Next come dry-storage shelves and a utility closet where your once-a-week servant stores brooms and vacuum.

The long wall around to the right is traversed for its full length by what looks like a doorless, blank-faced wall cabinet, with no way to get your hands on anything within. That's just what it is – it

houses counter-balanced storage shel[ves] that pull down to easy reach wh[en] needed.

And now we come to something you[´re] going to like: that standing white ca[bi-]net in the center of the wall is an ult[ra-]sonic dishwasher. Stack its rack w[ith] greasy dishes, with glasses that bear t[he] imprint of a lipsticky kiss, with eg[gy] knives and forks. Shut the door and [it] is bathed in water and bombarded [by] ultrasonic sound waves which remove [all] dirt. Next in the automatic dish-do[ing] cycle is warm-air drying and ultra-vio[let] sterilization. And now we're ready [to] put the dishes away – but we don't ha[ve] to. Relax. Light up. Talk to your g[irl.] Play a Stan Kenton recording. T[he] dishes stay right where they are, behi[nd] the panel, ready for their next use, si[nce] this machine also acts as a storage un[it.]

You'll notice a cantilevered wo[rk] counter runs the full length of the wa[ll] under the cabinets. It's clear except f[or] the foot-pedal sink – which need nev[er] be sullied by a dirty dish.

And now for the damndest isla[nd] counter you've ever seen. At one end [is] a radiant broiler-roaster. Here, und[er] the transparent dome, you can broil [a] four-inch sirloin or roast a pheasant [,] or a standing rib roast – to a turn, wi[th] all fumes drawn off and out of the hou[se] by a built-in blower which turns [on] when you turn on the heat. Lifting t[he] hinged dome automatically brings th[e] base of the unit to counter height. I[t's] our bet that the manipulation of th[e] broiler, and the sight through the dom[e] of a sizzling steak, will prove for yo[ur] guests a rival attraction to the best o[f] TV. And you'll be the director of th[e] show.

From the broiler on down the counte[r,] for about half its length, is a smoot[h] Carrara glass surface on which you ca[n] sit or lean – if you have no keys or coin[s] in your pockets or ring on your finge[r.] Because this, believe it or not, is you[r] stove, although there's not a burner i[n] sight and it's stone cold even when it[´s] on. That's because it heats only metall[ic] objects in its field, by induction; it's th[e] pots and pans that do the cooking, n[ot] the stove top and you can be mixing [a] cool salad right beside a hot pot of pot[a-]toes. Pilot lights beneath the transluc[ent] glass top wink on or off to show wha[t] cooks when you twiddle the dials on th[e] dashboard.

The rest of the counter is work surface[.] Because this is a cool, light kitchen, th[e] plant on it thrives.

Beneath the stove and work counte[r] is more storage space, hand-height uten[-] sil drawers and, down toward the vertic[al] freezer, a refrigerator to hold a few days[´] food, chilled mixers, beer and soft drinks[,] your pre-chilled Martini beaker and ver[-] mouth atomizer, canapés and cheeses[,] and an ample supply of ice cubes.

For further information on any aspec[t] of the PLAYBOY *penthouse apartment[,] write Playboy Reader Service, 11 E[.] Superior Street, Chicago 11, Illinois.*

NEXT MONTH:
THE BEDROOM, STUDY
AND BATH.

A MAN'S HOME is not only his castle, it is or should be, the outward reflection of his inner self — a comfortable, livable, and yet exciting expression of the person he is and the life he leads. But the overwhelming percentage of homes are furnished by women. What of the bachelor and his need for a place to call his own? Here's the answer, PLAYBOY's penthouse apartment, home for a sophisticated man of parts, a fit setting for his full life and a compliment to his guests of both sexes. Here a man, perhaps like you, can live in masculine elegance.

At first glance, it obviously looks like a hell of a fine place to live and love and be merry, a place to relax in alone or to share for intimate hours with some lucky lass, a wonderful setting for big or small parties — in short, a bachelor's dream place. It is all these, but it's more, too — thanks to the fact that it doesn't follow the conventional plan of separated rooms for various purposes. Instead, there are two basic areas, an active zone for fun and partying and a quiet zone for relaxation, sleep and such.

The living room, with its cozy shadow-box fireplace suggests a tête-à-tête on the couch — but it's just as inviting to a cordial crowd of fellow hi-fi enthusiasts. The electronic entertainment center, re-

BEDROOM

cessed in the giant storage wall that separates living room from foyer, contains binaural hi-fi, FM, TV, tape recorder, movie and slide projectors. And merely moving that blue Saarinen armchair makes living room and dining room one — for gala entertaining. Kitchen and dining room, too, may be used separately or together, thanks to the sliding Shoji screens which divide them. These areas comprise the apartment's active zone, which was described in detail last month.

A huge bed dominates the penthouse bedroom. This is a magnificent sleeping platform of veneer plywood on steel legs, 8 feet long and $4\frac{1}{2}$ feet wide. The 4" airfoam mattress stops short enough of the foot so that the platform's end serves as a bench on which to slouch while donning or doffing shoes and socks.

Casement windows stretch across one entire wall, framing an ever-changing, living mural of our man's city. In the corner nook formed by windows and the Modernfold door which closes off the study, is a charmed circle where a bachelor may have a romantic nightcap with

Above: Hidden by the brick wall in the illustration at left, the bedroom includes wall-hung, clear maple cabinets (Knoll #121, $249) with white lacquer innards fitted out as a bar. Below: Laminated walnut chair designed by Eames, made by Miller (LCW, $58) is part of the bedroom's lounge-area furniture grouping.

Below: Classic Noguchi table built by Miller (#50 IN, $350) has thick, clear glass top resting on black lacquer legs, is nucleus of bedroom lounge area. It is sturdy and, of course, alcohol proof.

Custom headboard-storage unit creates a dressing area.

a chosen guest. Grouped here are a Saarinen chair (the mate of the one in the living room), a walnut Eames chair and free-form Noguchi table. Across from you (but hidden in the illustration by the brick wall) is a hanging wall cabinet wherein is cannily concealed a built-in bar and small refrigerator, just large enough for ice cubes, mixers and mid-night snacks — a boon to the barefoot bachelor in PJs who's reluctant to trek to the kitchen for his good-night potation, or perhaps unwilling to interrupt the dulcet dialogue he's been sharing.

Now, we've sipped the nocturnal dram and it is bed time; having said "nighty-night" (or "come along, now, dearest") to the last guest, it's time to sink into

BATHROOM

the arms of Morpheus (or a more comely substitute). Do we go through the house turning out the lights and locking up? No sir: flopping on the luxurious bed, we have within easy reach the multiple controls of its unique headboard. Here we have silent mercury switches and a rheostat that control every light in the place and can subtly dim the bedroom lighting to just the right romantic level. Here, too, are the switches which control the circuits for front door and terrace window locks. Beside them are push buttons to draw the continuous, heavy, pure-linen, lined draperies on sail track,

which can insure darkness at morn — or noon. Above are built-in speakers fed by the remotely-controlled hi-fi and radio based in the electronic entertainment installation in the living room. On either side of the bed are storage cupboards with doors that hinge downward to create bedside tables. Within are telephone, with on-off switch for the bell, and miscellaneous bed-time items. Soft mood music flows through the room and the stars shine in the casements as you snuggle down.

• • •

At the start of a new day, the chime

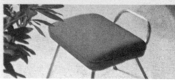

Top left: By all odds your chair of chairs will be this contour lounge set by Herman Miller (chair #670, footstool #671, $605 for both) which will hold you in free-floating luxury. Lower left: Knoll cabinets line the study's window wall; shown in walnut, available in other woods; in 4 and 6 foot lengths (#542, $264; #541, $381). Top right: Close-up look at texture of continuous carpet used in bedroom and study—a tweedy, wool-rayon mixture. Lower right: Desk is one of Knoll's #1500 series which offers 12 different pedestal arrangements, ranges from $450 to $550; the upholstered swivel chair is by Knoll (#71 S, $177).

STUDY

alarm sounds, morning music comes on and the headboard's automatic controls again prove their value: reaching lazily to the control panel, you press the buttons for the kitchen circuits and immediately the raw bacon, eggs, bread and ground coffee you did the right things with the night before (while the ultrasonic washer was doing the dishes) start their metamorphosis into crisp bacon, eggs fried just right, and steaming-hot fresh java. Now you flip the switch that draws the curtains and opens the terrace doors to let in the brisk morning air. Don't just lie there, man, rise and shine!

Just off the bedroom is the bath; you shave and shower and as you towel off you go back to the bedroom, but now you stay in the dressing area, behind the bed's seven-foot-tall headboard, which affords complete privacy and access to the bath without requiring you to cross any part of the bedroom proper — a blessing to the bachelor whose hospitality extends to a planned or impromptu overnight guest. On this side the unit is equipped with sliding doors (one of them mirrored) behind which are dustproof trays for haberdashery, a rotating tie rack and, below, a boot locker with a hand-height, suspended row of lever-operated shoe trees. The locker's hinged door, when open, forms a bench. Here, too, is the cedar-lined built-in blanket chest and, above it, storage shelves for linen. Opposite is an entire closet wall with separate compartments for winter wear, summer wear, sports clothes, dress clothes, and a guest closet with lighted, built-in vanity. The closet at the bathroom end of the wall is warm-air dried and has brass fixtures for hanging huge turkish towels and terry-cloth robes; the one at the opposite end has sliding shelves of cedar for flat-lying sweaters and knit T-shirts. Mirrors on the insides of the two center doors, which open in opposite directions, combine with the one on the head-board unit to form a three-way mirror.

The out-size bathroom is as practical as the more usual two-bath arrangement and carries out the apartment's feeling of spaciousness. The room actually comprises two areas, separated by a sliding screen of translucent glass, so that the one adjoining the bedroom can be completely private while the other remains accessible from the apartment's active zone. Suppose early guests arrive before their host is quite ready for them: with the sliding screen closed he can shower and dress undisturbed while they freshen up on the other side. The lavatory itself is completely enclosed, ensuring total privacy. In addition to the john, it has a bidet, magazine rack, ash tray and telephone. (Let's face it, there are bachelors, as well as some of their guests, who like to spend quite a lot of time in the throne room — maybe as a hangover from younger days of living at home, when it was the only place to get away from it all — hence we've made this posh head a comfort station in every sense of the phrase.)

The bathroom impresses with its size and colorfulness. With the screen rolled back, there's a continuous counter with two wash basins (one on either side of the screen) with backlighted mirror above. A row of compartmented drawers below, whose handles are towel racks, hold the potions, lotions, notions, sundries and other mysteries which ordinarily crown conventional medicine chests. One entire wall is decorated with bold and vigorous primitive paintings reminiscent of the prehistoric drawings in the caves of Lascaux. In the corner is a huge, rectangular, recessed tub which serves as the floor of the shower. The shower head — and the pipes leading to it — are concealed in massed foilage growing on both sides of the picture-window pane which divides this end of the bath from the dressing area of the bedroom. What with the cave paintings and the wall of greenery from which the spray descends, you may feel as though you're bathing under a waterfall in an exotic outdoor setting — an impression you can enhance if it strikes your fancy by turning on the sun lamps recessed into the ceiling. (Stravinsky's *Le Sacre du Printemps* — or the Chico Hamilton Quartet — tuned in loud on the bathroom hi-fi speaker will accentuate the mood.) For more serious sun bathing we've a Knoll slat bench with recessed sun lamps in the ceiling above it — provided with a foam-rubber mat covered in waterproof Naugahyde, it is a handy place to stretch out and luxuriate in a tropical glow all the year 'round.

• • •

Even a bachelor in his own domain needs a place like our apartment's study, where he can get away from the rest of the house and be really alone, where if he wishes he can leave papers on the desk in seeming disarray (actually in that precious disorder in which he alone can lay hands on just what he wants). This is the sanctum sanctorum, where women are seldom invited, where we can work or read or just sit and think while gazing into the fireplace.

Continuous storage cabinets range the full length of the study's window wall, providing ample storage for typewriter, dictaphone, stationery, office supplies, and hobby gear or scale-model collection. Imposingly jutting from these is the man-size desk, with comfortable swivel chair by Knoll (#71S, $177). On the other side of the desk is an easy chair (Miller #5484, $350). Here on special occasions you will seat the business guest with whom you want to work in your own surroundings and undisturbed — or as a rare exception, the admiring lass whose fond gaze makes poring over your papers more enjoyable.

Flanking the fireplace is an occasional table to hold pipes, humidor, books and magazines; and an enormously comfortable upholstered, contoured Herman Miller armchair with foot stool, a lord-of-the-domain chair reserved for you alone, which holds all of you evenly supported in the right places and fits in with your relaxed posture so that you and the chair are like twin spoons nested together. On the other side of the fireplace is a globe of the world, lit from within, craftily pinpricked so that major cities shine out as flecks of brightness.

The entire third wall is bookcase, floor to ceiling. The two bottom shelves are wide and deep enough to hold record albums, stamp albums, your biggest picture books and encyclopedias. The rest of the bookcase, on up, is shelves of normal width and depth, except that there is a space 20 inches high between the wide and narrow shelves, tube-lighted, providing a surface on which to lay open a dictionary or an atlas. At either end of this bookcase wall are binaural hi-fi speakers which connect with the sound equipment in the foyer wall. With a study like this, even the most dedicated pub crawler or theatre and nightclub buff will be tempted to stay at home of an evening, content within his own surroundings and savoring the city's glamour via the enchanted view from the window wall. But suppose the playboy master of the house decides that now, with the winter season starting, he wants to hold a real big shindig. By folding back that accordion door between study and bedroom the two are merged into one magnificent room, with the continuous carpeting from end to end and the matched draperies tying it all together. Now the whole apartment's a grownup's playground for rollicking, fancy-free fun 'til dawn lights the windows and it's time for prairie oysters and breakfast.

• • •

Throughout the apartment, its strikingly different atmosphere is achieved by the bold though harmonious use of solid color and interesting texture. Entering the bedroom from the living room we are immediately aware of the textural difference between the living room's cork floor and the luxurious wall-to-wall carpeting of the bedroom, which seems to invite a barefoot romp but which also bespeaks rich smartness. The dramatic brick wall between living room and bath projects into the quiet area, establishing visual continuity between the apartment's two zones and providing a sight barrier between the living room and the sleeping area of the bedroom, just as the headboard unit visually separates sleeping and dressing. Lighting — ample and glareless — is provided by those conical fixtures called "top hats," which are recessed into the ceiling at strategic locations. Lamps, which would impede the clean, open look of the place, are virtually dispensed with; there is a complete absence of bric-a-brac, patterned fabrics, pleats and ruffles.

• • •

This is the kind of pre-planning in design and furnishing which makes PLAYBOY's penthouse apartment a bachelor haven of virile good looks, a place styled for a man of taste and sophistication. This is *his* place, to fit his moods, suit his needs, reflect his personality.

For further information on any aspect of the PLAYBOY penthouse apartment, write Playboy Reader Service, 11 E. Superior Street, Chicago 11, Illinois.

Cadet Quarters, U.S. Air Force Academy,
Colorado Springs, Colorado
1958
SKIDMORE, OWINGS & MERRILL
ARCHITECTS

WALTER NORMAN TEAGUE ASSOCIATES,
INTERIOR DESIGNERS.

text by
JOHN LINDELL and JOEL SANDERS

View of Vandenberg Hall

View of Dormitory Hallway

View of Living Space

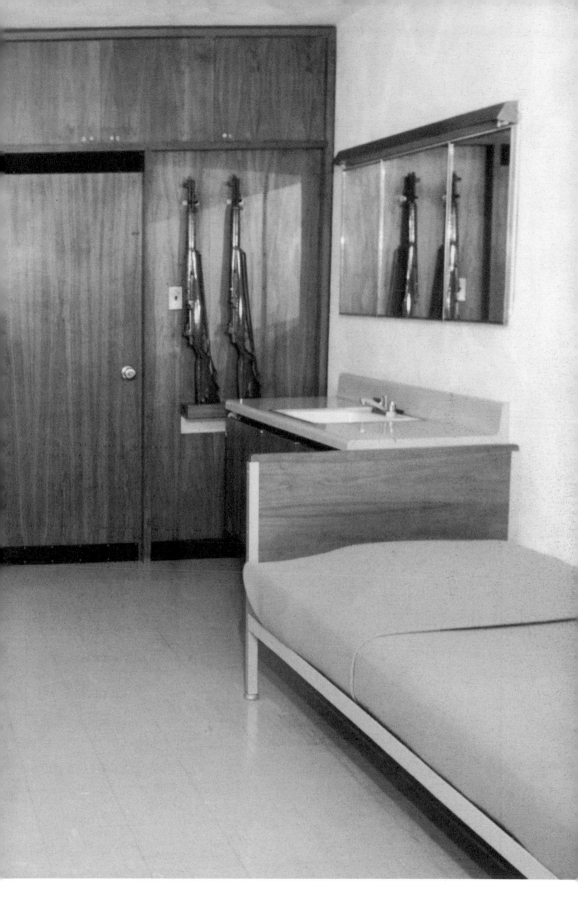

"BRING ME MEN"

MOTTO AT THE AIR FORCE ACADEMY ENTRY

The words "Bring Me Men" are incised in stone above the entrance ramp of Skidmore, Owings & Merrill's Air Force Academy. The inscription engendered a controversy when women were first admitted to this all-male academic institution; should the slogan remain or be removed? The decision of the female cadets to retain the motto demonstrates their recognition of the Academy as a site dedicated to the production of masculine subjects, irrespective of the soldier's biological sex. Within the campus, females as well as males train to become "men."

It comes as no surprise that the military would enlist architecture to shape and impart the masculine traits necessary to transform cadets into officers. Quite unexpected, however, was the military's decision in 1954 to deploy the language of modern architecture to achieve its goal.[1] The spirit of freedom associated with modernism's formal trademarks—spatial continuity and visual transparency—at first seemed antithetical to military values traditionally represented in classical styles. SOM's version of European modernism, refined in their commercial designs for American corporations, provided the appropriate medium for creating militaristic spaces of discipline and control.

From the disposition of buildings on the site to the layout of custom-designed aluminum framed furniture within the dorm rooms, SOM's campus plan depends on the quintessential modernist instrument—the grid. But unlike the prototypical modernist open plan, where Cartesian coordinates provide the framework within which forms dynamically shift and slide, at the Academy the grid regulates the articulation and static placement of every architectural element. In short, the grid serves as an architectural manifestation of the order and regimentation the cadets are subject to during their four-year stay. According to the project architect, Walter Netsch, the project's governing modules (28", 14", 3'-6", and 1'-9") derive from the 7'-0" dimension of a cadet's bed—the scale of the receptacle of the male body at rest. However, in the hands of SOM, the grid accomplishes more than simply insuring an image of regularity and control; exceeding the architects' intentions, it determines not only the organization of spaces but the movement of bodies within them. The scale of 1'-9" (a subdivision of 7'-0") stone pavers laid in a grid corresponds to the average shoulder width of a cadet. While designed by the architects to offer visual relief from the monotony of the vast plaza that organizes the campus, this geometric paving pattern has become institutionalized by the cadets, who now use it to mark the exterior pathways freshmen must adhere to when marching between buildings. Preventing direct diagonal movements, its formal structure enforces a rigid choreography of straight walks and 90-degree turns.

1 Impressed by the new university campus at Mexico City and Edward Durrell Stone's Hotel El Panama, Lieutenant General Hubert R. Harmon, in charge of planning for the Air Force Academy, was the first to suggest the viability of modernism for the new Academy's design. The Air Force ultimately awarded Skidmore, Owings & Merrill the commission in July 1954 after reviewing the qualifications of a number of large corporate applicants including Eero Saarinen, Pietro Beluschi, and Harrison and Abramowitz. However, after SOM presented their preliminary design to members of Congress and to the press, a public controversy erupted with regard to the appropriateness of the modernist language for representing this American institution. FOR A DETAILED ACCOUNT OF THE ARCHITECTURAL SELECTION PROCESS SEE KRISTEN SCHAFFER, "CREATING A NATIONAL MONUMENT," IN *MODERNISM AT MID-CENTURY: THE ARCHITECTURE OF THE AIR FORCE ACADEMY*, ED. ROBERT BRUEGMANN (CHICAGO: UNIVERSITY OF CHICAGO PRESS, 1994) PP. 16-54.

View of Closet

"WE WILL NOT LIE OR CHEAT NOR TOLERATE ANYONE AMONGST US WHO DOES"

The ground plane engenders virile behavior in other ways at the Air Force Academy. The collection of campus structures rests on an immense podium set against, and nearly indifferent to, its Rocky Mountain backdrop. This man-made base creates a relentless horizontal datum affording limitless views of the uninterrupted desert horizon framed between buildings. The plinth's excessive scale, panoramic views, and topographic indifference embodies in an exaggerated manner the Western conception of architecture as a vehicle for mankind's supremacy over nature. But if the campus's ground plane presents a legible world of truth and order against its immaculate surface, this membrane also functions as a mask. The Academy's "fifth facade" hides the underside of masculinity; a vast network of underground tunnels hidden by the plinth shelter unauthorized "spirit" activities—"unbecoming" conduct that the military recognizes as essential for the production of men.[2]

Moving from exterior to interior, horizontal to vertical, Vandenberg Hall (1958) also employs surfaces that both reveal and conceal. Dark stained wood paneling lines the dormitory corridors, evoking the ambiance of a corporate men's club. Within each room, shared by two cadets, the same wall treatment forms the discrete doors of built-in drawers, cabinets, and closets. However, unlike conventional domestic settings where closets function to hide their contents from view, these are meant to be opened. During daily inspections they reveal custom-designed uniforms by Hollywood director and designer Cecil B. DeMille placed in precise arrangements dictated by military protocol. Drawers contain underwear, socks, and shirts carefully folded around cardboard to prominently display logos and insignias. Shoes are stored in neat rows on a two-tiered shelf and their laces are hidden from view. Demonstrating how the wall dressings that shape a building work analogously to the clothes that outfit a body, these uniforms, when seen framed within closets and drawers, reinforce the image of masculine regimentation, hierarchy, and control symbolized by the outfits themselves.

However, the clothes the cadets actually wear on a regular basis are stored not in these wardrobes but in cardboard boxes in small cupboards above the closets and in a vanity that houses the sink.[3] It is tacitly understood that these storage areas will be overlooked during inspection. Unbeknownst to their designer, Walter Dorwin Teague, the carefully designed dorm room wardrobes inculcate the unspoken but essential masculine values of the military: appearance and duplicity.

"DON'T ASK, DON'T TELL, DON'T PURSUE"

2 BOYLE: You may not want this in the book but were there any kind of elements that made spirit missions (cadet activities that aren't supposed to happen but do) especially possible? **HOSMER:** Oh, the tunnels. The tunnels.... I was more interested in how you keep cadets out of the tunnels than how you get into them. **BOYLE:** That probably wasn't an easy job. **HOSMER:** No, it was impossible. You couldn't keep cadets out of the tunnels. (EXCERPT FROM AN INTERVIEW WITH LIEUTENANT BRADLEY HOSMER CONDUCTED BY ACADEMY ARCHITECT DUANE BOYLE PUBLISHED IN *MODERNISM AT MID-CENTURY*, P.194)

3 Plumbing in the cadet rooms includes only a sink; SOM's original scheme to outfit pairs of rooms with private bathrooms was rejected in favor of making cadets travel to ganged bathrooms located at the corner of each dormitory floor. This alternative represented a compromise between the architects' design and the military planner's intention of duplicating the facilities at West Point, where a common bathroom is located in the basement.

Cadets at Desk

A to Z
Domestic Prototypes

ANDREA ZITTEL

REFERENCE
INTRO, PAGE 16

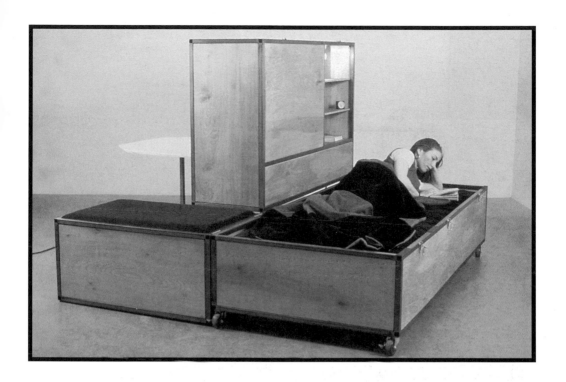

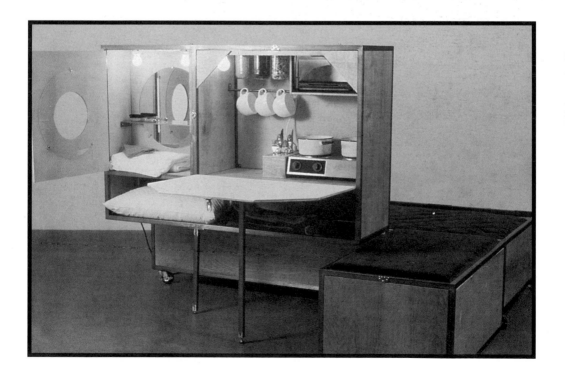

A to Z Living Unit
[1994]
Steel, wood, metal, mattress,
glass, mirror, lighting fixture,
stove, oven, green velvet
3 Views

Prototype for Processing unit
[1993]
Wood, metal, plexiglass, black vinyl,
A to Z Food Group sample, lighting
fixture, porcelain dishes, silverware
2 Views

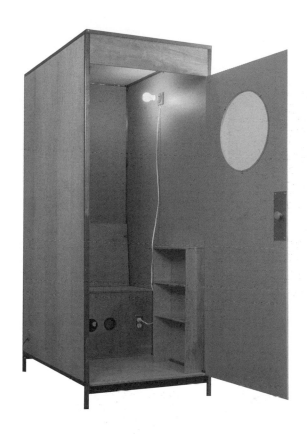

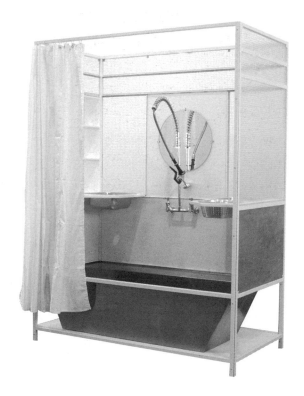

Prototype Warm Chamber
[1993]
Wood, steel, paint, heater,
and light

Prototype Cleansing Chamber
[1993]
Glass, wood, steel, paint, cotton
curtain

Carpet Furniture:
Drop Leaf Table
[1993]
Silk and wool dye
on wool carpet

Carpet Furniture: Dining Room Table
with Extra Seating & Carpet Furniture:
Couch with End Table (set of two)
[1993]
Silk and wool dye on acrylic carpet

**Prototype Designated
Dining Table**
[1993]
Wood, steel, paint, silver
plated copper

Chamber pot
[1993]
Spun aluminum

A to Z Food Group
[1993]
Rice, oats, couscous, chick peas, black beans, pinto
beans, broccoli, spinach, onions, mushrooms, bell
pepper, carrots, sunflower seeds, pumpkin seeds

Adjustable Wall
Bras,
1990-1991
VITO ACCONCI

An edition of six bras for the wall. This is a bra that is worn by a wall; the bra is the height of a conventional wall, and is made like a wall, skinned with a metal lathe and covered with a rough coat of plaster.

The bra is a multi-functional fixture for the home; it functions as lighting, audio-speakers, and furniture. From inside each cup, light spills out past the uneven plaster edges and through the metal lathe, onto the wall around it and into the room. The bra has its own sound: input from conventional sound-sources—radio, stereo system, television—is heard against the sound of heavy breathing that pans from cup to cup. Inside each cup a canvas backing, like the lining of a bra, forms a sling seat.

The bra serves as a wall-fixture or a room divider; the cups are hinged so that the bra can be adjusted to different positions relative to the wall—lines of cable act as shoulder straps that tie the bra to floor and ceiling, supporting the bra in its various configurations.

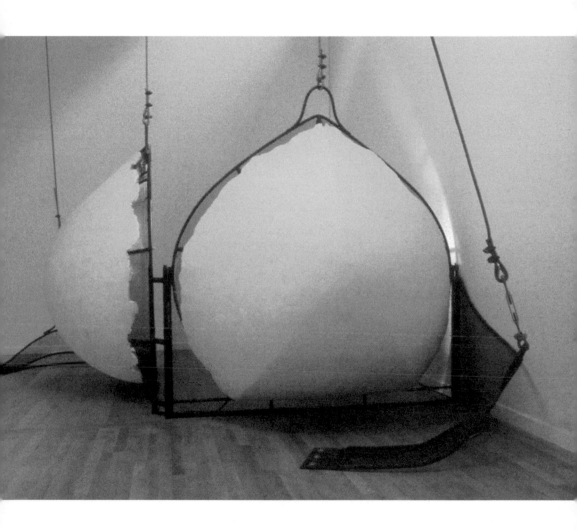

Adjustable Wall Bra
[1990]
steel lathe, plaster, cable, lights, audio
Corner Enclosure

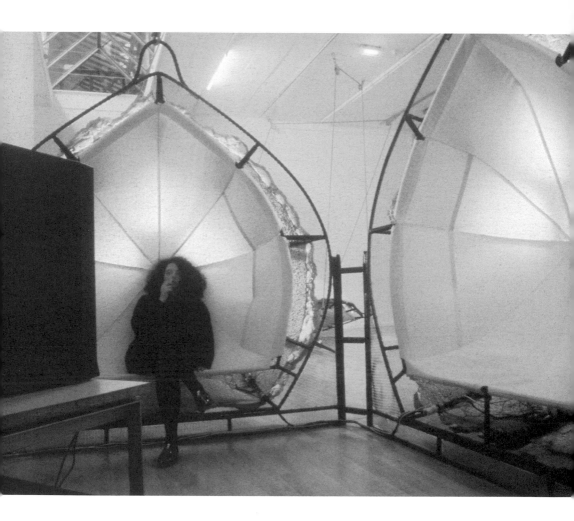

Double Chair

Lean-to Shelter

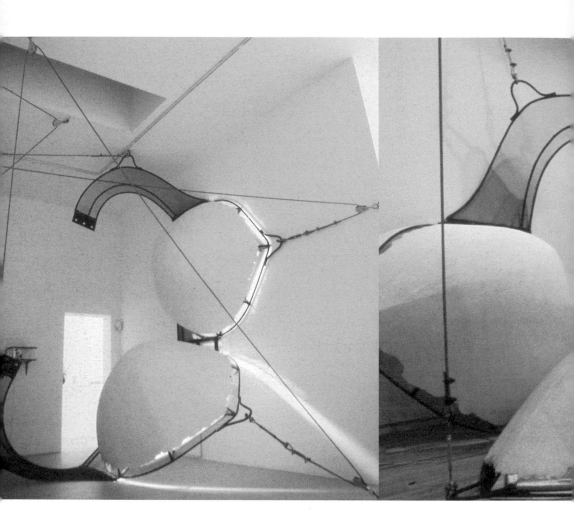

Room Divider

View of Installation

Tupperware

GEORGE

STOLL

REFERENCE
INTRO. PAGE 21

Untitled
[1995]
Beeswax, paraffin,
pigment

Untitled
[1995]
Beeswax, paraffin,
pigment

Untitled
[1995]
Beeswax, paraffin,
pigment

Untitled
(1995)
Beeswax, paraffin,
pigment

Untitled
[1995]
Beeswax, paraffin,
pigment

Collecting Well is the
Best Revenge:
**Commemorative Toile
Fabric, 1995**
RENÉE GREEN

FROM THE DOCUMENTS

"In 1565 in negotiations in Rouen and Dieppe it is imagined that Africans can be transported from the coast of Africa to the Americas for the exploitation of land. This trade possibility is publicly presented in 1592.

The ministry wishes the French navy and French commerce, in rivalry with Holland, to develop colonies and the Africans are in their eyes excellent instruments for work, the traffic in human merchandise being a possible source for serious benefits. They are in favor of this, thus in 1666 an action is passed by Parliament to buy and trade the Africans.

In 1684 the West Indies Company (Compagnie des Indes occidentales) was formed to conduct all of the commerce in the islands and in the Americas." HENRY-RENÉ ALLEMAGNE, *LA TOILE ET LES INDIENNES DE TRAITE*, (1942), P. 147; TRANS. RENÉE GREEN.

"The most beautiful of these fabrics, which the Indians termed *chittes* and the French merchants described as *perses*, were pro-

duced at Patna, at Seronge, at Tuticorin, at Madras, Negapatam, Palkot, and Sadraspatman.

From here they were shipped on the vessels of the Compagnie des Indes or sent by the Persian Gulf and carried over the caravan routes of Ispaham, Baghdad, and Asiatic Turkey. The gay colors, the striking decorative quality, and the exotic character of these delicate cotton prints created a furor. It was about the year 1658 when they first appeared at the Fair of Saint-Germain .... From this time on they were used as furniture covering and draperies; rooms were hung with them and they were fashioned also into dressing gowns. On every side there was such a demand for *Surates*, *Patnas*, and *Calancas* that the material became scarce and expensive. Some artisans, therefore, conceived the idea of copying the imported fabrics according to the process brought back by travelers in the Orient, and thus the native industry of French *indiennes* was created." HENRI CLOUZOT, *FROM PAINTED AND PRINTED FABRICS, THE HISTORY OF THE MANUFACTORY AT JOUY AND OTHER ATELIERS IN FRANCE 1760-1815* (1927), P.2.

PREVIOUS PAGE
Mise en Scène
[1991-1992]

ABOVE *Mise en Scène II:
Commemorative Toile*
Chair [1992]

Edict of 26 October 1686: "Manufacturers of silk, velvet, drapery, tapestry, haberdashery, trimming, etc., declared themselves ruined, because of the popularity of the *indiennes*. The Edict ordered the destruction of all blocks used in printing, prohibited the sale after 1 December 1687 of all printed cottons, whether Indian importations or French copies, and ordained that any such found in the shops be burned and the merchants fined 3,000 livres." IBID., P.4.

"An attempt to control Parisians and provincials was made by the issuance of more than thirty decrees from 1686 to 1750. Guards at the gates of the city disrobed delinquents; in a single day eight or nine hundred dresses were seized and burned in the streets, while women merely appearing at their windows dressed in contraband material were sentenced. *Jurés* of the weavers and silk manufacturers entered houses to seize the furniture. An edict of 1717 even threatened with the galleys persons found to have introduced contraband goods or to have given refuge to smugglers....Forbidden to display their costumes at the play or at the Tuileries, the *élégantes* wore them at their country houses. Madame de Pompadour furnished with *indiennes* an entire apartment at Bellevue, and the wives of the commissioners entrusted with the execution of the edicts were the first to parade their printed cottons. The total value of printed fabrics produced illegally or smuggled from abroad amounted in a single year to the incredible sum of sixteen million francs!

The question became a national one. The ministers, who in apartments furnished with imported prints deliberated on the wisdom of continuing prohibitive measures, at length decided to yield. November 9, 1759, all restrictions were officially removed. Factories opened everywhere in France. The passion for *indiennes*, developed under the prohibitive edicts, was so deeply rooted that, strange as it may seem, they retained their popularity despite the ease with which they could be obtained." IBID., P.6.

"Textiles to pay for slaves became so important...that in 1780 Nantes had more than 10 textile mills, employing 4,500 workers." MARLISE SIMONS, "NANTES JOURNAL: 'UNHAPPILY, A PORT CONFRONTS ITS PAST: SLAVE TRADE'," THE NEW YORK TIMES (17 DECEMBER 1993).

Mise en Scène II:
Commemorative Toile
Armchair [1992]

She is in the toile. Another
scene in the floating narrative. She wears a nun's
habit and her skin is dark as well. She sits on a stone
bench in a garden. A young Frenchman stands nearby looking cultivated and distressed. A slightly sinis-
ter-looking old woman appears in the background and
further in the distance is a monastery.

She is Ourika, as depict-
ed by Clara de Duras in a novel of the same name.
At the end of the novel Ourika dies in the monastery
to which she has banished herself because she
cannot fit into eighteenth-century aristocratic society. There was a "true" story of a black child
brought from Senegal just before the Revolution by
the chevalier of Boufflers and who had been raised
by his aunt, the princess of Beauvau, along with her
two orphaned grandsons. That formed the seed for
what became in 1824 a best-seller.

Those who are not famil-
iar with the story can still enjoy a familiarly styled
toile surface of intertwining floral vines on their
upholstery, which on closer viewing reveals in its
gaps a "strange fruit."

Mise en Scène:
Commemorative Toile
Detail [1991-1992]

end

Villa in Floirac, 1995

OFFICE for METROPOLITAN ARCHITECTURE

REM KOOLHAAS, JULIEN MONFORD, JEROEN THOMAS, YO YAMAGATA

A couple lived in a very old house in Bordeaux. Eight years ago, they wanted a new house, maybe, a very *simple* house.

They were looking at different architects.

Then the husband had a car accident. He almost died, but he survived. Now he needs a wheelchair.

Two years ago, the couple began to think about the house again. Now the new house could liberate the husband from the prison that their old house and the medieval city had become.

"Contrary to what you would expect," he told the architect, "I do not want a simple house. I want a complex house, because the house will define my world." They bought a mountain with a panoramic view over the city.

The architect proposed a house—or actually, three houses on top of each other. The lowest one was cave-like—a series of caverns carved out from the hill for the most intimate life of the family.

The highest house was divided into a house for the couple and a house for their children.

The most important house was almost invisible, sandwiched in between: a glass house—half inside, half outside—for living.

The man had his own "room" or, rather, "station"—a lift, 3 by 3.5 m., that moved freely between the three houses, changing plan and performance when it "locked" into one of the floors or floated above. A single "wall" intersected each house, next to the elevator. It contained everything the husband might need—books, artwork and, in the cellar, wine...

The movement of the elevator continually changed the architecture of the house. A machine was its heart.

View of Lift and Storage Wall
Exterior View

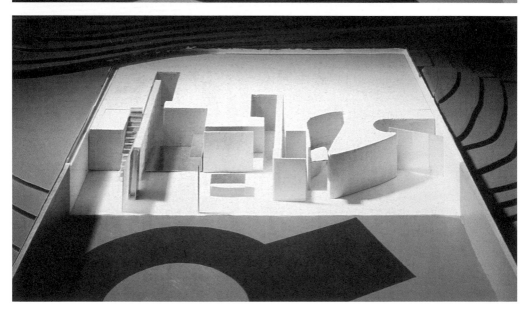

Model:
Third Level
Second Level
First Level

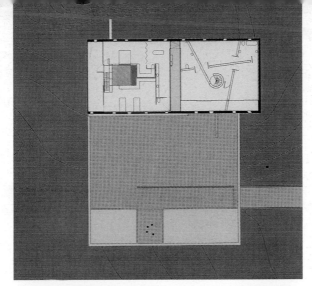

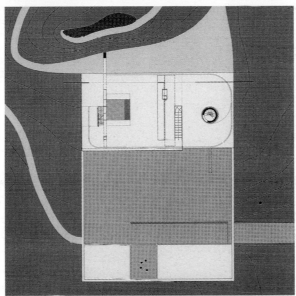

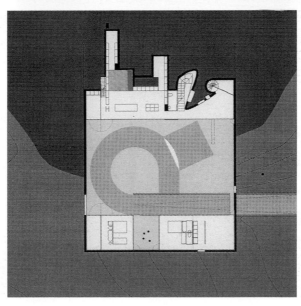

Plan:
Third Level
Second Level
First Level

View from Level 2
The Lift

ESSAY BY

DIANA FUSS and JOEL SANDERS

WORK BY

JOHN LINDELL

Berggasse 19: Inside Freud's Office
DIANA FUSS and JOEL SANDERS

In May of 1938, on the eve of Sigmund Freud's expulsion from Vienna and flight to London, Freud's colleague August Aichhorn met with the photojournalist Edmund Engelman at the Café Museum on the Karlsplatz in Vienna to make a proposal. Would it be possible, Aichhorn wondered, to take photographs of Freud's office and apartment without drawing the attention of the Gestapo who, since Hitler's annexation of Austria two months earlier, had been keeping the home of one of Vienna's most famous Jewish intellectuals under constant surveillance? The purpose of this photographic documentary was to provide an inventory of Berggasse 19 so exact that, as Aichhorn envisioned it, the home of psychoanalysis might be painstakingly recreated as a museum after the impending war.[1] Engelman, a mechanical and electrical engineer who ran a local photography shop on the Karntnerstrasse, agreed to try to provide a pictorial record of Berggasse 19. In the course of four days and using two cameras (a Rolleiflex and a Leica), two lenses (a 50mm lens and a 28mm wide-angle lens), and a light meter, and working without the aid of either flashes or floodlights, Engelman took approximately one hundred shots of Berggasse 19, focusing on the consulting room, study, and family living quarters.[2] These photographs, together with a short film segment of Freud's office taken by Marie Bonaparte in December 1937, provide the only extant visual record of the place where, for forty-seven years, Freud treated his patients, met regularly with his colleagues, and wrote his scientific papers and case histories.

Freud's biographers have written eloquently of his traumatic expulsion from his home in Vienna; cultural historians have studied in fascinating detail the peculiarities of Freud's domestic arrangements and the routine of his office schedule; psychoanalysts have analyzed at length the procedures of Freud's clinical practice; and art historians have recently begun to examine the meaning of Freud's extensive collection of antiquities and the links between psychoanalysis and archaeology. But we have yet to consider the significance of the site that housed these practices and objects. We have yet to fully enter, in other words, Berggasse 19. How might the spatial configuration of Freud's office, and the arrangement of furniture and objects within it, frame our understanding of psychoanalytic theory and practice? What might an architectural study of Berggasse 19 tell us about the play of vision, power, gender, and transference that structures the analytic scene?

Taking as its point of departure Engelman's black-and-white photographs, as well as our own architectural drawings gathered from site visits to Freud's offices in London and Vienna, this project traverses the porous boundary between the two-dimensional space of photography and the three-dimensional space of architecture. The convergence of

1 See Edmund Engelman, "A Memoir," which follows the published English-language version of the photographs, *Berggasse 19: Sigmund Freud's Home and Offices, Vienna 1938* (New York: Basic Books, 1976), p. 134. Rita Ransohoff's photographic captions visually orient the reader, while Peter Gay's preface to the volume, "Freud: For the Marble Tablet," provides an eloquent historical and biographical introduction. Readers might also wish to consult the more recent German edition of Engelman's photographs, *Sigmund Freud: Wien IX. Berggasse 19* (Vienna: Verlag Christian Brandstätter, 1993), which includes an introduction by Inge Scholz-Strasser, General Secretary of the Freud Haus.

2 Edmund Engelman, interview by the authors, 14 September 1995. Of these 100 photographs, 56 have been published in the English-language version of *Berggasse 19*, regrettably now out of print.

these two languages of space reflects the tensions that inform not only this essay but what it seeks to read, highlighting the confusion of surface and depth, inside and outside, subjects and objects, that characterize psychoanalysis's own primal scene. Until recently, questions of spectatorship have been theorized largely in terms of a subject's perception of a two-dimensional image (photography, film, television).[3] This essay explores the role of vision in three-dimensional space, examining how architecture organizes the physical and visual interaction of bodies as they move through the interior of Freud's professional office. Architecture and psychoanalysis come together here in a reading of the interior, for both are cultural discourses of the seen and the unseen, the visible and the invisible—of public and private space.

This collaborative project is impelled by a powerful fantasy, the same fantasy that drives Engelman's photographs— namely, the illusion that one can relive the experience of early psychoanalysis by retracing the footsteps of Freud's patients. But the space of Freud's office is a fundamentally irrecuperable one. The photographs of Berggasse 19, originally taken for the postwar construction of a Freud museum, have themselves become the museum—miniature sites of preservation and display. Today visitors to the consulting room and study in Berggasse 19 will find a space emptied of Freud's possessions (currently housed in the Freud Museum in London) but encompassed with enlargements of Engelman's photographs displayed on the walls. This highly unusual mode of museum exhibition insists on the mediating function of the photographs, while preserving the empty rooms of the office as a space of exile and absence: the place Freud was finally forced to flee at the end of his life "to die in freedom."[4] To the extent that our own research project is an attempt at recovery, at reconstituting from the fragments of history what has been buried and lost, our reading of Berggasse 19 is inevitably a work of mourning, framed by the same logic of memorialization that, we will argue in what follows, so pervasively organized the space of Freud's office.

I.   Engelman's photodocumentary opens with three exterior shots of Berggasse 19, motivated, as he was later to write, by a presentiment that the building itself would be destroyed in the war.[5] The façade of this typical late 19th-century Viennese apartment house comes into focus through a progressive sequence of long, medium, and closeup shots of the entry door. Exerting a kind of centrifugal force, the swastika placed over the door of Berggasse 19 by the building's Aryan owner pulls the camera in, gradually focussing and delimiting the social boundaries of the photodocumentary's visual field. What kind of space is the urban street space? For the European, the street is the place of chance encounters and accidental dramas. It is also, historically, the site of political uprising

3 An exception is Beatriz Colomina's analysis of spectatorship in the architectural interiors of Adolf Loos and Le Corbusier in her important book, *Privacy and Publicity: Modern Architecture as Mass Media* (Cambridge: MIT Press, 1994).

4 Freud, Letter to his son Ernst, 12 May 1938. In *Sigmund Freud, Briefe 1873-1939*, ed. Ernst L. Freud (Frankfurt am Main: S. Fischer, 1960), p. 435.

5 Engelman, "A Memoir," p. 136.

and counterrevolution—the birthplace of the modern revolutionary subject. But, as Susan Suleiman notes of the modern wayfare, "after 1933, any attempt to think politically about the street had to grapple with its profound ambiguity."[6] The street, formerly a place of collective resistance to state intervention, becomes, with the rise of fascism in Europe, a public venue for Nazi torchlight parades and other forms of national socialist ideology.

Engelman's three views of the street, taken with a wide-angle lens, capture a near-deserted Berggasse. Far from removing us from the sphere of political action, however, these daytime shots of a scarcely populated urban street illuminate, in visually arresting fashion, the realities of political occupation for the predominantly Jewish residents of Vienna's Ninth District. Most of the Ninth District's Jewish population were located on eleven streets, including the Berggasse which ran from the fashionable upper-middle class neighborhood of the University of Vienna at one, end to the junk shops of the Tandelmarkt owned by poor Jewish shopkeepers at the other.[7]

Though located just outside the Ringstrasse, the Berggasse was very much at the center of the German occupation. By the time Engelman embarked on his pictorial record of Freud's residence in May 1938, the image of a scarcely populated urban street operated as a potent indexical sign of political danger and social displacement. For Vienna's Jewish residents, occupation meant incarceration; to be "occupied" was to be exiled, driven out of the public space of the street and into the home.

Operating without the use of a flash ordinarily employed for interior shots, and continuing to use a wide-angle lens designed for exterior shots, Engelman transports the codes and conventions of street photography inside Berggasse 19. The building becomes an interior street as the camera's peripatetic gaze traffics through domestic space. Engelman begins his pictorial walking tour by bringing us across the entry threshold and into the lobby, a wide linear space which, with its cobblestone floor and coffered ceiling, resembles a covered arcade. At the end of the entry corridor, a pair of glazed doors—their glass panes etched with antique female figures—provides a view of an aedicule located, on axis, in the rear service courtyard beyond. These symmetrical semi-transparent doors establish a recurring visual motif that is progressively disrupted and finally displaced as we approach and move through the suite of rooms comprising Freud's office. Interestingly, Berggasse 19 wears its façade on the inside; those architectural elements normally found on the exterior of a building can be seen on the interior of Freud's apartment house. At the top of the switch-back stair, for example, we encounter a

6 Susan Suleiman, "Bataille in the Street: The Search for Virility in the 1930s," *Critical Inquiry* 21 (Autumn 1994), p. 62.

7 Hannah S. Decker, *Freud, Dora, and Vienna, 1900* (New York: The Free Press, 1991), p. 24. Bruno Bettelheim has speculated that Freud's choice to settle on this respectable but undistinguished street was motivated by a deep cultural ambivalence, as Freud sought to reconcile loyalty to his Jewish beginnings with competing desires for assimilationist respectability. See Bettelheim's *Freud's Vienna & Other Essays* (New York: Vintage, 1991), p. 20. Bettelheim argues in this review of Engelman's photographs that "studying the psychoanalytic couch in detail does not necessarily give any inkling of what psychoanalysis is all about, nor does viewing the settings in which it all happened explain the man, or his work" (19). Our own reading of Berggasse 19 suggests that just the opposite is the case: Engelman's photographs and the space of the office provide important clues not only to Freud's role as clinician but also to the historical development of psychoanalysis, a practice that evolved in response to the changing social, political, and cultural spaces it inhabited.

translucent window—an interior window that looks not onto an exterior courtyard but directly into the Freud family's private apartment. Illuminated from within, but draped with an inside curtain, Freud's interior window troubles the traditional distinction between privacy and publicity by rendering completely ambiguous whether we might be on the outside looking in or the inside looking out.

The architectural transposition of public and private space chronicled by Engelman's camera captures Freud's own relation to his work place, for although located at the back of the apartment and insulated from the street, Freud's office nonetheless operated as a busy thoroughfare. **[FIGURE 1]** Patients, colleagues, friends, family, and even pets moved in and out at regular intervals. When he needed privacy, Freud would seek refuge on the Ringstrasse where he would retreat for his daily constitutional, occasionally with a family member or friend to accompany him. For Freud, the interior space of the office and the exterior space of the street were seamless extensions of one another; both were places of movement and conversation, of chance words and surprise meetings, of accident and incident.[8] The commerce of everyday encounters constituted the primary source materials of interior reflection his patients brought to their private sessions with Freud. The transactions of the street quickly became the transferences of the therapeutic scene.

Inside Freud's consulting room and adjoining study, we are confronted with a confusing assortment of furniture and objects: couch, chair, books, bookcases, cabinets, paintings, photographs, lights, rugs, and Freud's extensive collection of antiquities. Freud displayed in the close space of his office the entirety of his collection, acquired mainly from local antique dealers with earnings set aside from his daily hour of open consultations.[9] The experience of viewing Engelman's photographs of Freud's office is like nothing so much as window shopping, as we are permitted to view, but not touch, the objects before us, many arranged in glass showcases. Ultimately, what Engelman seeks to document in these photographs is not just the objects but their particular sites of display. It is the very specific spatial arrangement of objects within the interior that constitutes the photodocumentary's visual field and that offers a blueprint for the future reconstruction of the office-museum.

The gaze of Engelman's camera is systematic, not random: it documents and surveys, inventories and catalogs. It moves from one corner of the room to the next, from wall to wall, window to window, memorizing the details of the office interior. This archival gaze is also a slightly manic one, obsessively traversing the same spaces, partitioning the office into a series of overlapping but discrete perceptual fields, at once contiguous and enclosed. The prosthetic eye of the camera attempts to take everything in, but finds its efforts frustrated by the very objects it seeks visually to preserve. The visual space becomes a carceral one as Engelman's camera repeat-

8 On the street as a site of "accident and incident," see Peter Jukes, A Shout in the Street: An Excursion into the Modern City (Berkeley and Los Angeles: University of California Press, 1990).

9 We might note in this regard Edmund Engelman's personal recollection of the ambiance of Freud's office, which he compares to the feeling of being "inside the storage room of an antique dealer." Interview, 14 September 1995.

[FIGURE 1]
Exploded Axonometric of Berggasse 19

The zone of rooms located immediately behind the protective surface of Berggasse 19's front façade buffers Freud's office (isolated in the back of the apartment) from the street. The office walls, outfitted with double sets of casement windows and lined with bookshelves and antiquities, heighten the impression of Freud's office as a sequestered, private, interior space.

[FIGURE 2]
Freud's Study
Courtesy of Edward Engelman,
Photographer

edly tries, and fails, to negotiate the crowded terrain of Freud's office, so cluttered with objects that many of the two thousand antiquities can be seen in these photographs spilling onto the study floor.[10]

Two months after his father's death in October 1896, Freud began assembling the antiquities that would transform his office into a veritable tomb. The debilitating illness and lingering death of Jakob Freud is generally recognized as the emotional crisis that galvanized Freud's compensatory interest in collecting. A father's demise is "the most important event, the most poignant loss, of a man's life" (4: p. xxvi), Freud famously opines in *The Interpretation of Dreams*, a book that has itself been read as an extended work of mourning, Freud's gradual coming to terms with the loss of his father. But it is not just his father whom Freud mourns through his accumulation of reliquary objects; it is also, in some profound sense, himself. Freud's self-described "death deliria"[11] played a central role in shaping the psychical and physical space of his office. Long before his father died, Freud was preoccupied with foretelling the exact time of his own future death. In a letter to Wilhelm Fliess dated June 22, 1894, Freud insists that although he has no scientific basis for his predictions, he "shall go on suffering from various complaints for another four to five to eight years, with good and bad periods, and then between forty and fifty perish very abruptly from a rupture of the heart."[12] As Freud moved into the period forecast for his "rupture of the heart," it was not his own death that occurred but that of his father, who fell fatally ill and died of heart failure short-

ly after Freud's fortieth birthday. "All of it happened in my critical period," Freud writes to Fliess a day after his father's funeral, "and I am really quite down because of it."[13] Freud apparently felt that his father died in his place, prompting a labor of self-entombment that exhausted itself only with Freud's own painful and prolonged death almost half a century later.

Like Osiris buried alive in his coffin,[14] Freud began surrounding himself with disinterred objects: Egyptian scarabs, Roman death masks, Etruscan funeral vases, bronze coffins, and mummy portraits.[15] The attempt to chronicle the space of Freud's office for the purposes of erecting a future museum upon its ruins was, by 1938, a touchingly belated act,

10 As early as 1901, only five years after beginning his collection, Freud writes of the shortage of space in his office study, already filled with pottery and other antiquities, and of his visitors' anxieties that he might eventually break something. See Freud's *Psychopathology of Everyday Life*, in *The Standard Edition of the Complete Psychological Works of Sigmund Freud*, trans. and ed. James Strachey, 24 vols. (London: The Hogarth Press, 1953-1974), 6: p.167. All citations from the *Standard Edition* hereafter cited in the text by volume and page number.

11 Letter to Fliess, 19 April 1894, in *The Complete Letters of Sigmund Freud to Wilhelm Fliess: 1887-1904*, trans. and ed. Jeffrey Moussaieff Masson (Cambridge: Harvard University Press, 1985).

12 Letter to Fliess, 22 June 1894.

13 Letter to Fliess, 26 October 1896.

14 Freud possessed many representations of Osiris, king of the underworld and god of resurrection. Osiris, in some accounts the first Egyptian mummy, was locked into a coffin by his brother and set adrift on the Nile. Three different bronze statues of Osiris (two complete figures and a large head fragment) adorn Freud's desk, testifying to the importance Freud accorded this particular Egyptian deity.

15 For a more complete discussion of Freud's antiquities, see the essays and selected catalogue in *Sigmund Freud and Art: His Personal Collection of Antiquities*, eds. Lynn Gamwell and Richard Wells (London: Thames and Hudson, 1989). John Forrester provides an especially fascinating reading of Freud's antiquities in his essay "'Mille e tre': Freud and Collecting," in *The Cultures of Collecting*, eds. John Elsner and Roger Cardinal (Cambridge: Harvard University Press, 1994), pp. 224-251.

for Freud's office was a museum long before Engelman arrived to document it. Like all museums, this particular memorial site doubled as a mausoleum, showcasing the self-enshrinement of a collector buried among his funerary objects. "Museum and mausoleum are connected by more than phonetic association," Adorno once commented; "museums are the family sepulchers of works of art."[16] Engelman's photographs dramatically capture what half a century of Freud commentary has overlooked: the location of the analytic scene within the walls of a crypt. When patients arrived at Freud's office, they entered an overdetermined space of loss and absence, grief and memory, elegy and mourning. In short, they entered the exteriorized theater of Freud's own emotional history, where every object newly found memorialized a love-object lost.

We might recall at this juncture that Berggasse 19 was not Freud's first professional office. Freud initially set up his medical practice in a new residential building erected on the ashes of one of Vienna's most famous edifices, the Ring Theater, which burned to the ground in 1881 in a spectacular fire, killing over six hundred people inside. Austria's Franz Josef commissioned the Viennese architect F.V. Schmidt to construct on the ruins an apartment house for the *haute bourgeoisie*, a portion of whose rent would be allocated to assist the hundreds of children orphaned by the fire. It was here, in an architectural monument to the dead of Vienna's Ring Theater, that psychoanalysis first took up residence. Not even the birth of the Freuds' first child, which brought the newly married couple an official letter from the Emperor congratulating them on bring-

16 Theodor Adorno, "Valéry Proust Museum," in *Prisms*, trans. Samuel and Shierry Weber (Cambridge: MIT Press, 1981), p. 175. Freud's office bears striking similarities to the house-museum of Sir John Soane in London. For a discussion of the museum as a place of entombment, see John Elsner's "A Collector's Model of Desire: The House and Museum of Sir John Soane," in *The Cultures of Collecting*, pp. 155-176. See also Douglas Crimp, *On the Museum's Ruins* (Cambridge: MIT Press, 1993).

17 For fuller accounts of the *Kaiserliches Stiftungshaus*, Freud's first home and office, see Ernest Jones, *The Life and Work of Sigmund Freud*, 2 vols. (New York: Basic Books, 1953), I: p. 149, and Bettelheim, *Freud's Vienna*, pp. 11-12.

ing new life to the site of such tragic loss, could completely erase for Freud the symbolic connotations of treating patients' nervous disorders in a place that came to be known as the *Sühnhaus* (House of Atonement).[17] Freud's psychoanalytic practice, from the very beginning, was closely associated with loss and recovery, the work of mourning.

II.   The patient's entry into Freud's office initiates a series of complicated and subtle transactions of power, orchestrated largely by the very precise spatial arrangement of objects and furniture. Freud held initial consultations, between three and four every afternoon, in the study section of his office.[FIGURE 2] Preferring a face-to-face encounter with prospective patients, Freud seated them approximately four feet away from himself, across the divide of a table adjacent to the writing desk. Located in the center of a square room, at the intersection of two axial lines, the patient would appear to occupy the spatial locus of power. As if to confirm the illusion of his centrality, the patient is immediately presented, when seated, with a reflection of his own image, in a small portrait-sized mirror, framed in gold filigree and hanging, at eye-level, on a facing window. As soon as Freud sits down at his desk, however, interposing himself between patient and mirror, the patient's reflection is blocked by Freud's head. **[FIGURE 3]** Head substitutes for mirror in a metaphorical staging of the clinical role Freud seeks to assume. "The doctor," Freud pronounces in *Papers on Technique*, "should be opaque to his patients and, like a mirror, should show them nothing but what is shown to him" (12: p. 118).

Freud's clinical assumption of the function of the mirror, and the substitution of other for self that it enacts, sets into motion the transferential dynamics that will structure all further doctor-patient encounters. In preparation for the laborious work of overcoming their unconscious resistances, patients are required to divest themselves of authority while seated in the very center of power. In a reverse panopticon, the most central location in Freud's study (the point from which the gaze normally issues) turns out to be the most vulnerable, as the patient suddenly finds himself exposed on all sides to a multitude of gazes. Viewed from both left and right by a phalanx of ancient figurines (all displayed at eye-level and arranged to face the patient), as well as from behind by a collection of detached antique heads and from in front by Freud's imposing visage, the patient is surveyed from every direction. Power in this transferential scene is exercised from the margins. From the protected vantage point of his desk chair, Freud studies his patient's face, fully illuminated by the afternoon light, while his own face remains barely visible, almost entirely eclipsed by backlighting from the window behind him.

"The process of psychoanalysis," Freud goes on to remark in *Papers on Technique*, "is retarded by the dread felt by the average observer of seeing himself in his own mirror" (12: p. 210). The analogy of the mirror, used to describe the process of psychoanalytic self-reflection, makes its first appearance in Freud's work in his reading of the memoirs of Daniel Paul Schreber. Mirrors figure prominently in Schreber's transvestic identification: "anyone who should happen to see me before the mirror with the upper portion of my torso bared—especially if the illusion is assisted by my wearing a little feminine finery—would receive an unmistakable impression of a *female bust*" (12: p. 33). And what did Freud see when, alone in his office amongst his classical heads and ancient figurines, he turned to face his own image in the mirror? Freud, too, saw the unmistakable impression of a bust—head and shoulders severed from the body, torso-less and floating, like the Roman head overlooking his consulting room chair or the death mask displayed in his study. His head decapitated by the frame of the mirror, Freud is visually identified with one of his own classical sculptures, transformed into a statuary fragment.

Looking in the other direction Freud also saw only heads. A wooden statue of a Chinese sage sitting on the table between Freud and his patient severs the patient's head in the same way Freud's head is decapitated by the frame of the mirror. From the vantage point of the desk chair, the patient's disembodied head assumes the status of one of Freud's antiquities, homologous not only to the stone heads filling the table directly behind the patient (the only table in the office displaying almost exclusively heads) but also to the framed photographic portraits above them, hanging at the exact same level as the mirror.

For Freud, every self-reflection reveals a death mask, every mirror image a spectral double. In his meditation on the theme of doubling, Freud remarks in "The 'Uncanny'" that while the double first emerges in our psychical lives as a "preservation against extinction," this double (in typically duplicitous fashion) soon reverses itself: "from having been an assurance of immortality, it becomes the uncanny harbinger of death" (17: p. 235). By captivating our image, immobilizing and framing it, the mirror reveals a picture of our own unthinkable mortality.

Yet, as Freud notes elsewhere, it is finally impossible to visualize our own deaths, for "whenever we attempt to do so we can perceive that we are in fact still present as spectators" (14: p. 289). The mirror that memorializes also reincarnates, reconstituting us as phantom spectators, witnesses to our own irreplaceability. The mirror thus functions simultaneously like a window, assisting us in passing through the unrepresentable space of our violent eradication, and helping us, in effect, to survive our own deaths. This was indeed the function of Etruscan mirrors (so prominent in Freud's own private collection) on whose polished bronze surfaces mythological scenes were engraved. By differentiating between pictorial space and real space, the frame of the Etruscan mirror offers the illusion of a view onto another world. These mirrors, originally buried in tombs, assisted their owners in passing through their deaths: the Etruscan mirror opened a window onto immortality.

Lacan saw as much in his early reflections on the mirror stage. Radically dislocating the traditional opposition of transparency and reflectivity (window and mirror), Lacan instructs us to "think of the mirror as a pane of glass. You'll see yourself in the glass and you'll see objects beyond it."[18] In Freud's office, the placement of a mirror on a window frame further complicates this conflation of transparency and reflectivity by frustrating the possibility of opening up the space of looking that both crystalline surfaces appear to offer. Normally, when mirrors are placed against opaque walls, they have the capacity to act as windows; they dematerialize and dissolve architectural edges, creating the illusion of extension and expanding the spatial boundaries of the interior. But in this highly peculiar instance of a mirror superimposed on a window, visual access is obstructed rather than facilitated. Unlike the glass panes on Berggasse 19's rear entry doors, which allow the viewer's gaze to pass easily along a central axis from inside to outside, the composition of Freud's study window, with the mirror occupying the central vanishing point, redirects the gaze inward.[FIGURE 4] By forcing the subject of reflection to confront an externalized gaze relayed back upon itself, the mirror on Freud's window interrupts the reassuring classical symmetries of self and other, inside and outside, and seeing and being seen that constitute the traditional humanist subject.[19]

18 Jacques Lacan, *Seminar I: Freud's Papers on Technique*, ed. Jacques-Alain Miller, trans. John Forrester (New York: Norton, 1988), p. 141.

19 For an excellent discussion of challenges to the traditional humanism of the architectural window, see Thomas Keenan, "Windows: of vulnerability," in *The Phantom Public Sphere*, ed. Bruce Robbins (Minneapolis: University of Minnesota Press, 1994), pp. 121-141. See also Colomina, *Privacy and Publicity*, esp. pp. 80-82, 234-238, and 283 ff. An earlier discussion of windows and mirrors can be found in Diana Agrest, "Architecture of Mirror/Mirror of Architecture," in *Architecture from Without: Theoretical Framings for a Critical Practice* (Cambridge: MIT Press, 1991), pp. 139-155.

[FIGURE 3]
**Study
Diagram**
*During the ini-
tial consulta-
tion with
Freud, the
patient, seated
at the center
of the square-
shaped study,
sees his reflec-
tion framed
within the por-
trait-sized mir-
ror on the cen-
tral mullion of
the window
behind Freud's
desk. Myriad
gazes, issuing
from Freud's
collection of
stone heads
and antique
figurines, sur-
vey the patient
from the
tables and vit-
rines that ter-
minate the
room's other
three axes.
When Freud
sits in his desk
chair, his head
blocks and
replaces the
patient's
image in the
mirror, initiat-
ing the trans-
ferential
dynamics gov-
erning future
therapeutic
encounters.*

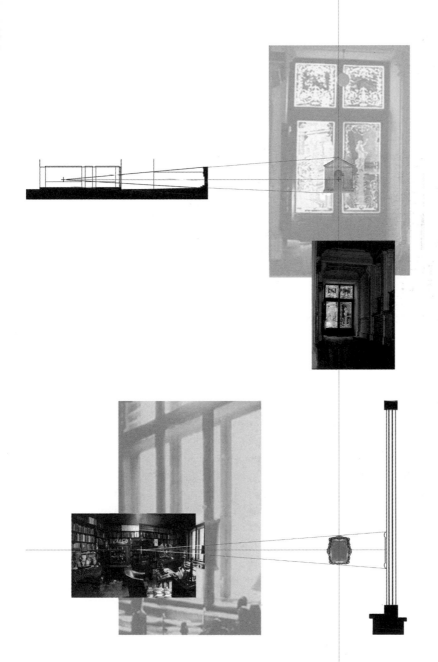

[FIGURE 4]
Sections through Entry Vestibule and Study Window
The window in Freud's study possesses certain compositional similarities with the building's rear entry doors. Seen frontally, both sites present us with a rectangular figure (pedicule and mirror) framed by a bifurcated glazed ground (door and window). But Freud's placement of the mirror before the study window inverts the traditional relationship of figure to ground. Disrupting the reassuring trajectory of a sovereign look (embodied by the transparency of the back entry doors), the mirror redirects the patient's gaze inwards, relaying the gaze back upon itself.

The architectonics of the Freudian subject depends fundamentally upon a spatial dislocation, upon seeing the self exteriorized. It is not only that when we look in the mirror we see how others see us, but also that we see ourselves occupying a space where we are not. The statue that confronts us in the mirror permits us to look not only at but through ourselves to the "object who knows himself to be seen."[20] The domain delimited by Lacan's *imago*, "the statue in which man projects himself,"[21] is thus a strangely lifeless one. As Mikkel Borch-Jacobsen pictures it in "The Statue Man," this mirror world is "a sort of immense museum peopled with immobile 'statues,' 'images' of stone, and hieratic 'forms'." It is "the most inhuman of possible worlds, the most *unheimlich*."[22]

What Freud sees in his mirror is a subject who is, first and foremost, an object, a statue, a bust. The "dread" of self-reflection that Freud describes in *Papers on Technique* appears to issue from a fear of castration, of dramatic bodily disfigurement. If, as Freud insists in "Medusa's Head," the terror of castration is always linked to the sight of something, then it is the sight of *seeing oneself seeing* that possesses lethal consequences for the figure in the mirror. Like Medusa, who is slain by the fatal powers of her own gaze reflected back to her by Perseus's shield, Freud's narcissistic gaze makes him "stiff with terror, turns him to stone" (18: p. 273). Self-reflection petrifies. Perhaps this is the knowledge that so frightened, and so fascinated, Freud: the realization that the subject's "optical erection" could only be achieved at the price of its castration, its instantaneous, fatal transformation into a broken relic.

20 Lacan, *Seminar I*, p. 215; see also p. 78.

21 Jacques Lacan, "The Mirror Stage as Formative of the Function of the I as Revealed in Psychoanalytic Experience," in *Écrits*, trans. Alan Sheridan (New York: Norton, 1977), p. 2.

22 Mikkel Borch-Jacobsen, *Lacan: The Absolute Master*, trans. Douglas Brick (Stanford: Stanford University Press, 1991), p. 59.

III.

As the clinical treatment moves from the initial consultation in Freud's study to the sessions on the consulting room couch, the distribution of objects in the room produces a new kind of body, and a reconfigured doctor-patient relation. **[FIGURE 5]** In the study, the patient, sitting isolated and exposed at the center of the room, occupied the point of maximum exposure; in the consulting room, the patient finds herself securely situated outside a circuit of visual surveillance. The arrangement of couch and chair, with their occupants facing outward at perpendicular angles, ensures that, once the analysis formally begins, there will never be an unobstructed line of vision between patient and doctor. The most intimate space in the room is thus also the most highly mediated, as if such close physical proximity between patient and doctor can only be sustained by the structural elimination of any direct visual transaction. **[FIGURE 6]** The placement of articles on and around the consulting room couch—the heavy Persian rug hung vertically from the wall and anchored to the couch by a matching rug, the chenille cushions supporting the patient's head, neck, and upper back, and the blanket and porcelain stove warming the patient's feet—all create the impression of a protected enclave, a room within a room, a private interior space.

The profusion of sensuous Oriental rugs and throw pillows, and the horsehair sofa in the consulting room in Berggasse 19 suggests the subtle encroachment of "female" domestic space into the public sphere of the office. Freud's professional office as a scene of domestic comfort is precisely how the Wolf Man remembers it thirty-eight years after the completion of his formal analysis:

> I can remember, as though I saw them today, his two adjoining studies, with the door open between them and with their windows opening on a little courtyard. There was always a feeling of sacred peace and quiet here. The rooms themselves must have been a surprise to any patient, for they in no way reminded one of a doctor's office . . . .
> A few potted plants added life to the rooms, and the warm carpet and curtains gave them a home-like note. Everything here contributed to one's feeling of leaving the haste of mod ern life behind, of being sheltered from one's daily cares.[23]

23 *The Wolf Man, by the Wolf Man*, ed. Muriel Gardiner (New York: Noonday, 1991), p. 139. Sergei Pankeiev also takes note, as all Freud's patients did, of the many objects in the room: "Here were all kinds of statuettes and other unusual objects, which even the layman recognized as archeological finds from ancient Egypt. Here and there on the walls were stone plaques representing various scenes of long-vanished epochs. . . . Freud himself explained his love for archeology in that the psychoanalyst, like the archeologist in his excavations, must uncover layer after layer of the patient's psyche, before coming to the deepest, most valuable treasures" (139). For more on the dominance of the archeological metaphor in Freud's work, see Donald Kuspit, "A Mighty Metaphor: The Analogy of Archaeology and Psychoanalysis," in *Sigmund Freud and Art*, pp. 133-151.

24 H.D., *Tribute to Freud* (New York: McGraw-Hill, 1975), p. 132. Hereafter, abbreviated "TF" and cited in the text. H.D.'s autobiographical account of her psychoanalytic sessions with Freud provides us with the most complete recollection we have, from the point of view of a patient, of Freud's consult ing room. Her memoir offers a narrative counterpart to Engelman's photographs, describing, in surprisingly rich detail, the view from the couch and the sounds, smells, and objects around her.

25 Max Schur, *Freud: Living and Dying* (New York: International Universities Press, Inc., 1972), p. 246.

In her autobiographical work, *Tribute to Freud*, the American poet H.D. recalls Freud's office in similar terms, emphasizing the feelings of safety and security generated by the space encompassing the consulting room couch: "Today, lying on the famous psychoanalytical couch, . . . [w]herever my fantasies may take me now, I have a center, security, aim. I am centralized or reoriented here in this mysterious lion's den or Aladdin's cave of treasures."[24]

H.D. goes on to describe the "smoke of burnt incense" (TF, p.23) and the "fumes of the aromatic cigar" (TF, p.132) that waft above the couch, emanating from the invisible corner behind her. Freud considered his passion for collecting "an addiction second in intensity only to his nicotine addiction."[25] The air in Freud's treatment room, densely humidified by ceramic water tubes attached to the Viennese stove, hung heavy with the smell of Freud's favorite cigars, which he often smoked during analytic sessions. Reading the visual record of Freud's office alongside these verbal accounts, a carefully staged orientalist scene insistently begins to take shape. Reclining on an ottoman couch, cushioned by Eastern car-

[FIGURE 6]
Consulting Room Diagram

The position of Freud's treatment chair behind the head of the couch effectively prohibits any direct visual exchange between patient and doctor. While Freud's corner chair offers a view of the entire consulting room, as well as the study desk in the adjoining room, the couch directs the reclining patient's gaze to the bare corner above the Viennese stove, the only surface in the office uncluttered by artifacts.

pets, and wreathed in pungent smoke, patients find themselves at home in a late Victorian fantasy of the opium den.

In Europe's *fin-de-siècle* fascination with the East, oriental interiors—especially the smoking room—were closely associated with leisure and relaxation. The bright dyes, luxurious textures, and bold designs of increasingly popular Persian carpets were instrumental in importing into the bourgeois Victorian home a stereotypical aura of Eastern exoticism. In fact, the last decades of the nineteenth century found Europe in the grip of what one German design historian has called "Oriental carpet fever."[26] The first major European exhibition of Oriental carpets took place at the Imperial Austrian Trade Museum in Vienna in 1891, the very year Freud moved his home and office to Berggasse 19. For Freud, these Persian carpets and Oriental fabrics may well have reminded him of his father, by profession a wool merchant who traded in Eastern textiles. For Freud's patients, the enchantment and mystery of these Oriental rugs further sequestered them in the interiorized, reclusive space of the consulting room couch—a place of private fantasy and quixotic danger: "[a] mysterious lion's den or Aladdin's cave of treasures."

As if in compensation for the risks that must be taken there, Freud envelops the patient on the couch in all the comforts of a private boudoir, ordinarily the most interior and secluded room of the Viennese home. Freud's office, in fact, is located in the back wing of what was originally designed to be part of a domestic residence, in that area of the apartment house typically used as sleeping quarters.[27] It is the sexual overtones of the famous couch—the sofa as bed—that most discomforted Freud's critics and, if Freud himself is to be believed, no small number of his patients.[28] In one of the few essays to take note of the spatial organization of the scene of analysis, Luce Irigaray has pointed out that the sexual connotations of lying supine can vary dramatically, depending on the sex of the patient. A woman reclining on her back with a man seated erect behind her finds her relation to the doctor inevitably eroticized.[29] The same could be said for Freud's male patients, whose daily sessions of private sex talk with their male doctor tacitly homoeroticized the clinical encounter. "Some men," Freud once commented, "scatter small change out of their trouser pockets while they are lying down during treatment and in that way pay whatever fee they think appropriate for

26 Friedrich Spuhler, *Oriental Carpets in the Museum of Islamic Art, Berlin*, trans. Robert Pinner (London: Faber and Faber, 1988), p.10. See also David Sylvester, "On Western Attitudes to Eastern Carpets," in *Islamic Carpets from the Joseph V. McMullan Collection* (London: Arts Council of Great Britain, 1972); Kurt Erdmann, *Seven Hundred Years of Oriental Carpets*, ed. Hanna Erdmann, trans. May H. Beattie and Hildegard Herzog (London: Faber and Faber, 1970); and John Mills, "The Coming of the Carpet to the West," in *The Eastern Carpet in the Western World, from the 15th to the 17th Century*, ed. Donald King and David Sylvester (London: Arts Council of Great Britain, 1983). For a more detailed treatment of orientalism in the context of Western architecture and interior design, see John M. MacKenzie's *Orientalism: History, Theory and the Arts* (Manchester: Manchester University Press, 1995). While many of the older carpets on display in the Vienna exhibition came from mosques, Freud's newer carpets were woven in Northwest Persia, most likely in court workshops.

27 Freud's first office in Berggasse 19 was located on the building's ground floor, beneath the family apartment, in three rooms formerly occupied by Victor Adler. Freud conducted his practice here from 1891 to 1907, when he moved his offices into the back rooms of the apartment immediately adjacent to the family residence.

28 Freud admits towards the end of *Papers on Technique* that "a particularly large number of patients object to being asked to lie down, while the doctor sits out of sight behind them" (12: p.139).

29 Luce Irigaray, "The Gesture in Psychoanalysis," in *Between Feminism and Psychoanalysis*, ed. Teresa Brennan (New York and London: Routledge, 1989), p. 129.

the session" (6: p. 214). The association of lying down with scattered change—in short, of sex with money—invokes the specter of (male) prostitution, a connection that Freud appears to intuit here but not fully register.

What is being staged, or restaged, around the privileged, centralized, over-invested figure of the consulting room couch? "I cannot put up with being stared at by other people for eight hours a day (or more)," Freud acknowledges, defending his mandate that all patients, without exception, assume a reclining position on the couch. But why a couch? The couch turns out to be yet another museum relic—a "remnant," Freud calls it, "of the hypnotic method out of which psycho-analysis was evolved" (12: p. 133). While Freud abandoned his early hypnotic practice of placing patients into a somnambulistic sleep, he retained the couch as a serviceable memorial to psychoanalysis in its infancy. The couch, given to Freud as a gift by his former patient Madame Benveniste around 1890, operated as a nostalgic reminder of his professional past.

But there is more to this couch than its store of personal memories for the doctor; the analytic couch served a mnemonic function for the patient as well. The following anecdote, recounted by Freud in *The Psychopathology of Everyday Life*, provocatively suggests a different way of thinking about the prominence of the consulting room couch:

> A young lady suddenly flung open the door of
> the consulting room though the woman who preced-
> ed her had not yet
> left it. In apologiz-
> ing she blamed her   **30** Ibid., p. 128.
> 'thoughtlessness'; it
> soon turned out that she had been demonstrating
> the curiosity that in the past had caused her to
> make her way into her parents' bedroom. (6: p. 214)

What is being subtly replayed here, across the threshold of two rooms, is none other than the spectacle of the primal scene. The patient in the waiting room, hearing sounds through the consulting room door, bursts into Freud's office, propelled by the same "curiosity" that drew her, as a child, to cross the threshold of her parent's private bedchamber. Freud's intruding female hysteric sees all too clearly the highly eroticized choreography made possible by the very particular configuration of consulting room couch and chair, so closely juxtaposed that if one were to remove the arm of the couch and the arm of the chair behind it, the patient's head (formerly propped at a thirty-five degree angle) would fall nearly into Freud's lap. Shortly after this incident of analysis *interruptus*, Freud soundproofed his consulting room by adding a second set of doors lined with red baize. The sound barrier between treatment room and waiting room now insulated the analytic couple, whose muffled voices previously risked transporting the patient in the next room back to the trauma of the primal scene, to that interior place of fantasy where "uncanny sounds" are registered but only belatedly understood.

Freud's own placement in this scene is by no means a simple one; the question of the analyst's identificatory position is far more complicated than Irigaray's "orthogonal"[30] pairing of prone patient/erect doctor might suggest. Significantly, Freud chooses to assume a passive position in his exchange with the patient. Advising against the taking of notes during treatment sessions, a practice that prohibits the doctor from maintaining a posture of "evenly suspended attention" (12: p. 111), Freud recommends that the analyst "should simply listen, and not bother about whether he is keeping anything in mind." This passive listening technique represents the exact correlative to the fundamental rule of analysis for patients, the injunction to say anything that enters one's head "without selection or censorship" (12: p. 112).[31] The analyst must never engage in the work of scientific research while involved in the clinical act of listening. He must instead make himself vulnerable and receptive; he must "lay . . . [himself] open to another person" (12: p. 116); he must allow himself "to be taken by surprise" (12: p. 114).

> To put it in a formula. he must turn his own unconscious like a receptive organ towards the transmitting unconscious of the patient. He must adjust himself to the patient as a telephone receiver is adjusted to the transmitting microphone. Just as the receiver converts back into sound waves the electric oscillations in the telephone line which were set up by sound waves, so the doctor's unconscious is able, from the derivatives of the unconscious which are communicated to him, to reconstruct that unconscious, which has determined the patient's free associations. (12: pp. 115-116)

31 Freud's own practice was to take notes from memory after all his sessions that day had been completed. For particularly important dream texts, the patient was asked to repeat the dream until Freud had committed its details to memory (12: pp. 113-114)

32 Neil Hertz, "Dora's Secrets, Freud's Techniques," in *In Dora's Case: Freud, Hysteria, Feminism*, eds. Charles Bernheimer and Claire Kahane (New York: Columbia University Press, 1985), pp. 229 and 234.

Opening himself to the risk of feminization, Freud assumes the role of an orifice, a listening ear, while the patient becomes a mouth, an oral transmitter. Freud, as office receptionist, opens a direct line to the patient, adjusting the patient's unconscious to the frequencies of his own psychical interior. This interconnection between patient and doctor, transmitter and receiver, mouth and ear, sets up a technology of oral transmission: transference operates telephonically.

The gratification Freud derived from the "electric oscillations" of the transferential line suggests that at the center of psychoanalysis's primal scene is a performance of what Neil Hertz has dubbed "oral intercourse in that other sense of the term." Freud's choice of a telephone to describe the intimate exchanges between doctor and patient highlights the "epistemological promiscuity" that characterizes psychoanalysis's therapeutic practice.[32] The very arrangement of couch and chair facilitates an erotics of voice, privileging sound over sight, speech over spectatorship. In the consulting room, telephone replaces mirror as the governing topos of the doctor-patient relation.

However, like the mirror on the window, Freud's imaginary telephone immediately connects us to the place of mourning. This indeed is the lesson of Avital Ronell's *The Telephone Book*, which reminds us that the telephone has always been involved in a hermeneutics of mourning, in a call to an absent other: "like transference, the telephone is given to us as effigy."[33] Invented originally as a device for the speech impaired, the telephone works as a prosthesis to co[...] radical loss. Freud, partially deaf in his right ear, detected i[...] speech of the telephone the soft reverberations of distant connections, the sound of the unconscious. A powerful transmitter of disembodied presence, Freud's telephone was capable of summoning the very spirits of the dead—modulated voices from beyond the grave.[34]

IV.

In one respect, the arrangement of bodies in the consulting room bears a certain disquieting resemblance to a wake, with Freud holding vigil over the body of his patient lying immobilized on the couch, most likely enshrouded (mummy-like) in the blanket provided, and surrounded by hundreds of funerary objects. *Eros* and *thanatos* turn out to be comfortable bedfellows as Freud's analytic couch doubles as not just a bed but a bier. Occupying the space of an off-screen presence, the analyst's listening ear and ventriloquized speech offer the patient the promise of re-establishing a tenuous connection to the Other who has been lost. By assuming the position of telephone receiver, the one who accepts the call to the Other, Freud thus finds himself addressing the patient from the borderline between presence and absence— the threshold between life and death.

In the minds of his patients, Freud was not only healer, prophet, and shaman but gatekeeper to the underworld, "patron of gate-ways and portals" (TF, p. 106). Like the stone Janus head on his office desk, Freud "faced two ways, as doors and gates opened and shut" (TF, p. 100).[35] A modern-day Hermes or Thoth, Freud keeps vigilant watch over the dangerous passage across the invisible borders of past and present, memory and forgetting. "'In analysis,'" Freud once explained to H.D., "'the person is dead after the analysis is over,'" to which H.D. responded, "which person?" (TF, p. 141) With characteristic acuity, H.D. troubles the notion of physician as mourner, alluding to the possibility that it is Freud himself who is mourned, Freud who may already find himself on the other side of the portal. In the journey through death staged by the work of analysis, the question of who is the traveler and who the guide remains, at the very least, open.

In one of Freud's most interesting metaphorizations of the scene of treatment, he imagines doctor and patient as fellow passengers on a railway journey. Tutoring the patient on the technique of free association, Freud recommends: "Act as though . . . you were a traveler sitting next to the window of a railway carriage and describing to

33 Avital Ronell, *The Telephone Book: Technology, Schizophrenia, Electric Speech* (Lincoln: University of Nebraska Press, 1989), p. 84.

34 Ibid., esp. pp. 88-96. Freud lost much of the hearing in his right ear after his surgery for oral cancer in 1923. Peter Gay writes that Freud actually moved the couch from one wall to another so he could listen better with his left ear. See Gay, *Freud: A Life for Our Time* (New York: Anchor Books, 1988), p. 427.

35 Psychoanalysis generally reads the space of the doorway as a symbol of change and transition, but in at least one instance the doorway became for Freud a powerful image of arrested movement. In a letter to Minna Bernays dated 20 May 1938, written as he anxiously awaited permission to emigrate, Freud compares the experience of impending exile to "standing in the doorway like someone who wants to leave a room but finds that his coat is jammed." Cited in *The Diary of Sigmund Freud, 1929-1939*, trans. Michael Molnar (New York: Charles Scribner's Sons, 1992), p. 236.

someone inside the carriage the changing views which you see outside" (12: p.135). The train, associated throughout Freud's work with death and departure, carries doctor and patient along the same track, advancing the familiar genre of the travelogue as a model for the talking cure. The picture of easy companionship and leisurely conversation that Freud paints for his patient clearly seeks to domesticate what threatens to be a terrifying venture. Yet what is particularly striking about Freud's scenario of the fellow train travelers is his own severely circumscribed role within it, for Freud is the passenger whose vision is impaired, who can only imagine the view outside the window that his companion is invited to describe. While doctor and patient are located on the same side of the window, the patient alone is visually empowered while Freud is functionally blinded. Freud can listen but he cannot see; hearing must compensate for a radical loss of vision. Once again, then, Freud imagines himself as a passive, responsive organ: "two open ears and one temporal lobe lubricated for reception."[36]

In depriving himself of visual authority, Freud assumes the role of the blind seer, the one who "sacrifices sight . . . with an eye to seeing at last."[37] Through his figurative self-blinding, Freud inserts himself into a long line of blind healers and sightless soothsayers: Oedipus, the guilty son, who achieves wisdom by putting out his own eyes; Tiresias, the prophet of two sexes, who suffers blindness at the hands of the goddess Hera after testifying to women's greater sexual pleasure; and Tobit, the man of last respects, who never stops asking his sons to close his eyes as the time approaches for his own burial. It is impossible to forget the dream Freud had on the night after his own father's funeral—a dream about closing the eyes. Freud dreamt that he was in a place (in one account, a railway station) where a sign was posted that read: "You are requested to close the eyes." Late for his own father's funeral, Freud reads this dream as an expression of guilt for his failure to give his father a proper burial. Freud explains that "the sentence on the sign has a double meaning: one should do one's duty to the dead (an apology as though I had not done it and were in need of leniency), and the actual duty itself. The dream thus stems from the inclination to self-reproach that regularly sets in among survivors."[38]

"You are requested to close the eyes" refers to the literal act of performing a burial rite and to the symbolic necessity of taking one's leave of the dead. As Didier Anzieu perceptively notes, however, the request to "close the eyes" is also one of the instructions Freud habitually gave to his patients when beginning an analytic session.[39] The clinical rehearsal of this particular ritual provides what is perhaps the clearest illustration of the

36 Letter to Fliess, 30 June 1896.

37 Jacques Derrida, *Memoirs of the Blind: The Self-Portrait and Other Ruins*, trans. Pascale-Anne Brault and Michael Naas (Chicago and London: University of Chicago Press, 1993), p. 30. In this elegant book Derrida traces a tradition of prints and drawings depicting figures of blindness, including three of the visionary blind men alluded to here: Oedipus, Tiresias, and Tobit.

38 Freud recounts this dream both in the letter to Fliess cited here, dated 2 November 1896, and later, in slightly altered form, in *The Interpretation of Dreams* (4: pp. 317-318). See also Freud's analysis of another death-bed dream, "Father on his death-bed like Garibaldi" (5: pp. 427-429).

39 Didier Anzieu, *Freud's Self-Analysis*, trans. Peter Graham (Madison, CT: International Universities Press, 1986), p. 172.

extent to which Freud envisioned the work of psychoanalysis as an elaborate funeral rite. Freud eventually discontinued the practice of enjoining his patients to close their eyes,[40] but vision and blindness continued to define for Freud the core dynamic of the therapeutic relation. Eyes now open, the patient on Freud's consulting room couch encounters the penetrating look of Gradiva, a plaster cast bas-relief hanging on the wall at the foot of the ottoman, carefully positioned to stare directly down at the patient. It is Wilhelm Jensen's Gradiva—for Freud the very incarnation of immortality—who offers patient and doctor (eye and ear) a new set of instructions: "look, but not with bodily eyes, and listen, but not with physical ears. And then . . . the dead wakened" (9: p.16).

In Freud's theater of inversions, where a healing ritual can lull the living into a nether world of dreams and a funeral rite can waken the dead, subjects and objects are also transposed. When H.D. first enters the office in Berggasse 19, it is the objects, not their owner, that seize her attention: "The statues stare and stare and seem to say, what has happened to you?" (TF, p.110) There are more sculptures in Freud's vast collection of antiquities than any other kind of art object, figures with a more immediate and anthropomorphic presence than either painting or photography.[41] Apparently these statues are endowed with the vision that Freud himself is denied; the figurines, their faces and their sight animated, stand in obverse relation to Freud, his face composed and his eyes veiled. In one of H.D.'s only physical descriptions of Freud, she describes him as though she were appreciating a piece of statuary, sculpted by an expert craftsman:

[40] According to Anzieu, Freud discontinued this practice in 1904; ibid., p. 64.

[41] Lynn Gamwell has noted that "almost every object Freud acquired is a figure whose gaze creates a conscious presence." See her "The Origins of Freud's Antiquities Collection," in *Sigmund Freud and Art*, p. 27.

> *His beautiful mouth seemed always slightly smiling, though his eyes, set deep and slightly asymmetrical under the domed forehead (with those furrows cut by a master chisel) were unrevealing. His eyes did not speak to me.* (TF, p. 73)

The portals of Freud's eyes are closed to his patients, as if he himself were an inanimate statue. By prohibiting the patient from looking at him during analysis, Freud, ostensibly seeking to ward off the possibility of idolatry, actually lays its foundations. Positioning himself in the place of "the one who must not be looked at," Freud immediately assumes the status of an otherworldly presence, concealed behind the inscrutable exterior of a powerful and mysterious graven image.

Is this why the view from Freud's consulting room chair resists all attempts to reproduce it technologically? And why Engelman's camera, when it attempts to see the space of the office through Freud's eyes, is effectively rendered blind? "I wanted to see things the way Freud saw them, with his own eyes, during the long hours of his treatment sessions and as he sat writing," Engelman concedes in his memoir, "[but] I couldn't . . . fit my bulky tripod into the tight space between Freud's chair at the head of the couch and the little table covered with an oriental rug on which [were] set a half-dozen fragile looking Egyptian statuettes."[42] Unable to simulate the view from the analyst's chair, Engelman finds that he must redirect his gaze back to the perspective of the patient. The consulting room chair stands as a fundamentally uninhabitable space, a tribute to the imposing figure of the analyst who remains, even to the searching eye of the camera, totally and enigmatically other.

V.

"Tucked" away in his "three-sided niche" (TF, p. 22), Freud once again can be seen to occupy a spatially marginalized position. But while Freud's physical mobility in the consulting room may be more severely restricted than that of his patient, his field of vision is actually far greater. From his treatment chair, Freud can see not only the cabinet of antiquities below the now famous reproduction of Pierre Albert-Brouillet's engraving, *La Leçon clinique du Dr. Charcot*, but also the room's two main apertures (window and door) that frame it on either side. While from this position he is capable of monitoring any movements in or out of the consulting room, Freud's view of the entry door is partially obscured by a set of fully intact antiquities displayed on the table in front of him, a double row of figurines that, like the patient on the couch, are carefully arranged on a Persian rug. Are we to see these unbroken antiquities as visual surrogates for Freud's patients ("there are priceless broken fragments that are meaningless until we find the other broken bits to match them," H.D. writes [TF, p. 35]; "I was here because I must not be broken" [TF, p. 16])?[43] Or are we to see Freud's patients as simply another part of his collection, a conjecture reinforced by the photographs of Marie Bonaparte and Lou-Andreas Salomé, two of Freud's former patients, placed on the study bookcases alongside Freud's other antiquities?

It seems likely that the relation between Freud's antiquities and his patients is more complex than either of these two possibilities allows. Notably, the Egyptian statues in front of the consulting room chair are visible to Freud from the side, like the figures in profile found on the Egyptian papyrus hanging on the wall closest to Freud's immediate line of vision. This particular mummy covering, which depicts a scene of embalming,[44] holds a privileged place amongst Freud's antiquities, its location next to the treatment chair permitting hours of careful study. For Freud, interpreting a patient's dream is like deciphering an Egyptian hieroglyph. Pictographic script emblematizes the work of dream interpretation, offering a visual analog to the template of the dream text, the "picture-language" (13: p. 177) of the unconscious.

From his consulting room chair, Freud also has an unobstructed view of the desk in the adjoining study, where he will adjourn late in the day to take notes on his sessions and to write up his research. "One of the claims of psycho-analysis to distinction is, no doubt, that in its exe-

42 Engelman, "A Memoir," p. 137.

43 H.D. saw immediately the significance of Freud's reliquary objects, their mirror relation to the patients who came to Freud every day to be "skillfully pieced together like the exquisite Greek tear-jars and iridescent glass bowls and vases that gleamed in the dusk from the cabinet" (TF, p.14).

44 C. Nicholas Reeves identifies this particular piece of ancient cartonnage as a frontal leg covering from the mummy of a woman. The two lower panels once again depict Osiris, king of the underworld. For a fuller description of this Egyptian mummy covering and its hieroglyphics, see *Sigmund Freud and Art*, p. 75.

cution research and treatment coincide" (12: p.114), Freud remarks, immediately qualifying that it is, in fact, unwise to begin scientific research on a case while treatment is still in progress. The architectural design of the office accordingly splits the interior in two, artificially divorcing the space of listening from the space of reflection. But the strict methodological barrier Freud erects between study and consulting room is nonetheless breached by the two doors that remain, like listening ears, perpetually open between them. [FIGURE 6] A single axial line links desk chair to treatment chair, reflection to reception. While Freud listens to the patient from his consulting room chair, he has a clear view of the desk that awaits him, and a vision of the work of analysis towards which the clinical session aspires. Similarly, while Freud composes his scientific notes and theoretical papers at the study desk, consulting room couch and chair stand before him like an empty stage set, a visual reminder of the drama that has recently unfolded there in which Freud himself played a prominent role. The centers of knowledge in these adjoining rooms are thus visually continuous: treatment anticipates research; research rehearses treatment.

The immediate view from Freud's desk chair is no less phantasmatically staged, with many of Freud's favorite figurines lined up in a row on his desktop like so many members of a "silent audience."[45]

Freud's desk, the most interior place in the office and the most difficult to access, is also the site of greatest structural fortification. Surrounded on three sides by three wooden tables, Freud's work area marks out yet another protected enclave, more confining yet more secure than the interior room created for the patient on the couch. It is at his desk that Freud makes the perilous transition from listening to writing; it is at his desk that he enters into dialogue with his professional demons; it is at his desk that he struggles to put his own manuscripts to rest. Visible in Engelman's photographs of the study desk are the spectral outlines of Freud's *Moses and Monotheism*—Freud's last completed work that, he confesses, "tormented me like an unlaid ghost" (23: p.103).

45 Gamwell in *Sigmund Freud and Art*, p. 28.

46 Letter to Jung, 16 April 1909, in *The Freud/Jung Letters*, ed. William McGuire, trans. Ralph Manheim and R.F.C. Hull (Cambridge: Harvard University Press, 1988), p. 218. This story of the haunted steles appears in the same letter in which Freud analyzes another episode of his death deliria (the superstition that he will die between the ages of 61 and 62) and where he makes reference to what he identifies as "the specifically Jewish nature of my mysticism" (220).

In what sense might Freud's office, and the clinical encounter that takes place there, be read not just as an elegiac space but as a haunted one? Freud, it appears, was forever exorcising ghosts. A year after moving his office into a wing of his living quarters, Freud writes to Carl Jung of what he calls his "poltergeist"—a cracking noise issuing from the two Egyptian steles resting on top of the oak bookcases. Believing at first that these ancient grave-markers are possessed by spirits whenever Jung is in the room, Freud only reluctantly relinquishes his fanciful superstition when the steles continue to groan in his friend's absence: "I confront the despiritualized furniture," Freud laments, "as the poet confronted undeified Nature after the gods of Greece had passed away."[46]

But the Greek gods are not the only apparitions haunting the furniture and antiquities in Freud's office; for Freud's patients, these possessions operate as spectral doubles for the analyst himself.

At least once in every analysis, Freud explains, the patient claims that his free associations have stopped; however, if pressed, he will admit that he is thinking of the objects around him—the wallpaper, the gas-lamp, the sofa: "Then one knows at once that he has gone off into the transference and that he is engaged upon what are still unconscious thoughts relating to the physician" (18: p.126).[47] A transferential force emanates from Freud's possessions; these overinvested forms operate, for the patient, as shadowy substitutes for the analyst who must not be seen. Whether or not Freud's patients actually related to their physician's objects in this way is perhaps less interesting than the revelation of Freud's own deeply cathected relation to his things, which his theory of animation implicitly betrays. For this quasi-mystical account of the patient's transference onto the doctor through the medium of surrogate-objects is based on Freud's ready presumption that these inanimate possessions *could* somehow function as versions of himself.

The possibility that Freud may identify with these objects, may actually see himself as a part of the vast collection amassed around him, finds ironic visual confirmation in the last of Engelman's office photographs. In the only office photograph that includes a human figure, Freud's upper torso and head appear behind the study desk like yet another classical sculpture.[FIGURE 7] Captured in a moment of statuary repose, Freud's imperturbable facial features appear to imitate the bust of him sculpted seven years before by the Yugoslavian artist Oscar Némon. This final image of Freud amidst his collection provides eloquent testimony to Jean Baudrillard's claim that, while "a given collection is made up of a succession of terms, . . . the final term must always be the person of the collector," for in the end "it is invariably *oneself* that one collects."[48]

The very medium of the photograph participates in the process of memorialization that so deeply permeates the space of Freud's office. Theorists of photography inevitably return to the camera's technological capacity to objectify the subject, to turn the image of the living into a memorial to the dead. "The home of the photographed is in fact the cemetery," Eduardo Cadava writes; "a small funerary monument, the photograph is a grave for the living dead."[49] Engelman's camera captures that moment, identified by Roland Barthes, when the one who is photographed is neither subject nor object but a subject becoming an object, a subject who is truly becoming a specter.[50] The photograph of Freud amongst his relics mortifies its living subject—it embalms Freud in a tomb he spent over forty years preparing. It is a suit-

47 On the subject of a patient's transference onto the doctor through the medium of objects, see also Freud's *Papers on Technique*: "[the patient] had been occupied with the picture of the room in which he was, or he could not help thinking of the objects in the consulting room and of the fact that he was lying here on a sofa . . . . [E]verything connected with the present situation represents a transference to the doctor, which proves suitable to serve as a first resistance" (12: p.138).

48 Jean Baudrillard, "The System of Collecting," in *The Culture of Collecting*, p. 12.

49 Eduardo Cadava, "Words of Light: Theses on the Photography of History," in *Fugitive Images: From Photography to Video*, ed. Patrice Petro (Bloomington and Indianapolis: Indiana University Press, 1995), pp. 223 and 224.

50 Roland Barthes, *Camera Lucida: Reflections on Photography*, trans. Richard Howard (New York: Farrar Straus & Giroux, 1981), p. 14.

able memorial to the man who seemed to glimpse, more assuredly than anyone, the many elusive ways in which our deaths anticipate us and our lives encrypt us.

Photography might be said to haunt psychoanalysis in another way, for a principle of photographic likenesses, of double exposures and exposed doubles, animates and reanimates the transferential scene. Insofar as the mechanism of transference works precisely by means of a double exposure—a superimposition of one figure onto another—the process of psychoanalysis can be seen to operate as a form of photographic development. Like photography, the technology of transference performs a kind of spirit work in which the phantoms of missing or lost others come back to life in the person of the analyst. In "Introjection and Transference," Sandor Ferenczi refers to the physician as a "revenant" in whom the patient finds again "the vanished figures of childhood."[51] Freud, as object of his patients' transferences, was just such a revenant, the living image of an absent person. Psychoanalysis, in this respect, was never very far from the schools of nineteenth-century spiritualism it so vigorously sought to bury. The ghost of the spirit medium speaks through the psychoanalyst every time the patient, through the agency of transference, communes with the dead.

A year and four months after Engelman took his clandestine photographs of Freud's Vienna office, Freud died of cancer in his new home at 20 Maresfield Gardens in London. He died in his office, a room that had been renovated by his architect son Ernst and arranged by his maid Paula Fichtl to reproduce, as closely as possible, the office at Berggasse 19. In this, the most painful period of his sixteen year battle with oral cancer, Freud's

[51] Sandor Ferenczi, "Introjection and Transference," in *Sex in Psychoanalysis* (New York: Basic Books, 1950), p. 41.

office became his sickroom. It was here that Freud slipped into a coma after Max Schur, at Freud's request, administered the fatal doses of morphine that would end Freud's life on 23 September 1939. Cremated three days later, Freud's ashes were placed, according to the family's wishes, in a Greek urn—a red-figured Bell Krater presented to Freud as a gift by Marie Bonaparte. One might say that Freud at last found a resting place amongst his beloved antiquities.

This essay is part of a longer book-length project on the space of Freud's office. We would like to thank the many curators who made this research possible: Lydia Marinelli of the Freud Haus in Vienna; Erica Davies and J. Keith Davies of the Freud Museum in London; and Christian Witt-DörIn of the MAK (Österreichisches Museum für angewandte Kunst) in Vienna. We also thank Kim Yao, who assisted in the production of the architectural drawings. Most of all, we extend our gratitude to Edmund Engelman, who graciously agreed to be interviewed for this essay.

[FIGURE 7]
Freud at Study Desk
Courtesy of Edward Engelman,
Photographer

end

Untitled

JOHN LINDELL

REFERENCE
INTRO. PAGE 16

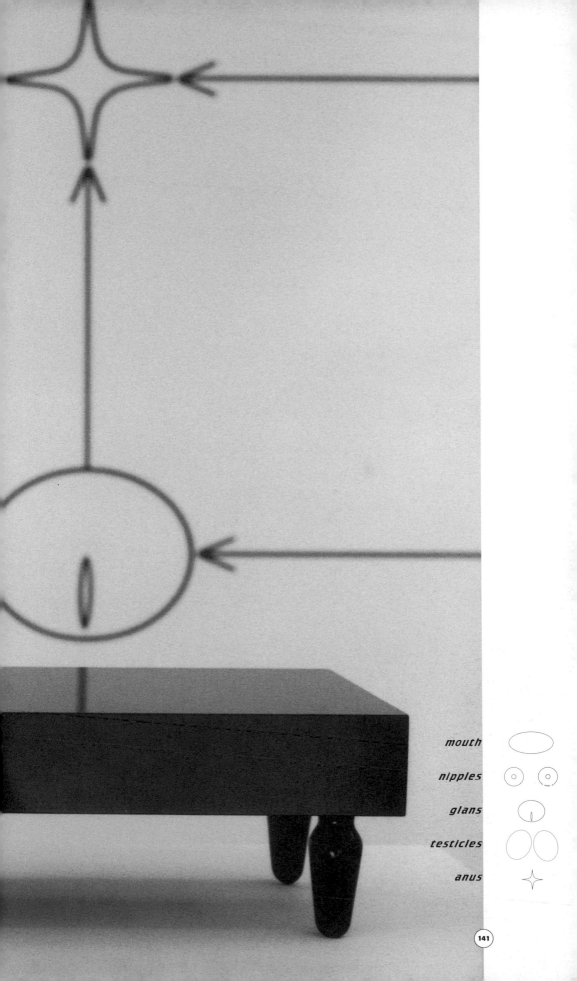

mouth

nipples

glans

testicles

anus

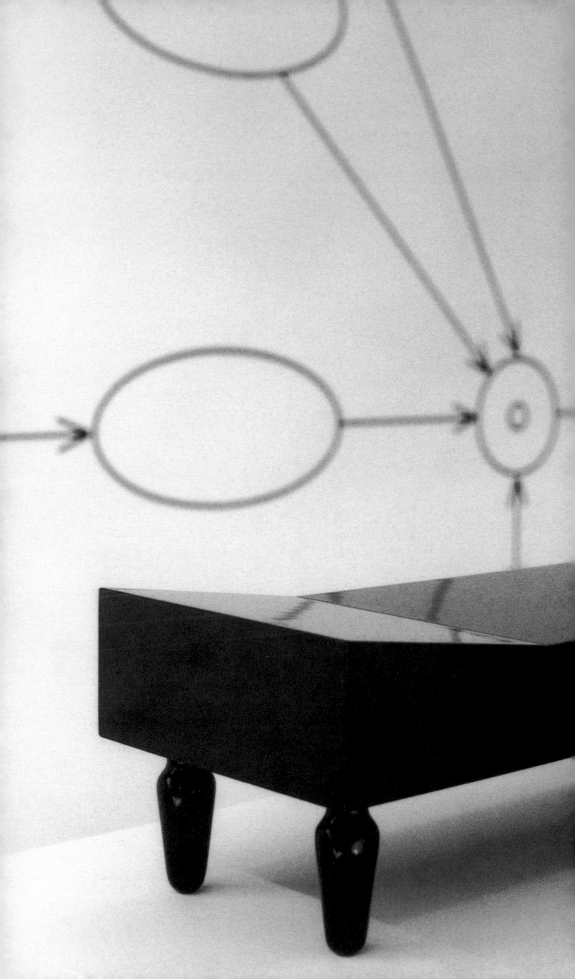

mouth

nipples

glans

testicles

anus

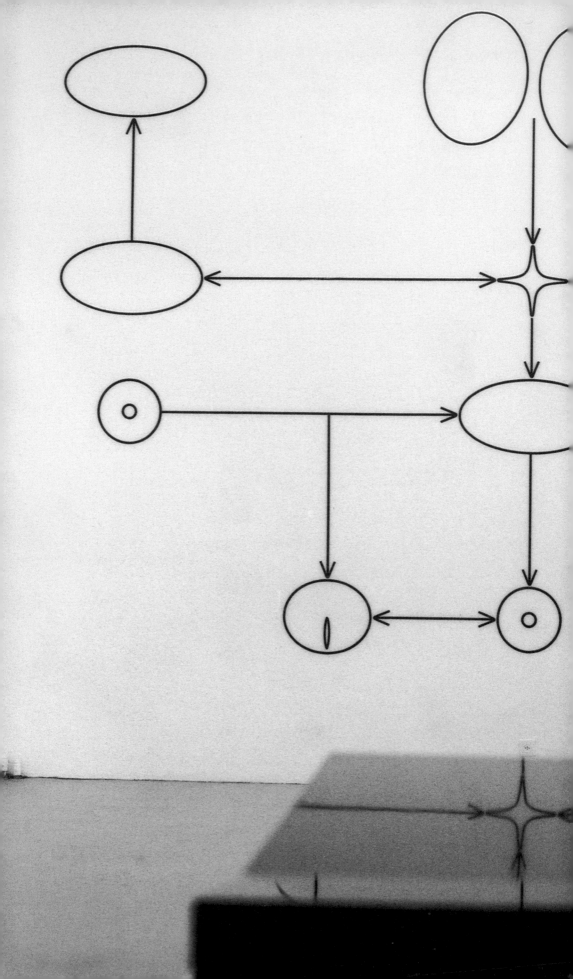

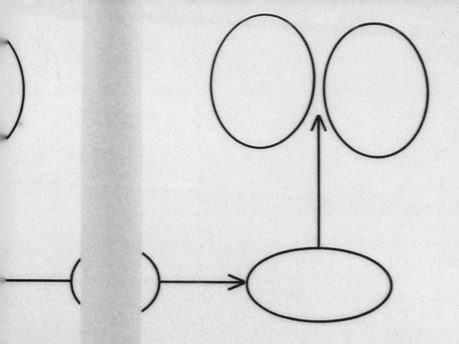

mouth

nipples

glans

testicles

anus

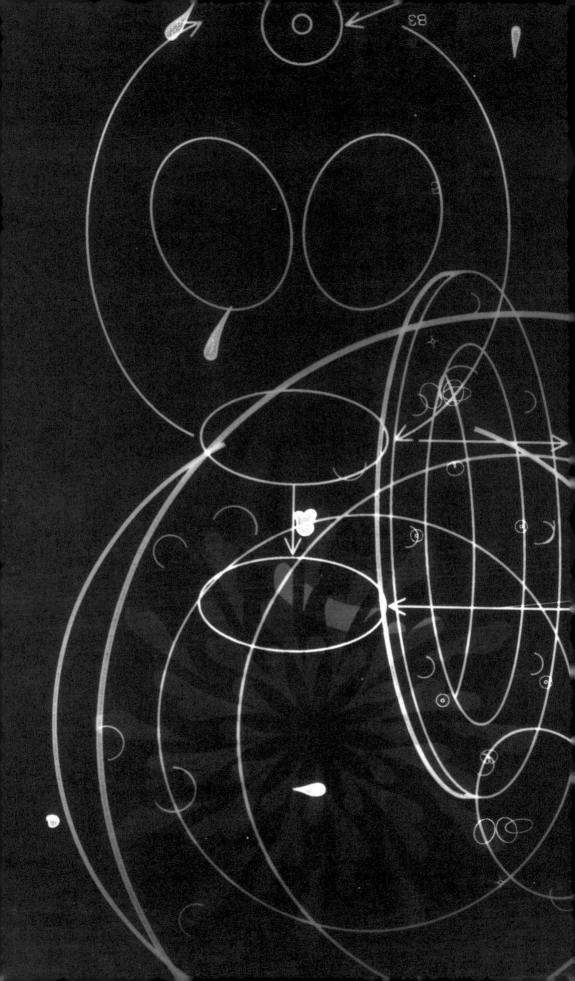

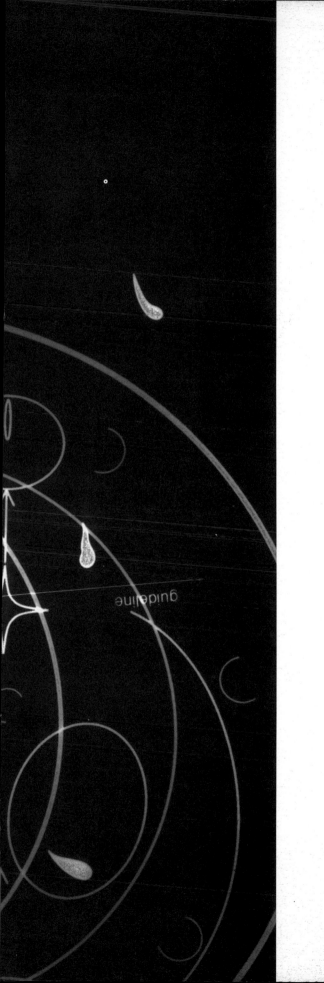

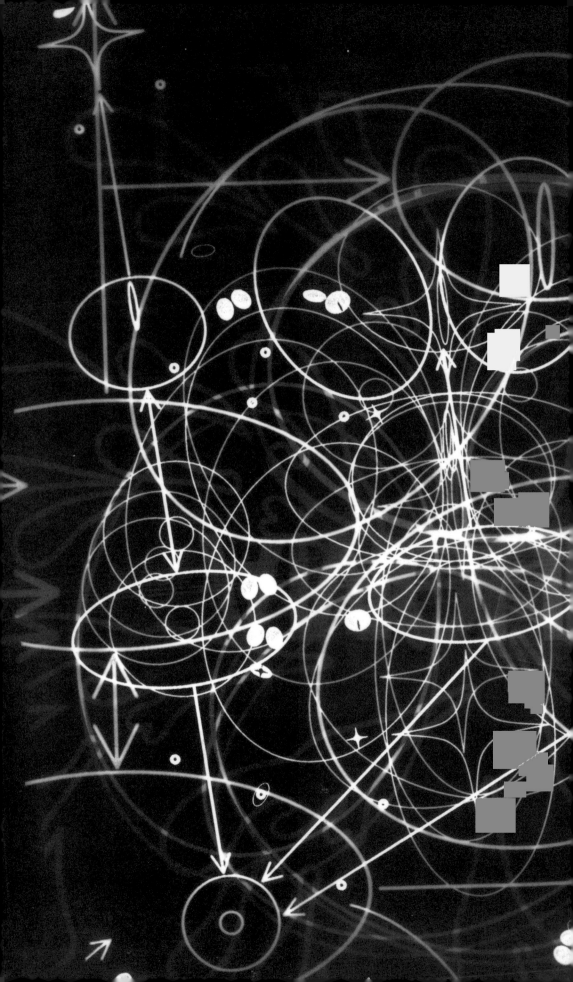

ESSAY BY

LEE EDELMAN

WORKS BY

INTERIM OFFICE OF ARCHITECTURE

KENNEDY AND VIOLICH ARCHITECTURE

ROBERT GOBER

PHILIPPE STARCK

Men's Room
LEE EDELMAN

I.   ***The public*** men's room, archi-
tecturally speaking, is rarely a room
with a view—or rarely, at least, a room that affords a view outside itself. Like
the closet, to which it is near allied (both as "water closet" and as site of
bodily relations discursively tabooed), the men's room tends to lack windows. And on those occasions when windows do figure as part of its structural design, the glass, more often translucent than transparent, generally
precludes any visual commerce between the areas without and within.
Substituting mirrors for windows, satisfying the eye's desire for depth of field
by returning its look to itself, the men's room, through a segmentation of
space that can justly be called self-reflexive, gestures, despite the accessibility of that space to a subset of the "public," towards an idea of interiority,
towards a principle of containment, implicit in the architectural imperative
that shapes the subject—forming and informing him as the subject of ideology—in its own monumentalizing image, modeling the subject as container of
space through the articulation of structural, because structuring, identities.

Closed in on itself as if to exemplify the
very notion of constructed space, but always, of course, designed to permit
exchanges between inside and outside analogous to those that would seem most
successfully arrested by its circumscription of the visual, this locus of functional
attention to culturally abjected bodily functions always necessarily functions in
excess of a logic of mere functionality. The men's room, that is, though clearly
conceived as a technological response to the hygienic concerns associated with
bodily necessities, constitutes a social technology in itself to necessitate a certain relation between the male subject and his body. The design of the men's
room, simply put, has palpable designs on men; it aspires, that is, to design them.
As a site of representation, as a space intended to "serve" the subject it collaborates to call into being, the men's room gives the male subject his body in its relation to symbolic space—effectively locating him within his body as he is located
within space itself—by allowing him, before the only public, the male one, whose
witness can matter, to enact, as if in a theater, the law of its mandatory closeting.
I refer, with this, not only to the law of (heterosexual) masculinity as we know it—
the law that reads the male body, in its potential to be seized, overwhelmed, by
erotic stimuli not provoked by the "proper" object (a woman) or centered in the
"proper" place (the genitals), as requiring consignment to a psychic space analogous to a closet—but also to the law whereby the straight male body becomes a
closet itself: a spatial enclosure for an autonomous subject able to imagine inhabiting his body only by conceiving his body simultaneously as container and thing
contained; as *being* and *needing* a closet; as bestowing upon him the social protection, the cultural shelter, it uniquely affords within our patriarchal sex-gender
system, but only so long as he performatively shelters the structural flaw that
opens his body, by way of its multiple openings (ocular, oral, anal, genital), to the
various psychic vicissitudes able to generate illicit desires. As a prime arena for
that performance, for that enactment of the body's compliance with the cultural
regulation of desire, the men's room marks a critical stage both for and in the
solicitation of masculine subjectivity.

II. But just as soliciting the subject can define the social project of the men's room, so it also names the threat against which the solicited subject must be sheltered. However much the men's room may prompt the performers within it to heed its own subjectifying call—the call it slyly assimilates to the irresistible call of nature itself—it allows for the possibility of error, for what the penal code calls soliciting for the purpose of committing unnatural acts. And the habitual structuring of the men's room to ensure the possibility of this error makes clear that whatever shelter it provides requires the presence of the threat its very design apparently solicits.

The men's room, set apart as it is to provide a culturally designated "privacy" in which to respond to the body's demands, houses two highly differentiated spaces that reestablish within it the consequential distinction between public and private zones, mapping each of those attributes onto specified zones of the male subject's body. Thus, the genitals, though figured as the "private parts," acquire, through the openness of the urinal, a relatively "public" status here, while the anus and its functional necessity bear weightier burdens of social embarrassment.[1] In the men's room the norms of male bodily display reverse the values that the laws of *pudeur* assign to the privatized portions of male anatomy in the world outside: you don't show your ass in the men's room; and you don't conceal your dick. The partition that distinguishes the privacy of the stalls from the exposure of the urinals and sinks, therefore, defines the men's room, like the U.S. Congress, as strategically bicameral, allowing each part of its legislative body to hold the other in check. As *camera lucida* and *camera obscura* at once, the men's room might simply come out and proclaim as its motto "I am a camera" were it not that it operates more saliently as a factory for turning into cameras themselves all those who enter to confront, as if *in camera*, the unblinking eye of the law that keeps watch, through every patron's eye—including, signally, their own—to see that what is publicly displayed is never directly observed.

III. The law of the men's room decrees that men's dicks be available for public contemplation at the urinal precisely to allow a correlative mandate: that such contemplation must never take place. The performative bravado, "naturalized" only

1 These sentences condense an argument I have made at greater length in "Tearooms and Sympathy; Or, The Epistemology of the Water Closet," in my *Homographesis: Essays in Gay Literary and Cultural Theory* (New York and London: Routledge, 1994), pp. 148-170. Since I will focus in this essay primarily on the significations informing the logic of the urinal, I cite here, by way of contextualization, a passage from "Tearooms and Sympathy" that may help to trace the lineaments of my argument concerning the space of the stall:

"I want to suggest that the men's room . . . is the site of a particular heterosexual anxiety about the potential inscriptions of homosexual desire and about the possibility of knowing or recognizing whatever might constitute 'homosexual difference.'

"This can be intuited more readily when the restroom is considered not, as it is by Lacan, in terms of 'urinary segregation'—a context that establishes the phallus from the outset as the token of anatomical difference—but as the site of a loosening of sphincter control, evoking, therefore, an older eroticism, undifferentiated by gender, because anterior to the genital tyranny that raises the phallus to its privileged position. Precisely because the phallus marks the putative stability of the divide between "Ladies" and "Gentlemen," because it articulates the concept of sexual difference in terms of 'visible perception,' the 'urinary' function in the institutional men's room customarily takes place within view of others—as if to indicate its status as an act of definitional display; but the private enclosure of the toilet stall signals the potential anxiety at issue in the West when the men's room becomes the locus not of urinary but of intestinal relief. For the satisfaction that such relief affords abuts dangerously on homophobically abjectified desires, and because that satisfaction marks an opening onto difference that would challenge the phallic supremacy and coherence of the signifier on the men's room door, it must be isolated and kept in view at once lest its erotic potential come out" (pp. 160-161).

by virtue of cultural insistence, implicit in taking one's dick in one's hand in the presence of other men similarly engaged, depends upon one of two governing assumptions: either that such a display can occur because the space that permits it is consecrated, more or less explicitly, to the purposes of gay male sex, or that the display itself contemptuously—or apotropaically—declares its refusal to allow that such a space could possibly be one where gay men, or gay male desire, might appear. Oscillating between these two assumptions, the logic of the men's room compels the normative enactment of a vigilant nonchalance that responds to the disciplinary pressure that the men's room exerts upon visual relations. Though the open display of the glans at the urinal disavows its capacity to occasion desire, the vector of the gaze, however oblique, remains alert to observe the glance that exposes any interest at all in the glans thus exposed. Where better to discern the full force of aggression implicit in the question—"Are you looking at *me*?"—that condenses our pervasive male cultural anxiety about the capacities of gay men to transform, or to queer, the consistency of the reality produced and assured by the gaze of the symbolic? And if, in response to that question as posed by a man at a urinal taking a leak, another patron, so occupied or not, should answer, unapologetically, "yes," or if he should urge his irate companion to seek out the cloistered protection of a stall if he so dislikes being looked at that way, then how could the first man respond to this blatant defiance of the law so cunningly built into the architectural disposition of this space but with what he must view as an *equivalent* violence, whether it be verbal—as in, for instance, the clarion-cry, "Faggot!," with which certain straight men imagine they display a triumphant acuity in unveiling what was staring them in the face all along—or physical—as in the numerous blows with which, in response to this discovery, they try to consign to oblivion all those of whose type they resent their inability to be, for so much as a moment, oblivious themselves.

At the urinal, then, the ritualistic indifference that must seem to accompany, and must seem to greet, each act of genital display aspires to conceal the constant scrutiny bestowed by every sidelong glance on every sidelong glance. Whereas women may retreat to the powder room—alone or even, to the comically theatricalized befuddlement of heterosexual men, in pairs—to attend, as its very name suggests, to the question of how they look, men, upon entering the men's room, focus instead on how they are looking, or, more precisely, on how their looking may be looked upon in turn. If the men's room offers no windows through which the eye can escape its locale, and if it prohibits the eye from alighting on what the design of the urinal insists nonetheless on publicly drawing out, then its space might properly be interpreted as the very site of the symbolic gaze, as a space that monitors the circuitry of visual relations propping up a "reality" in which each look of the subject is filtered through the gaze of a symbolic order that, in every sense of the word, solicits him. Consider, after all, that however much the men who stand shoulder to shoulder at the urinal may study the eyes of their neighbors through the corners of their own, the frontal force of their attention will fall, most often, upon their own member and the arc of what it voids. And what, in such a case, can the eye be looking for, or at, if not a look, if not a *way* of looking, that either will confirm the symbolic gaze that solicits the subject as heterosexual through the phal-licization—which necessitates the ocularization—of the penis, or else will threat-en, shake, solicit the coherence of the heterosexual subject through the recog-nition of another desire, another solicitation, superimposed upon the images that parade as solid social reality like distorting ghosts rudely conjured by interfer-ence in video reception when the signals from two adjoining channels are both displayed at once. His penis, that is, must be seen by the straight male subject as what sees him and hence, like the antenna of a television set, as what enables him to see: as the visible gaze of the symbolic, the part of his body least his own, that takes *his* measure and grants him a privileged place in the structure of social meaning as it justifies his place within the room set aside for men. But should its sublation into the phallic eye be put on the blink by the glance of a man who, seeming to meet what should be its gaze, seemingly gazes back only at meat, such justifications may vanish and, with them, the subject's own solidi-ty, his place in the social architecture, as he and the images shaping his world themselves fade into ghostliness, unexpectedly picking up frequencies they had been programmed not to receive so as to keep their focus singularly fixed on the channel that common wisdom receives as the site of public access.

IV. The following, written by Monique P. Yazigi, appeared under the title, "What Do Men Want? Perhaps, Says a Restaurant, Private TV?," in the "City" section of the *New York Times* on 23 October 1994:

> *The American Renaissance Restaurant, at 260 West*
> *Broadway, has inset two 13-inch Mitsubishi television*
> *sets above the two black porcelain urinals in the men's*
> *bathroom. "You would have to be a man to understand*
> *why we did it," said John Aron, the manager of the*
> *restaurant, giggling. "Men usually have nothing to look*
> *at and they certainly don't want their eyes to wander."*

Tellingly, the entrance to the men's room here first passes, at least allusively, through Freud's interrogation of *female* desire—as famously expressed in his much cited query, *"Was will das Weib?"*: "What does woman want?"—as if to con-firm a complementarity, like that of paired lavatory doors, that disavows any seri-ous doubt about what men *really* want. Though the surety of that knowledge lets the title relax into the cultural stereotype, comically deployed, of the success-fully domesticated heterosexual man whose desire has been channeled by—and toward—the channels on his TV, that humor can barely distract from the static introduced by conceiving the men's room as a place in which men's desires, sus-ceptible to rechanneling as they thus appear to be, might plausibly find satisfac-tion. Indeed, when the restaurant's owner, accounting for the televisions in terms at a variance—strategically unremarked—from those of the manager cited above, explains that, "We want people to feel like they're at home," one might reason-ably reflect on Freud's well-known analysis of the homelike and the unfamiliar, the *heimlich* and the *unheimlich*, which disconcertingly come together as the double-edged shadow of the uncanny cuts its way across the can to cancel any and every assurance about where men may feel at home.

For Freud, of course, the uncanny names the experience of derealization provoked by some threat to the ego's integrity that recalls the time before the ego had fully detached itself from the world. Bound up, therefore, with a sense of doubleness as the subject, in a vertiginous rupture of the ground on which he stands, senses himself unexpectedly observed and all at once starts to view himself through the eyes of another person or thing that seems, improperly and unnaturally, to usurp his subjectivity, the uncanny always manifests itself in a troubling, which can take specific form as a doubling, of the gaze. The subject, in *its* grip, will always feel that he is losing *his*, finding himself no longer at home in the world he thought he knew; for this alarming disappearance of the sense of "at home-ness," which occurs, however paradoxically, with a certain sickening familiarity, signals a toppling of the walls within which the subject has been constructed and through which he has realized the imaginary architecture of a self. The uncanny, then, might be understood as a distinctive type of "home-sickness" that, like dwellings inadequately vented to allow air to circulate in and out, produces a sickness of and in the home that occasions a nostalgic longing for the sense of safety that "home" once assured.

Only in such a context should one interpret the claim that TVs in the men's room help patrons to "feel like they're at home." Some men, to be sure, determined to catch every moment of excitement as they watch The Big Game, may leave the door to the bathroom ajar—or open—when they make their needful retreat to use the facilities at home, but very few would count among the tell-tale signs of "home-liness" the luxury of having a television set available in the john. Although the "meaning" of the television may be colored by its connection to the life men live in the living room, its association with the *heimlich* turns *unheimlich* in the bathroom, which is never to be conceptualized as a room wherein life could be lived. After all, as anyone who has ever placed or read a real−estate advertisement knows, bathrooms are not even numbered as rooms when describing the size of a home. Rather than make the space of the men's room as comfortable as one's own home, therefore, placing televisions above the urinals reflects an awareness that it only heightens in attempting to occlude: that the men's room is an uncanny space where the gaze of the symbolic order sees male bodies into social meaning, thereby establishing the men's room as a nodal point, ground zero, in the cultural compaction of masculinity into a logic of visual relations.

The manager of the restaurant comes closer to this truth in his mini-meditation on the customary misfortunes of the men's room and men's eyes. Just as the owner can only address the uncanniness that structures the men's room, however, through his representation of the television sets as making the space more like "home," so the manager can only identify the double vision the men's room induces by contradictorily insisting, on the one hand, that it offers those using it "nothing to look at" while recognizing, on the other hand, a temptation within it fully capable of enticing their eyes "to wander." But this contradiction resolves into clarity once the visible dicks at the urinal, toward which their eyes might incautiously turn, are understood to carry, as if by legislative decree, a sort of Surgeon General's warning that labels them precisely *as* "nothing to look at," thus granting them all the power, and danger, of Yahweh rising up before Moses from out of another sort of bush. And just as the prohibition against glimpsing Yahweh's face coincided with a prohibition against speaking his name, so here, for the manager and owner both—as, indeed, for the culture they inhabit—the law that prohibits the gaze of a man from resting on his neighbor's dick suffers under prohibition itself as something that every man must know but none must ever pronounce. "You'd have to be a man to understand," as the manager rightly puts it, alluding to the homophobic commandment of the men's room that solicits the subject into manhood as unmistakably as the voice of Yahweh called Moses to his destiny before the Law.

V.   The televisions above the urinals, commanding the attention of men with the intelligence to read the writing on the wall, stand in for, and thereby figure, the thing, the "nothing," they must not view. Just as a quasi-Lacanian doctrine would have it that wherever the imaginary, dyadic relation between man and TV set holds sway, it must always yield to the rule of the symbolic through the intrusion, both regular and regulatory, of an inevitable third term, the remote control, so in this less customary configuration, the man who has taken his dick from his pants, like the stranger who stands there beside him, glues his eyes resolutely to the video monitor not only to keep his gaze under control, but also, and more crucially, to display that control for the other who monitors *him*. If the thing in his hand still functions, nonetheless, as an instrument of remote control, then surely it is he who is subject to control by virtue of having been "subjected," as it were, into a position of control by it. The two screens staring from the lavatory wall may evoke a binocular vision designed to enthrall men's looks like the ocellated patterns on a predator's outspread wings, but they merely unfold the phallic gaze into which the dick, like a lowly caterpillar becoming a butterfly, turns. And any man who turns towards his neighbor to witness that transformation risks suffering a transformation himself, becoming, as a certain slang would have it, a different sort of "butterfly," thus earning a punishment similar in kind to the heavier lot that befell Lot's wife in return for her furtive, backward glance at the spectacle of Sodom's end.

As the television, for the subject in this symbolic enclosure, comes to occupy the position of the phallicized dick—which is always the dick of the Other; and as his own dick comes to assume the position of the disciplinary gaze; so he in turn can only come across as one more image traversing the screen, carefully programmed by the culture that sponsors him to flesh out its shadowy "reality" with the endlessly rerun drama that screens his situation's comedy from view. Pinned within this triangle whose protection he flashes as ostentatiously as an enameled flag on his lapel, this subject resists, as if he gave no thought to it at all, the fourth term flashed by his neighbor, the dick eroticized *as* dick, which threatens to bathe the triangle an embarrassing shade of pink, or, worse, to reshape it as the diamond that is only, he knows, a *girl's* best friend.[2]

VI.   Who could envy the person on whom this lesson has been lost when, positioned before the urinal, having, admittedly, let the ray of his gaze be bent away from the television screen by a glimmer of someone's family jewels on view across the way, he hears their rightful owner call out, to every man in the men's room save, as he soon finds out, himself: "I thought this was where the dicks hang out; who let this pussy in?" Dicks, as in the schema above, take the place of male subjects here; and if they acquire the status, figuratively speaking, of so many birds of a feather, then "pussy" names the luckless cat caught wanting to swallow the canary. For just as the penis in the men's room undergoes phallic ocularization, so the eye regresses to a more primitive stage of oral incorporation. And since, in this always uncanny space, the subject, as if reenacting his primal encounter with the symbolic gaze, finds himself sundered into subjectivity, alienated into an identity always at a distance from the representation by which he totalizes himself, the devouring eye will connote at once his ravenous desire to appropriate the image that would heal his symbolic wound—the wound that is, itself, the symbolic—and his aggressive anxiety lest he be devoured by the annihilating, appropriative gaze of the Other.

All of which means, more simply, that in the men's room, looking sucks. So long as no one can see him, of course, a man who thinks himself straight may allow, on occasion, for one whom he thinks of as bent to

2 When it underwent remodelling recently, Splash, a popular Manhattan gay bar, similarly had television monitors installed above the urinals in its men's room. Unveiling on its screens, however, exactly what those of the American Renaissance Restaurant attempt, as visual magnets, to displace, Splash offers its patrons images of eroticized male bodies that function like the go-go guys who dance and disrobe in the bar: they appeal to the gay male desire to see what the norms of straight culture conceal while providing the reassurance of a screen to keep that desire from demanding, too nakedly or aggressively, a reciprocal response.

bend, in fitting and proper homage, before an uprightness not solely embodied in the posture the straight man maintains; but letting himself be eyeballed where others might witness his acquiescence to the heavy-lidded, almost feline look that takes in whatever hangs out can only expose him to a questioning in which the very part exposed will hang in the balance, suspended in doubt, as if in the process of opening his trousers so as to gain access to his dick he had unwittingly let the cat—that is, the pussy—out of the bag.

The bullying voice at the urinal so quick to terrorize any look not fixed unswervingly straight ahead—and hence any look not unswervingly straight—thus articulates the logic of the men's room in the process of animating the male subject, speaking through him its accusatory language of a sexual (Charlie) McCarthyism. And the men's room, when all is said and done, knows only the one word, "pussy," though it comes in a striking variety of forms and has so many more than nine lives. All appearances to the contrary, the secret truth of the men's room for straight male subjects is simply this: there can be no dicks within it (they fail to register on straight men's screens) only "pussies" and those who are not "pussies," only those who are out to look and others who are ever on the lookout for them. In effect, then, however paradoxical, the men's room signifies effeminization insofar as it appears to demand a disavowal, a renunciation, of visual desire even while necessitating that men confront, in the mind's eye, if nowhere else, the image of what they must not see if they wish to continue to have.

Small wonder, then, that this space should occasion so general and widespread an anxiety that the owners of the American Renaissance Restaurant would install TVs above the urinals in a well-considered effort to forestall discomfort in the comfort station. But if those machines for the reception of images seek to overcompensate for the image of the dick that no male orifice can properly receive, then perhaps it makes sense that the *New York Times* included in the news it deemed fit to print the fact that each of the television screens measured exactly "13-inch[es]," a size that is hardly noteworthy where only *television sets* are concerned.

VII.   That something *more* than television sets might be at issue, however—that the "13 inch[es]" on which men's eyes, like the piece in the *Times*, must focus could double for the something *less* whose average length, as medical research calculates, it slightly more than doubles—comes out with the word the article uses to evoke the manager's affect while asserting that one would "have to be a man to understand why" the restaurant owners chose to put the TVs in the men's room. Such a statement, after all, when uttered by one represented, while doing so, as "giggling," would seem to exclude from the zone of understanding the very one who makes it; for "to giggle," as the *Random House Dictionary* notes, is "to laugh in a silly, often high-pitched way. . . as from juvenile or ill-concealed amusement or nervous embarrassment." More than merely girlish—though that, in the context of the men's room, would surely count as indictment enough—the giggle is downright sissified, even bordering on camp, its onomatopoeic origins making the word itself an embarrassment and calling to mind such equally effeminizing motions of the body as, for example, the jiggle or the wiggle to which, by way of the signifier, it is, at least in English, metonymically linked.

"Silly," "high-pitched," "ill-concealed," "nervous": why not just call a cat a cat and crown the giggle the undisputed closet queen of mirth? Expressing a pleasure it self-consciously tries, and audibly fails, to restrain, the giggle, whenever it escapes from a man, reveals, if not the homo, then at the very least the homunculus: the little man, the juvenile, the boy inside who won't grow up, who still resists the necessity of embracing responsibility—which is also to say, a wife—in order to assume his status as censorious adult. Like some contemporary fountain of youth, the water closet seems to effect this miraculous rejuvenation as it confronts us with bodily movements for which there is scarce an adult vocabulary and to which, no matter what our age, there can be no adult relation. Perversely, then, the men's room, in the same way it effeminizes, also, like a time machine, turns grown men into boys. And how could it do otherwise, designed as it is to return them not only to the site of the symbolic gaze, but also to the public performance of bodily functions that carried a libidinal charge when first placed under surveillance by a keen parental eye in order to call forth the subject as he who internalizes cultural power by learning to display an efficient control (one that parents will blithely call "his") both *over* his turbulent body and, that mission accomplished, *through* it.

The gruffest taunt at the urinal, as such a public display of control, may strive to defend against it, but can no more escape the infantilizing logic that literally structures the men's room than the manager's giggle can hide the extent to which the very idea of that space seems to plunge him, as indeed it must plunge us all, deep in a mental echo chamber vibrating still to the sound of words such as "pee-pee," "wee-wee," and "poop." Like the densely-packed days of his youth, the young boy's functions may be numbered, but they stretch in their binary rotation to the very crack of doom, carrying with them the power to revive, unconsciously, the first solicitation of the men's room: that bittersweet moment when watchful eyes, well pleased, bent into approving smiles and the lavatory's surfaces rang with praise—"Now there's a good little man!" For some that scene will be replayed before the days of their youth are done, winning a similar approbation, though with other acts and for other eyes than those that glowed with parental pride at their, and the child's, success; but that first solicitation is sufficient to assure that no one who steps into the men's room will ever do so as a man, or leave it without a sense of relief more profound than he lets himself know.

VIII.   So they stand at the porcelain urinals, the various patrons of the men's room, effeminized or infantilized, reduced to giggles or gibes when not preserving a safer silence that lets them pour from themselves, like a chorus replacing the voices they dare not raise, the sound of many waters, each bright stream as much a tribute *to* as tributary *of* the law that flows through each and every one as though they were its channels. And if their obedient eyes are fixed, in one *particular* rest room, on a channel that they can never change on a TV set they can never turn off, will anyone really believe that this architectural innovation does more than allegorize the general principles that underlie and shape the public men's room—and, with it, men? Much like a television set itself, the manager's claim that the TVs serve to keep men's eyes from wandering must be understood as a screen through which a strategic window on a cultural truth may well, in fact, be opened, but only in the process of lowering across it a curtain—almost, but not quite sheer—that filters the truth from view.

Surely, after all, if lowering a blind, and thereby assuring a certain blindness, had really motivated the designers of this space, a plain partition, even if fashioned from the finest black porcelain to match the urinals, would have proven far more effective as a visual prophylactic and have done so, just as importantly, at considerably lesser expense. But the urinal, and in this the American Renaissance men's room offers a lesson, aims not to enforce a blindness, but to induce it in vision itself: to intensify and heighten responsiveness to visual stimulation, but to displace it from the "nothing" that is there most saliently on display to the very mechanics of looking into which that "nothing" is absorbed. The most Miltonic of structures, the urinal not only institutionalizes the disciplinary gaze with which, long ago, our first parents—those on whom we bestowed the name before they gradually faded within it, diffused into the social functions we didn't realize they already were—enjoyed what they saw as our triumphs and bemoaned what they saw as our shames, but also maintains as its doxa that all men sufficient to stand before it must always in turn be free to fall: free, that is, to fall precisely into the shame of a visibility fitting as punishment for the stolen glance that attempts to see beneath the veil, that precious invisible cloth, by means of which the naked dick is tricked out in phallic drag.

The urinal's golden temple works to make all of us men of that cloth, celebrants at a sacred fount before which we gather, dicks in hand, to show our faith in the machinery of our ideological redemption. And the mystery of the faith is this: whether focusing raptly on the television screen or attending singlemindedly to the parabola of our piss, our salvation depends on our failing to see that these things are done in parables; directly reversing St. Mark, that is, we are only saved insofar as in seeing, we may see, and *not* perceive. By this truth the men's room reconciles the contradictory tenets, both of them palpable lies, in which all who would pass for men must show, by deed and not word, their belief: there is nothing to see at the urinal and those who use it have nothing to hide. The dicks that hang out in the men's room may hide themselves in plain sight, but in doing so they stretch, unawares, toward an inversion of the Pisgah sight that Moses was allowed. Assuming the name of the father, all those who clutch their dicks like drooping flags assert a claim to their rightful place in the privileged realm of "men" towards which, one might say, from before the beginning their steps were always turned; but if they, unlike Moses, gain entry into the land that they were promised, it is only on the condition that they, unlike Moses, will never be permitted to see it—will never, at any rate, see what it is that, by seeing, they would be missing, since the single article of faith, the only thing in the whole of the men's room that must unfailingly be observed, is the doctrine on which the revelation of the dick at the urinal always relies: seeing is *not* believing. The men's room demands that we take it—and thus that we take it out—on faith; let us call it the faith of the fathers, the faith that makes all of us wholly ghosts, mere images of the images that pass across the screen, haunted still by a memory, vague and almost irretrievable—if not a screen itself—of being taken, against our will, hand writhing in mother's larger hand, to do our business where even then we knew we had no business: the *other* room that would cast its shadow, as cutting as that of the uncanny, forever after across our vision of the business of being a man.

Two Public Toilets

The Public Bathroom Project,
Boston Center for the Arts,
Boston, MA, 1993

KENNEDY and VIOLICH
ARCHITECTURE

The Latrine Project,
Headlands Center for the Arts,
Sausalito, CA, 1987-1988

INTERIM OFFICE of
ARCHITECTURE
(IOOA)

**Interim Office of
Architecture**
*View of Non-
Functioning Urinals*

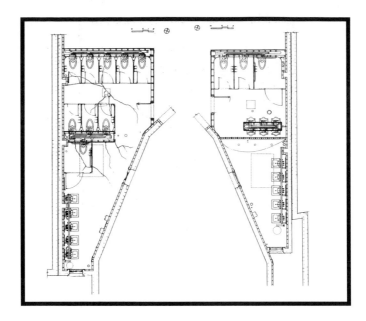

Both Interim Office of Architecture (Bruce Tomb and John Randolph) and Kennedy and Violich Architecture use commissions to renovate public bathrooms in urban arts centers as pretexts for exposing and subverting the architectural codes that shape and regulate sexual identity.

The programmatic necessity of modifying pre-existing gender assignments drives both firms' designs. Within the 1920s Cyclorama Building now occupied by the Boston Center for the Arts, existing plumbing configurations, budget constraints, and space requirements compelled Sheila Kennedy and Frano Violich to construct the new women's room in the space formerly occupied by the men's room and the new men's room in the space that previously housed the women's room. Similarly, at the "Latrine Project," Interim Office of Architecture reconfigure a 1940s single-sex army latrine to form a coed public lavatory for the Headlands Center for the Arts in Sausalito, California.

Conventional bathroom architecture confirms and naturalizes gender distinctions by segregating the sexes within rigidly contained spaces. Subscribing to the popularly held belief that lavatory design responds to the functional demands of anatomical difference, the public restroom perpetuates the notion that gender rests squarely on the foundations of anatomy. In their projects, both teams highlight and debunk this myth by emphasizing the interchangeability of these supposedly site-specific spaces. Adopting strikingly similar design strategies, they expose and preserve traces of existing infrastructure, identified with one gender, in new spaces now designated for the other. At the Boston Center for the Arts, floor drains—the severed remains of old urinals—are paired with new sinks in the women's room. Holes of toilet stacks once enclosed in the women's stalls mark a threshold to the urinal chase in the men's room. In its original state, the Headlands military latrine possessed a line of sinks and open showers, a row of exposed urinals, and a cluster of unpartitioned toilets; men would urinate, defecate, and wash within an undifferentiated space. This was

> For a discussion of how public bathroom architecture participates in the construction of sexual difference, see the Introduction to this volume.

Kennedy and
Violich Architecture
*Floor Plan of Women's
and Men's Rooms*

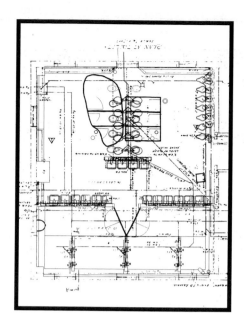

obviously an inappropriate condition for a contemporary coed bathroom. In their conversion, IOOA respects the spatial order and material austerity of the room's past. Faucetless sinks and fixtureless urinals are now dispersed among the working fixtures. In both projects, the dysfunctional remnants of toilet fixtures disturbingly refer to the emasculation of once manly spaces.

In addition, both teams of architects call attention to the abject functions of the biological body accommodated within but suppressed by the hygienic white surfaces of the public bathroom. Kennedy and Violich expose the chase, the space discretely contained within the wall that conceals the clean and waste water pipes that conduct bodily waste and fluids. According to the architects, in its etymological relation to the old French *chas* and the Latin *capsa*, the chase is associated with chastity and enclosure. Disturbing the seamless porcelain shell of the chase that masks the space of the abject, Kennedy and Violich use quarter-round tile coves to produce an involuted and puckered surface. In addition, they inscribe images and texts excerpted from Plumbing Standards on the ceramic glaze. Exposing not only the space but the sound of the abject at the Headlands, IOOA employ those architectural elements that normally conceal bodily functions to reveal them. Expectations of privacy afforded by 1/4"-thick steel plate toilet partitions are undermined by mounting them too high off the ground. The materials of the lavatory make noise, amplifying even the most delicate of bodily sounds. The steel doors to the toilet stalls creak. Plumbing lines, hung from the ceiling, make audible the sound of rushing water: when the toilets are flushed, their flexible, braided steel tubes (actually, aircraft fuel lines) wiggle under high pressure, causing the rush of fluids to resound throughout the space.

Making the user aware of the ways in which the ostensibly functional architecture of the restroom perpetuates social attitudes about gender, hygiene, and propriety, both renovation projects disclose how, contrary to our expectations, biology is not destiny in the public bathroom. —*J.S.*

Interim Office of Architecture
Floor Plan of the Latrine

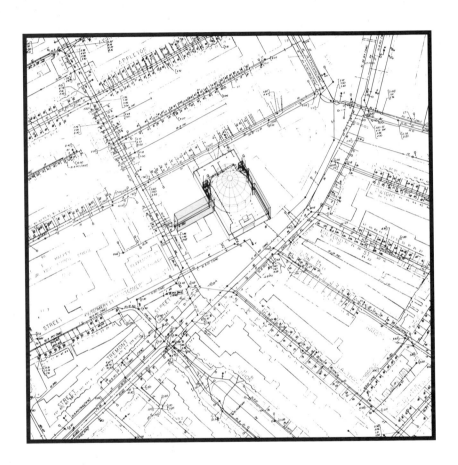

**Kennedy and
Violich Architecture**
Site Plan

Kennedy and
Violich Architecture
Urinal Fragment
Below Sink

**Kennedy and
Violich Architecture**
*Women's Bathroom and Detail of
Puckered Tile and Drain Microbe Tile*

**Kennedy and
Violich Architecture**
*Men's Bathroom and Detail of
Text Tile from Building Code*

**Interim Office of
Architecture**
*View of the Sink Wall
with Lights Above*

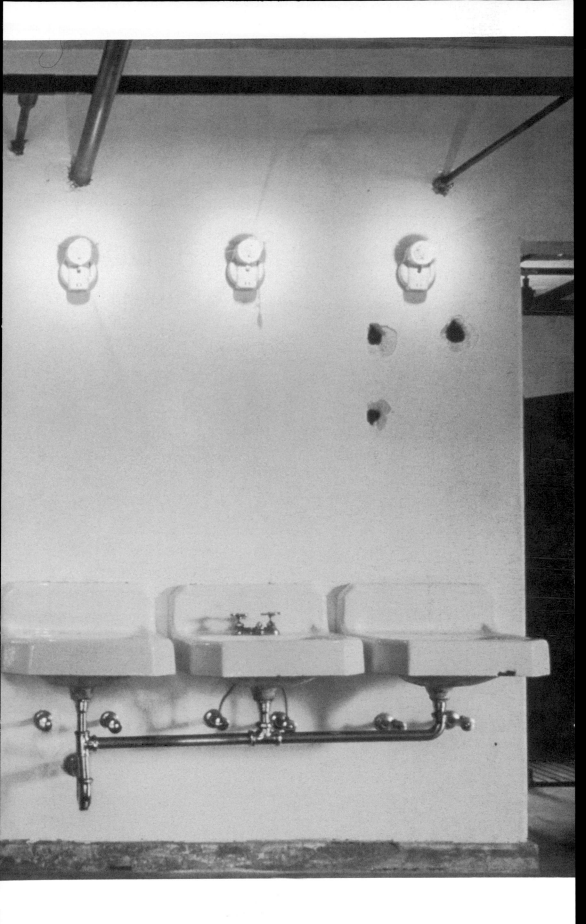

**Interim Office
of Architecture**
*View of Existing Porcelain Toilet with
Braided Stainless Steel Supply Hose*

**Interim Office of
Architecture**
*View of Privacy Stall with
Steel Supply Hose*

Untitled

ROBERT GOBER

REFERENCE
INTRO. PAGE 20

Drain
[1989]
Cast pewter

Two Urinals

[1986]

Wire lath, plaster, wood,
semi-gloss enamel

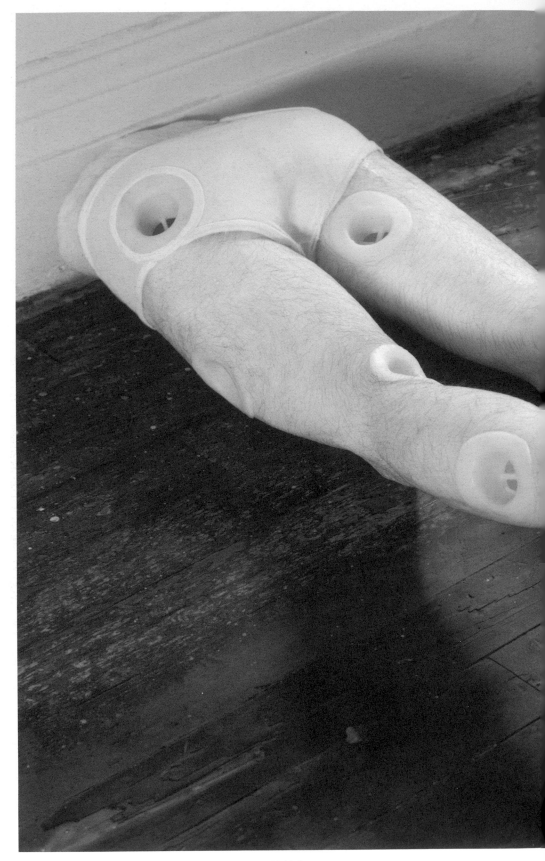

Untitled
(1991-1993)
Wood, wax, human hair, fabric,
fabric paint, shoes

Selected Bathrooms

PHILIPPE STARCK

REFERENCE
INTRO. PAGE 18

Men's Room,
Royalton Hotel,
New York City
Communal Sink

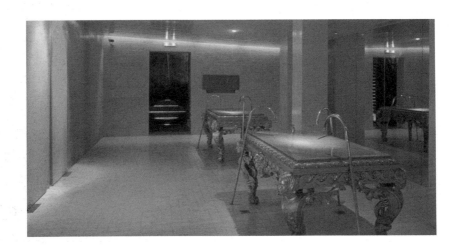

Teatriz, Madrid
*View of Bathroom and
Sink Detail*

*View of Cubicle and
Door Detail*

ESSAY BY

MARCIA IAN

WORKS BY

THANHAUSER AND ESTERSON

MATTHEW BANNISTER

MATTHEW BARNEY

When Is a Body Not a Body? When It's a Building
MARCIA IAN

I.

"The gym is full of social people, and that's not even counting the pencilnecks whose main purpose in the gym is to follow thongs around—or the thongs whose main purpose is to ignore the pencilnecks and follow good-looking bodybuilders around."[1]

The bodybuilder labors to erect a building on the site that was his body. As a sport, as an art, as a compound noun masquerading as a complex concept, bodybuilding relies first and foremost on an architectural metaphor. The motivation behind bodybuilding is the will to build a better, or at least a different, body. Also implicit in this compound of "body" and "building," however, is a wish to equate the two, and thereby elide the distinction between the organic and the inorganic. I would even claim that to treat the body as inanimate, to turn something merely alive into a perdurable thing, is the true purpose of bodybuilding as a "practice." The bodybuilder treats his own flesh as if it were material he can redesign, reconfigure, and reshape from the ground up, as if to liberate his own inner building. In bodybuilding lingo, he trains and diets in such a way as to "shred" his muscles in order to "tear down" the existing structure, to substitute the "rock hard" for the soft, the monumental for the human, and the masculine for the feminine.[2] The only natural limitation the hard-core body-builder—he for whom the slogan "No Limits" is not just the logo on a brand of gymwear but also a kind of religious belief—will acknowledge is what he reverently terms "genetics."

The Apollon Gym is always full, even when no one is there; the Apollon Gym is always empty, even when it is full of people. It is a typical gym insofar as it functions equivocally as a social and anti-social space. In this respect the Apollon can serve as a model gym, its form and function ideally suited to eliminate the difference, or space, between flesh and metal. Paradoxically, the gym is a space designed to eliminate space and it does so, I would argue, by negating, or at least by denying, interiority. By "interiority" I refer to the inner precincts of body and mind as well as the physical space created by the walls of a room or building. The present site of the Apollon, in Edison, New Jersey, used to be an auto body shop; it is now a human body shop. The building fronts a busy commercial street lined with warehouses; huge tractor trailers rumble up and down the street at all hours. On this site, our flesh is both forced into dangerous proximity with senseless metal, and not forced, because we bring our bodies there in order to make them as hard as possible, to approximate or proximate the inanimate.[3]

1 Tom Platz in *Ironman* (October 1995).

2 In my experience, this is equally true for the serious female bodybuilder. Moreover, defining the qualities (and quantities) connoted by the term "masculinity," as well as identifying how, when, and even if, ideal masculinity may be distinguished from femininity, is a crucial issue for female as much as for male bodybuilders.

3 By "we" I refer to the population of "serious" lifters, confirmed "gym rats," and others who find it necessary to work out hard, heavy, and often.

Entering the front door of the Apollon, one passes through a small vestibule with glass on both sides. To the left is the glass door (always locked) to the tiny pro shop, which is crammed with racks of muscle shirts and pants designed to show off the "gorilla physique." The right-hand wall of the vestibule houses a display case in which cans of protein powder and other dietary supplements (to help build the "gorilla physique") are ranged for sale. The small office where the gym owners sit, talk on the phone, look at magazines, and sell various beverages is located behind this case. The office opens out via a door and a walk-up window into the main gym area. Having passed through this area, one enters an undivided space measuring approximately 6000 square feet, whose right-hand and rear walls are cinderblock, painted white but almost entirely covered with mirrors. The left-hand wall is comprised of four garage doors big enough to admit tractor trucks. These doors are frequently opened for ventilation or to allow exercise equipment to be moved through them, but one of them is blocked off with mirrors. Heating ducts and other accenting structures, such as the staircase leading upstairs to the men's and women's shower rooms, which form a second story over the pro-shop and office, are painted the color of fresh blood, as is much of the exercise equipment. The floor is covered almost entirely with thick, hard, black rubber matting.

Facing the back of the room, one sees an illuminated sign that also hung in the gym's previous location, a dank basement in the nearby borough of Highland Park. The sign is about five feet high and displays the gym's name and symbol—the cartoonish figure of a mustachioed, dark-haired white male in a leopard-spotted circus performer's leotard (not exactly a Greek god), who jauntily holds a preposterously overloaded barbell that bends with the weight overhead. The word "Apollon" is poised above him, and he stands on the letters of the word "Gym," which are made to look like cinderblocks exploding beneath his feet from the stress of his mighty lift. Beneath the exploding block letters the sign reads, "Established in 1975," "Open 7 days," and "Co-ed." The term "co-ed" is of course anachronistic and politically incorrect; furthermore, it professes that which is manifestly not the case.

Unless it is between 5:00 P.M. and 7:00 P.M. on a weekday, I am more often than not the only female working out. This has been true for the eight years that I have worked out at the Apollon almost daily. (There may be a "thong" or two, the gym equivalent of female groupies, hanging about.) If there happen to be a few other women there, they are most likely using the treadmills or stairclimbers, the "butt-blaster" or chest machines, while I am the only one pursuing a serious bodybuilding regimen. (Diane, a female power-lifter, used to work out at the Apollon's old location in the mornings, but I have not seen her for at least six years. And for a few months Marge, a female welder and sculptor, trained here in Edison, but I have not seen her in six months.) Even on weekends the population of this gym is overwhelmingly male, "working class"—police officers, teamsters, construction workers, sanitation workers, utility workers—and heterosexual. (Racially, however, the population is heterogeneous and amicable; race will not be an issue here.)

A sign similar to the one on the inside back wall stands outside near the road. It is an advertisement to passersby for the hyperbolic masculinity presumably available inside the body shop. The picture bears a striking resemblance to Frank, a well-built mustachioed Italian-American who used to manage, if not own, the gym. Although he always talked as if the gym were his, it was unclear whether Frank or the equally cagey, but spindly and edgy, Jewish-American Mark, or both, owned or managed the gym. Recently, Manoli and his Greek-American family bought the place from him, or from them, and the question became moot. As long as Frank and Mark were in charge, certain gym members indulged in loud lewd speculation as to what the "real" relationship between them might have been. Since the larger of the two signed and trained new members, acquired new equipment, spun tales about improvements he planned to make, and told everyone racy anecdotes about women, while day in and day out his partner cleaned the place, swept the floor, and whined, Frank and Mark fit right into the kinds of homophobic stereotypes the "real men" working out in the gym deployed with gusto. "Husband" and "wife" were the pejoratives most frequently used to describe the pair. Oddly, the objects of these remarks never seemed to mind.

By the time Frank and Mark sold the gym, it was jammed full of old and new weight-lifting equipment, machines, benches, weight racks, and so on, reputedly acquired by "the husband" with "the wife's" money. It is especially difficult to maneuver when the gym is crowded. Weaving in and out carefully between pieces of exercise furniture not placed far enough apart to allow me (and I am not large) to pass without banging into things while on my way from bench to rack carrying dumbbells weighing eighty pounds each, I might, for example, encounter someone similarly loaded down and *en route*. We would then have to unload, back up, or turn aside, like two water buffalo face to face on a narrow bridge. We joke and grumble about this situation as we work out; at home we discover bruises and cuts where we have banged our flesh into metal.

In gym culture it is a compliment to call someone a machine, a brute, an animal, or a monster; a behemoth, a colossus, or a fucking Greek statue. Gym language is a compendium of mixed metaphors, and the more—the bigger, the louder, the stronger, the bulkier, the more outrageous—the merrier. There is, however, a hierarchy of mixed metaphors, the highest order of which engages a vaguely classical vocabulary used to connote transcendent excellence. In the pages of muscle magazines, male bodybuilders whose physiques are particularly impressive are routinely compared to a variety of (highly masculine) aesthetic forms, among them Greek statuary, Davidian figures or Rodin sculptures, ancient gods of various persuasions, classical heroes. The titles awarded in America's most prestigious bodybuilding competition, the Mr. and Ms. Olympia, are another case in point. (The first contest I entered—and won— was the "Neptune Classic.") Admittedly, no one ever calls another bodybuilder a building. Rather, the bodybuilder thinks of himself as a builder, who is also the object under construction. Bodybuilders and gym rats routinely ask each other, "Are you building?" by which they mean, "Are you in a phase of training where you are trying to add more lean muscle to your physique in one target area or another?" What he is building is a machine, a rock, an animal, a behemoth, a colossus, a fucking Greek statue; or a building with no space left inside, because it has been transformed, according to the body-builder's fantasy, into a thing made entirely of dense, hard muscle.

In his "classic" on classicism—the ancient and seminal text of *The Ten Books of Architecture*—Vitruvius cites the form and mathematical symmetry of the human body as a paradigm for design: "Without symmetry and proportion there can be no principles in the design of any temple; that is, if there is no precise relation between its members, as in the case of those of a well shaped man."[4] As the "highest" and most nearly perfect earthly creation, man's body is a natural microcosm of universal harmonies; therefore, the architect should design the temple in the image of man. Vitruvius advises the architect to design structures in which the proportions of part to part, and of part to whole, mimic and serve as analogies to those obtaining among the human face, the body, the limbs, and so forth. In bodybuilding, however, the converse of this relation is more often the case. The well-shaped man should resemble a building, and not just any building, but a *fucking* Greek temple. Or, better yet, make that a *fucking* Greek COLUMN, made of muscle hard as marble. Okay, with a head atop the column. A capital (*caput*-al) musclehead.

In other words, a male bodybuilder's body ideally has no interior. It is to contain no space, but be solid, lean meat. The term "musclehead," a colloquial and non-

4 Vitruvius, *The Ten Books of Architecture*, trans. Morris Hicky Morgan (New York: Dover, 1960), p. 72.

pejorative synonym for "serious lifter," even suggests that his head be equally dense. The language muscleheads speak in the gym is, furthermore, low on content but high on performativity. It is routinized and, among men, often homophobic. That is, it is explicitly phobic about the interiors of men's bodies, such that it creates and maintains uncrossable yet tense and tensile boundaries between the outsides of men's bodies. The more amiable of these verbal routines take the form of terse exchanges accompanied by hand-shaking, shoulder-patting, and head-nodding intended to greet one another upon arrival or say good-bye when leaving; exhort one another to work harder, "stay tight," or pile on more weight; acknowledge the success or failure of an attempt at a lift; or critique or mock technique, attitude, virility, or style. This is a minimalist masculine language of gesture and gesticulation that can be described as pragmatic, performative, and relatively void of content. I take various kinds of pleasure in using it. Most of the men in the gym accept me as a serious lifter ("Hey! You're as strong as me! Do you compete?") and will interact with me accordingly.

At times I feel like a primatologist who is grateful that the apes she chooses to live with accept her. Some males, however, prefer, month after month and even year after year, to avoid acknowledging my presence in the potentially intimate space of the gym, and instead watch me continually in the mirrors, and discuss my progress and puzzling identity among themselves. ("What's *her* deal?") Some persist in reminding me that I am female by commenting on my appearance, flirting or angling for eye contact, offering various gallant services such as moving my weights or benches for me (as *if*), or expostulating, especially if I am stronger than they, about how strong I am "for a girl." (A recent example: "That's a lot of weight for a girl. Aren't you afraid you're going to split wide open?") Often they seek my attention in order tell me how their training is going, especially if they are feeling "weak" and want to be reassured that they will get back in the groove. They commence these narratives whether I happen to be in the middle of lifting, pacing back and forth like the big guys, or just standing there, scowling, with my walkman headphones on. I guess I have certain responsibilities as resident female.

Such ritualized exchanges contribute significantly to the atmosphere of the place, and, along with the banging of metal plates, grunts and groans, help create a hypnotic atmosphere of mechanical and repetitive physical, social, and psychological noise. Sociality in the gym, then, depends as much on repetition, ritual, provocation, and performativity, as does physical training. Gym sociality is even more repetitious than weight training. Weight training is supposed to, and can, produce "results" in the form of a new physique and its attendant psychological effects.[5] Gym discourse plays its part by helping to fill social "space" in such a way as to all but eliminate social intercourse and evacuate mental space in order to make pure "action" possible. In its unintended Zen wisdom, it prevents thinking about what one is doing to a degree that may prevent doing it. To make it through a tough work-out requires a fixed and delimited focus on one's inward or outward image or, rather, on making the inward and outward congruous and identical, canceling the space or the incongruity between them; it requires the temporary elimination of the vagaries of consciousness, and the reduction of "reflection" to the image in a mirror.

[5] Repetition without content is not all that goes on, of course. Friendships, sexual liaisons, and other kinds of liaisons are often initiated in the gym, though they are usually conducted outside the space of the gym to escape the scrutiny of gym regulars. Among the interactions I have most enjoyed in the gym are the regular conversations over many years, thanks to which I have gotten to watch several fellow lifters grow up. Rascally teen-agers when I first met them, they are now proud police officers, managers, and delivery men. I have watched tattoos spread up and down their legs and across their backs. They have seen the growth of my t-shirt collection and my various hair colors. We have amicably traded opinions on such subjects as sex, religion, politics, art, and so forth, and still do.

In a bodybuilding gym, one's consciousness and the gym can become concentric non-spaces. One goes inside the gym to fill up, extirpate, or deny the inside: this is the paradoxical essence of the hyperbolic masculinity available inside the gym. Femininity is unwelcome in the gym except in its capacity as an admiring audience of the spectacle of phallic masculinity. Femininity represents the spectacle, or the specter, of interiority, a reflection of oneself as penetrable and vulnerable with which the male bodybuilder does not wish to identify. From it he must distinguish himself. Outside the gym, masculinity may be in crisis insofar as men may be discovering their feelings, their subjectivities, their rectums, all of which are signs of the "woman" in them, as Shakespeare put it in *Hamlet*, a play about how consciousness makes a man passive enough to "lose the name of action."[6] Inside the musclehead gym, however, masculinity reassures itself that it is exactly what it appears to be: a body with no interior, and no aperture. A typical "conversation" in the gym constitutes a kind of anti-cruising, a form of verbal warning sign (Trespassing Strictly Prohibited) and goes something like this:

> *"Hey. What's up. What you workin' today?"*
>
> *"Legs."*
>
> *"I'm doing back. I did legs Tuesday."*

Thus do we locate each other in space and time, where we are in the week's, or the day's, training ritual. More than that, we identify ourselves to each other *as* pure location and, therefore, as a point without dimension, a site that is a body part or, rather, a part of a body part—namely, a muscle group. Today I am legs. Tomorrow I will be chest. Therefore I am neither you nor I, at least not here, not now. So get out of my face.

II.

KNOWING YOUR ASS FROM YOUR ELBOW: WHY THE GYM IS NOT A MALE SPACE

"First and foremost, the judge must bear in mind that he/she is judging a women's bodybuilding competition and is looking for an ideal feminine physique. Therefore, the most important aspect is shape. . . . The other aspects are similar to those described for assessing men, but in regard to muscular development, it must not be carried to excess where it resembles the massive muscularity of the male physique."[7]

6 At 4.7.186-190, Laertes addresses his drowned sister, the excessively feminine and submissive Ophelia: "Too much of water, hast thou, poor Ophelia, / And therefore I forbid my tears; / but yet / It is our trick; nature her custom holds, / Let shame say what it will: when these are gone / The woman will be out."

7 Ruling in the IFBB Professional Guidebook for Athletes, Judges, and Promoters reiterated in an "advisory" November 20, 1991; reprinted in *Flex* (July 1992), p.115. These guidelines had long been in effect, were made explicit before 1987, and were summarily reiterated and enforced at the Ms. International competition in Columbus, Ohio, 1992, causing much confusion and controversy within and among judges, competitors, and fans. This issue of *Flex* described the events at the Ms. International; all but one of the writers seem to support the guidelines.

The International Federation of Bodybuilding sent the advisory quoted above to the judges of the February 1992 "Ms. International" competition in Columbus, Ohio, warning them that the injunctions against masculinity in female bodybuilders would be "strictly enforced." These injunctions make it clear that, even in bodybuilding, the one sport and the only sub-culture that ostensibly values muscle for muscle's sake, muscle means man, while women are at best second-class citizens. It is not that women *can* not become as muscular as males—they can, and do—but that they *must* not. Male bodybuilders are supposed to emulate or concretize mythical models such as Zeus, Hercules, Arnold, or Apollon (?!), while women are supposed to incarnate a far more elusive abstraction: femininity. Femininity, equated here with "shape," might seem like a vacuous Platonic tautology, a category without content, except that in this case the "content" implied by "shape" is cushy body fat—and space, space for the phallus.

To appear solidly and massively muscular is to be masculine. Such an appearance, meritorious in a male, is by definition in "excess" if not monstrous in a female (never mind that many outside bodybuilding consider it such in a man as well). For a bodybuilder to appear massively muscular to the judges, he must not only build muscle, but make its anatomical detail visible by dieting away as much subcutaneous and intermuscular fat as possible. (Tanning, shaving, and oiling are other, cosmetic aids to visibility.) It is the radical reduction of body fat that makes women's tits and ass shrink, and it is this particular detumescence that alarms men in bodybuilding, perhaps because they associate it with detumescence of the phallic kind.

For the male or female hard-core lifter, tumescence, or engorgement of the muscles, is without doubt the goal of every training session. Ya hafta get a good pump goin'. But it is difficult not to see the engorged muscular physique as a giant potent penis, and difficult not to think that that is precisely what it is *supposed* to be, to mean, to represent. The male physique athlete is to embody and perform "the phallic mystery rearing itself like a whirling dark cloud," and "to raise a great pliant column, swaying and leaning with power."[8] Not surprisingly, increasing numbers of female bodybuilders are getting breast implants in order to reassure the judges that they are feminine despite their muscle. Women feel obligated to hang on to or install pockets of softness that will make them identifiable as women, while men struggle to eliminate as much as possible from their own bodies the fat that in the bodybuilding world signifies the "feminine."

In this respect, at least, bodybuilding is certainly "classical."

According to Thomas Laqueur, until the end of the eighteenth century the female sex was understood as a lesser form of the male, rather than as a different kind of human. A one-sex model ruled, and that sex was male. Laqueur writes, for example:

> The learned Galen could cite the dissections of the Alexandrian anatomist Herophilus, in the third century B.C., to support his claim that a woman has testes with accompanying seminal ducts very much like the man's one on each side of the uterus, the only difference being that the male's are contained in the scrotum and the female's are not. . . . For two millennia the ovary, an organ that by the early nineteenth century had become a synecdoche for woman, had not even a name of its own.[9]

8 D.H. Lawrence, *The Plumed Serpent* (New York: Vintage, 1992), pp. 308 and 309.

9 Thomas Laqueur, *Making Sex: Body and Gender from the Greeks to Freud.* (Cambridge and London: Harvard University Press, 1990), p. 4. Not until the 19th century, argues Laqueur, does a two-sex model appear. The complexities of this subject preclude my treating it seriously here. It seems clear to me, however, that the two-sex model, far from supplanting the one-sex version, is characteristically used to support it. Current studies of sex difference, focusing on statistical samples and questionnaires, tend merely to read degree *as* kind. If a certain percentage of women answer a question a certain way, this permits conclusions to be drawn about women's "nature." Two sexes are just not enough.

Male and female were seen to differ in degree, the male being "higher" than the female because, ironically, she was flesh personified whereas he was possessed of superior cognitive and spiritual faculties. His flesh was more ethereal, less material, than hers, because less tied to reproduction. In the one-sex model fundamental to bodybuilding, the "lesser" that must characterize the female is the smaller quantity of muscle she is allowed to possess. According to classical medicine and philosophy, "men and women were arrayed according to their degree of metaphysical perfection . . . along an axis whose *telos* was male."[10] In the case of bodybuilding, wherein muscle is idealized, muscularity is the physical index of metaphysical perfection. Fat, on the other hand, is its negative axis.

On the night of the 1992 Ms. International competition, a fabulously muscular British woman named Paula Bircumshaw challenged this *telos*. If this contest had been judged according to the standards for male bodybuilding, namely muscular thickness and definition, symmetry, etc., Bircumshaw would have won, or at least placed very high. But the judges followed the IFBB guidelines and considered the bodies on stage as belonging to women, not to physique athletes. They eliminated Bircumshaw from competition early on, a discriminatory act that was met by loud derision from the audience; in praise of bodybuilding's audiences, let it be said that they are there to see muscle. Enraged by her mistreatment and excited by the crowd, Bircumshaw popped back on stage when she was supposed to be gone, and apparently directed an obscene gesture at the judges. She continued mugging and gesticulating as she made a grand exit from the auditorium. (She was later suspended from the Federation for two years for her "unprofessional" conduct.)

10 Laqueur, *Making Sex*, p. 6.

Writing in *Flex* about this competition, held in conjunction with the Arnold Schwarzenegger Classic, Julian Schmidt describes the event as the "Columbus Uprising"—the occasion of a "battle for a new world order" between, on one side, "the very soul of political correctness," namely the "covetous" feminists and pro-native American protesters who were on the scene and, on the other side, a noble army of the "hearty folk who settled this territory." In language that sent me scurrying to the OED—this was the first time a muscle magazine ever sent this pencilneck scurrying to the OED—Schmidt first praises Arnold, host and commandant of this hearty folk army, and then slams the covetous upstarts. As for Arnold, "what better oriflamme to lead the battle, then, than Arnold Schwarzenegger, himself a gonfalon of success who can take every one of the PC-ers' craven planks and shove it down their whining throats?" But this perfection was tainted, Schmidt writes, when:

> As I took my seat for the last half of the men's contest, my stomach revolted from an aporrhoea [stench] emanating from a nearby seat. Its occupant wore a skirt, high heels and makeup. This bromidrotic [stench-ridden] beast had removed its jacket, allowing the stench to escape and revealing an upper body that

would give a Mack truck fits in a posedown. Its legs were easily the equal of those [of the men] onstage. There was no need for me to comment. The judges had already done so by their votes in the Ms. International. . . .Their message had all the subtlety of a train wreck: Women's bodybuilding must either lose its tribades [lesbians] or lose the sport.[11]

There is no way for the reader to know whether the woman near Schmidt actually stank or whether the poor man was suffering from olfactory hallucinations. In any case, however, it is clearly his opinion, an opinion by no means unusual among either male or female bodybuilders, that women whose muscularity rivals that of men are not women, nor men, but beasts, things, Mack trucks, perverts. Ironically, these epithets are compliments when applied to a male bodybuilder by a muscle enthusiast.

In his book, *Little Big Men: Bodybuilding Subculture and Gender Construction*, Alan M. Klein presents what might be described as an ethnographic study of gym sub-culture based on first-hand experience in California's bodybuilding gyms and plentiful interviews with bodybuilders.[12] The book title describes Klein's conclusions in a nutshell, and they come as no surprise: male bodybuilders by and large, he argues, are narcissistic and insecure men driven to compensate for their feelings of inadequacy by uncritically fashioning themselves into cartoonish figures of hypermasculinity. Driven by "authoritarian personalities," they are primitive proto-fascists who embody and enact the "hegemonic masculinity" of our culture. The male bodybuilders Klein interviewed in California, like those at the Apollon (and at gyms in New Jersey and Virginia where I have trained), are mostly "blue-collar" and relatively uneducated, unlike the women he met, who were more educated, more liberal, more self-aware and confident.[13] Most of all, says Klein, these men tend to be both homophobic and femiphobic:

The fear of appearing female, or effeminate, is what I have been calling femiphobia; it is perhaps the most important ingredient in the fashioning of hegemonic masculinity. Unlike narcissism and fascism, femiphobia is a gender-negative construction, in being a barometer of what not to be (for example, not weak, or not appearing flaccid).[14]

Femiphobia, according to Klein, "fuels hypermasculinity, homophobia, and misogyny," all "way[s] of responding to the anxiety generated in the North American male's search for masculinity."[15]

[11] *Flex* (July 1992), pp. 55-57

[12] Alan M. Klein, *Little Big Men: Bodybuilding Subculture and Gender Construction* (Albany: State University of New York Press, 1993).

[13] Klein also claims the women were more supportive of each other, and less competitive, and that men should be more like them; ibid., pp. 184-185.

[14] Ibid., p. 269.

[15] Ibid., p. 270.

Particularly significant in the present context is the inextricability for these men of femiphobia with homophobia. Klein observes that in the bodybuilding world:

> The most prejudiced attitudes were typically reserved for women. . . . [F]emale bodybuilders were often seen as threatening. One judge at a small local contest was confronted by the parents of a woman who had placed low. His response to them was as candid and astonishing as I'd ever heard: "She's got no tits, no ass. I wouldn't fuck her, so whadaya expect?"[16]

Another "gym insider" remarked to Klein that he couldn't admire a woman "like C., whose back is bigger than mine. . . I mean, what the fuck!. . . . I just don't have the propensity for it. I mean, that would be like holding another man."[17] Being a gym insider seems to mean being the kind of guy who can get inside the kind of woman this kind of guy wants to get inside of. Inside the gym world as elsewhere it is the woman who must connote interiority, which is in turn represented visually by tits and ass. Muscle, by contrast, connotes exteriority, the exteriority of the phallus. A woman with a back like a man's *is* in effect a man; the bodybuilder is afraid of her insofar as she might turn out to *be* "another man," a penetrable man, or one who could penetrate him. The fear of muscular women, the fear of a woman as "another man," is more homophobic than it is femiphobic. This would accord with what Klein writes about hustling in California bodybuilding gyms. Many male bodybuilders who think of themselves as straight permit gay men to perform oral sex on them in return for money, which they use to support the bodybuilding life style. That this goes on is common, and common knowledge, but not much talked about. Because there is no penetration, and thus no feminization, involved, such sex acts do not in any way interfere with these bodybuilders' conceptions of themselves as straight men.

For a man to be penetrated, to have an interior, is to be a "woman." We know this from prison movies; we know this from Plato; we know this from Catherine MacKinnon. To be attentive to the inner world of feelings, emotions, sentiment, and subjectivity, is conventionally to be feminine; to be active, interactive, objective, competitive, and outward-bound, is conventionally to be masculine. Historically the man's world has been

> where the action is . . . where one becomes fully human or achieves self-realisation; it is where heroic exploits and daring deeds are done; it is where "culture" flourishes in the form of abstract ideas . . . it is where Nature is mastered; it is where males run kingdoms and Empires, wage wars, conduct politics or manage businesses . . . . It is the realm of important things.[18]

The man's world is causal; it is where he does things and things happen; it is a mythical non-domestic space (though his home is his castle) of unbounded pos-

16 Ibid., p. 224.

17 Ibid.

18 Jean Crimshaw, *Philosophy and Feminist Thinking* (Minneapolis: Minnesota University Press, 1986), p. 72.

sibility. Woman herself is supposed to *be* (her) place, a domestic space. ("Hi honey, I'm home.") From the beginnings of Western thought woman has been identified metaphysically with, and as, space itself. For this reason, some taint of femininity will necessarily haunt the gym or any other supposedly "male" space, rendering the straight men who congregate there a tad suspicious of each other. Joke-telling and towel-frisking may result.

Insofar as space denotes interiority, it is feminine because it denotes the negative of the masculine. It is the upward thrust, and not the inner space, of a skyscraper that makes it phallic. Luce Irigary's discussion of the gendering of Western philosophy and epistemology by way of Plato's "myth of the cave" has as much as proved this point.[19] As a metaphor for subjectivity—"as a metaphor of the inner space, of the den, the womb or *hystera*"—this myth can be read "not only [as] a silent prescription for Western metaphysics but also, more explicitly, [it] proclaims (itself as) everything publicly designated as metaphysics, its fulfillment, and its interpretation."[20] Just as, in physical terms, space requires walls or limits to define it as form, in metaphysical terms "the *'interior'* . . . circles back around the *'exterior'* of an invisible but impenetrable paraphragm. Plato's *hystera*, [the] closure-envelope of metaphysics"[21] is the interior that is ever defined as the potentially entrapping "other," capable of wrapping itself around the "exterior" and the "impenetrable." Above and beyond and outside the feminine, loom wisdom, knowledge, the reflexive auto-logic of the Father, creating man in His own image, the image of an absolute beauty unsullied by the cave, the earth, by woman, by fat.

19 Luce Irigary, *Speculum of the Other Woman,* trans. Gillian C. Gill (Ithaca: Cornell University Press, 1985), pp. 243-364.

20 Ibid., p. 243.

21 Ibid., p. 320.

For masculinity to be sure of itself, to know itself as itself, as an identity or a recognizable sameness over time, means to be itself and not an other, an other that must also be constructed and used (like a fetish) to protect the familiarity of self. In Irigaray's argument, the potentially unpredictable and threatening fluidity of femininity (an ocean capable of eroding male identity) must be plugged up by the rigid Phallus, and subjected to, or cast under, the ontological ground of Western self-knowledge. This act, which delineates the boundaries of the subject by means of the subjection of the other, simultaneously creates the distinction between exteriority and interiority as one of its effects, institutionalizing the equivalence of the masculine with the external and the feminine with the internal.

For Irigaray this is not so much an anatomical distinction between the phallus and the womb as a form of political tyranny that justifies itself biologically. In bodybuilding subculture, as elsewhere, the subjection of woman is effected by enforcing the equivalence of femaleness (a set of physical characteristics) with femininity (a set of "qualities" such as weakness, passivity, receptivity). In the gym, at bodybuilding competitions, and in the pages of muscle magazines, this equivalence is asserted and re-asserted *ad nauseam.* Astonishingly, few women have publicly protested this nonsense. In effect there is no livelihood for bodybuilders outside the self-promoting and self-perpetuating institutions—the gyms, the magazines, the shows that made their way into the mainstream in the 1970s—established in the late 1930s by Ben and Joe Weider and their acolytes, who run their feudalistic kingdom like a "family," expelling upstarts and iconoclasts. Would-be champions tend ponderously to toe the line. Paula Bircumshaw is a notable exception.

Another exception (who proves the rule) is Laura Creavalle, who has won the IFBB Ms. International title three times and the 1988 Women's World Amateur Championships, and who, according to many on-lookers, should have won last year's Ms. Olympia over Weider favorite and returning champion, Lenda Murray. Creavalle is gradually withdrawing from the bodybuilding spotlight. She and her husband now host a "camp" on the coast of Maine for individuals and couples seeking relaxation, personal training, and nutritional counseling, and she plans to retire soon from competition. Recently interviewed in the *NPC News*, Creavalle agrees with other competitors who "think the judging criteria should be changed or maybe . . . some of the pro judges . . . keeping three or four of the top judges and switching some others."[22] Creavalle, who has competed in the Olympia competition seven times, has been judged by pretty much the same people for seven years; one of them told her that he knows her physique "with [his] eyes closed." Creavalle points out that this means that "he has a preconceived idea of what [her] physique is all about," making it difficult to see how she and others may have improved or changed, let alone to revise outmoded or inappropriate ideas about women's physiques in general.

22 *NPC News: National Physique Committee* , 9, no 1995), pp. 51-55. The quotations that follow are a from these pages.

Creavalle thinks that the judges may never allow her to win the Olympia competition because her persona on stage may be "a little bit too aggressive" for them. "Aggressiveness seems to be good for the men, but if you're aggressive as a woman it's perceived as negative." She seems apologetic, assuring the interviewer that she is "not aggressive backstage towards anyone"; her friends know her to be a "comedian most of the time." The interviewer reminds her that "they're supposed to be judging physique, not personality," but this is not always easy to remember when self-assertiveness is punished. Creavalle, who says she is "not a feminist," nevertheless speaks pointedly about how bodybuilding continually thwarts women in the sport and insults "females in general." For example, the first place prize in the Arnold Classic is one hundred thousand dollars, while the women's prize in the Ms. International, its companion competition, is twenty thousand dollars. The promoters claim that this is because the men "draw" that much more than the women, but the women are never promoted comparably. They are not offered as estimable idealizable potential role models. Female bodybuilders are almost never featured on the covers of muscle magazines, for example. The women on the covers, if not simply top-heavy models or gym bunnies, are underpaid "fitness" competitors who perform competitive aerobics routines outfitted as gym bunnies, complete with breast augmentation, big hair, and so on, all meant to please those manly judges.

Some of these "fitness girls" come to Creavalle for advice. She isn't sure what to tell them: "How do you become a better fitness competitor? Is it bigger boobs or is it who can do the best back flips?" As for the current tendency to feature fitness women on magazine covers, Creavalle comments:

> I think about it a lot. I'm not a feminist, I just think that it's so sad how the more things change, the more things stay the same. You have a big guy [on the cover] and women are on their knees pulling at him. It's just women in a subservient role all over again. We're just bimbos and we just love your body. Nobody wants to look like that. . . . [It's unjust] not only to the female bodybuilders, but females in general. How are women going to have any self esteem when their self esteem has to be tied to a man's perception of them. . . It's sad for women. Just put the man on the cover alone instead of having a big boobed woman with two little pasties standing there and smiling. It's really sad that everything you do has to get approval from a male.

The "big boobed woman with two little pasties standing there and smiling," or on her knees "pulling at" the "big guy" embodies the hyperbolic femininity needed to establish the "normality" of the larger-than-life male bodybuilder.[23] The cover model reassures men, in Creavalle's words, that "we [women] just love your body," and she does so by means of conspicuous convexities that suggest complementary and presumably enticing interiorities. In this sense, hyperbolic femininity is a cipher, a place-holder for masculinity, a mirror in which masculinity cannot see itself. This may not come as news to those of us who already think of masculinity and femininity as forms of masquerade, but to most inhabitants of the bodybuilding world it might as well be Greek.

Today it is 6:00 P.M. when I arrive at the gym; it's peak hour, and likely to be extremely crowded. It is certainly crowded on the outside. I turn into the parking lot and check along the sides and rear of the building for an available space, only to find myself pulling out of the lot onto the street again. There is nowhere to park. There is even a car (a hot little number with four-wheel drive) parked right by, and partly blocking, the front entrance. I may have to park next door in the lot of the pizza parlor. Officially, however, bodybuilders don't eat pizza much, especially since nutritional experts no longer advise bulking up during the off season (when not preparing for a competition). It could be said that bodybuilders are dedicated to not eating pizza. I try to brush aside the ethical quandary of parking in the lot of an establishment to whose existence I oppose my own. Luckily, a space opens up in the gym lot; relieved, I park the car, taking with me my wrist straps, personal stereo, and water bottle. Once

23 This big-boobed woman serves as an icon of and an advertisement for masculinity. Over the years, however, I have observed that the big guy tends actually to mate with a petite, fluffy woman—the contrast makes him seem even bigger—or else to a conspicuously matronly woman, whose appearance provokes speculation of other sorts too arcane to go into here.

inside I scan the gym and find the usual crowd of at least fifty men, some of whom I have seen almost daily for eight years, and a few women.

Does the preponderance of males in the gym make it a male space? Where "muscle" is equated with "maleness," and "space" with "femaleness," can there be such a thing as a male space? Can the dedication of the gym to muscle building and strength training, to the increase of physical mass and power, the continual mobilization of aggression, the sweating and swearing, the heaving and hauling of barbells and dumbbells, the hulking bulky bodies shuffling to and fro from pillar to post, from power rack to drinking fountain, *make* this a male space? Is the gym a social space, or an anti-social space, given the fact that it houses—domesticates—what is in many ways an anti-social, even anti-human, activity? Is it a "space" at all, or a war zone where masculinity strives blindly to eradicate its own interiority?

III.

THE LITTLE TOILET THAT COULDN'T

The/a woman never closes up into a volume.
The dominant representation of the maternal figure as volume may lead us to forget that woman's ability to enclose is enhanced by her fluidity, and vice versa. Only when coopted by phallic values does the womb preclude the separa-tion of the lips. [24]

24 Irigaray, *Speculum of the Other Woman*, p. 239. Emphasis original.

In its previous, base-ment location, the Apollon had a men's locker room just inside the front door, complete with showers and toilets, but the only facility women could use was a water closet across the corridor which men used too. It was as if the Apollon gym were trying to enforce an antique one-sex model by offering facilities for one gender only. The Apollon Gym was enacting its femiphobia in the most crass material way. Ostensibly devoted to physical culture and the life of the body, the Apollon "forgot" that women had bodies complete with excretory functions that it was their responsibility to accommodate. This architectural amnesia was not simply a consequence of the design of the Highland Park building; if it had been, one could have excused the lack of women's facilities as "not their fault." On the contrary, when the Apollon moved to its new site, Frank and Mark supervised the entire process of converting the auto body shop into a health club, and lo and behold produced another health club with no private facilities for women. The design and construction of the new gym in Edison recapitulated a femiphobic insistence upon a one-sex model in such a way as to provide an architectural objective correlative, a symptom, for the pathological atavism I am describing.

The amenities Frank promised that Apollon members would find in the new gym included complete and comfortable locker room facilities for males and females. But the new Apollon opened with no locker rooms at all. There was one private bathroom (toilet and sink) accessible from the main floor, designated as "men's," and nothing at all for the women. Inside and to the rear of the little office space was a bathroom intended for the gym managers who worked in the office; this the women were invited to share. The office, however, was usually occupied by the managers and an assortment of their male gym cronies who liked to hang out there with them. To make one's way through their midst to the toilet and then urinate or whatever in such close proximity, always within earshot, was willy-nilly to publicize one's private rituals. (Admittedly, exhibitionism is a "perversion" intrinsic to bodybuilding; however, pissing for men I can't see is not my thing.)

Over the course of the next two years a kind of loft space was constructed over the front office area and was divided into men's and women's locker rooms, neither of which had lockers (although several sets of different sorts of lockers, including some painted hot pink, have since come and gone). Shower stalls appeared, though it was a *long* time before water was piped in, and eventually a couple of sinks were installed, but no toilets. I complained continually about this to Frank, explaining that the female gym members found the situation in the office embarrassing. Each time he would say, "But I've already got the toilet! I just need someone to put it in." (Gee. Perhaps "putting it in" is itself the problem.) One day, almost three years after the gym had opened, a shiny new toilet appeared in middle of the shower room. There was no stall around it, nothing separating it from where it stood in the middle of the shower room—nor any door between the shower room (which therefore was not a room) and the dressing room, which was easily visible from the hall between the two locker rooms. In other words, a woman sitting on the toilet would be entirely visible to anyone passing by whenever the door to the "locker room" (in which there were no lockers) was open.

I nagged some more; six months later, a door was installed between the shower room, in the center of which sat the toilet, and the locker room that had no lockers. The door had no knob on it, just a hole where the knob should be, and what looked like part of a locking mechanism. I inquired, and was assured by Frank that he had the knob, but needed someone to "put it in." Meanwhile, one day I went to use the toilet and shut the door behind me. To my dismay, it locked, and when I was done I couldn't get out. The work-out music was blaring downstairs, so that no one could hear me banging on the door. So, naturally, I punched the door down, ripping the moulding from the wall with it, and went downstairs. Some months later, Manoli, who was working there and in the process of buying the place, replaced the door and installed a doorknob with a lock.

No toilet was installed in the men's shower room because, said the gym's one female staffer (who got pregnant and quit), "the men are pigs; every time they take a shit they flood the toilet." From her point of view, at least, men and women are distinguishable by their respective toilet habits, cloacal analogs for sex difference insofar as the women wanted a separate bathroom space inside the club, while the men could take their excreta outside as easily as they could whip out their dicks. One day when I walked out the front door of the gym and turned to go to my car, I saw Nick about to urinate right by the entrance—not in the back near the dumpster, not on the side where passersby on foot or in vehicles or gym members going in or out of the building would not notice him. Upon seeing me frown at him, he stuffed his cock back in his pants and sauntered with a snicker back into the gym.

Nick's dick display underscored, again in material terms, that simple-minded equivalence between masculinity and exteriority upon which the "logic" of bodybuilding is based, together with an exhibitionistic disdain for interiority itself.[25] There is no room for interiority at a place like the Apollon (no matter how big the building), which represents itself as a construction site for "straight" masculinity. The bathrooms and showers for both sexes are set up so that same-sex cruising is all but impossible— not than any one, particularly a male, would want to risk getting caught doing such a thing in so violently heterosexual an environment. Moreover, the saga of the women's toilet suggests a phobic inability to respond to the ways in which women have their own interiorities (as opposed to those that they represent to and for men) to which they need to attend. Elsewhere, masculinity may be in crisis. Here, however, in the world of bodybuilding, it is definitely in stasis, although to maintain this stasis requires herculean efforts.

Bodybuilding flaunts this stasis in the gym and on the stage as a kind of *tableau vivant*, an apotheosis of stereotype as archetype. In truth, there are not many opportunities in our culture for "straight" men to display their flesh publicly. Men's clothing has always concealed far more than it reveals to the eye, unlike women's wear, which now more than ever constitutes a continuous soft-core advertisement for pussy (or rather, titty). Male self-expression in general is notoriously buttoned-up and out-of-touch, when it is not out of control, necessitating group excursions into the woods in search of tender feelings. But in the world of bodybuilding, where hardness is all and it is one's job to "stay tight," the softer side of the male is all but invisible, packed deep in a suit of fleshy armor. The bodybuilder's display exposes to view a baroquely developed exteriority ("I'll show you my gun / My Uzi weighs a ton")[26] as if to say, "This is all there is. What you see is what you get."

By way of contrast, I want to talk very briefly about another site of masculine, mainly heterosexual, display and acting out—namely the heavy metal music scene. Perhaps surprisingly, it makes room for its own interiority. In lieu of a lengthy disquisition on the gender politics and poetics of metal and hard-core music, suffice it to say that, despite certain often-observed similarities between some heavy metal performance styles such as "glam" and the stylistic practices of certain other ex-centric performers such as drag queens, by and large metal performers and their fans embrace and express traditionally masculine qualities like explosive anger, aggressivity, egoistic self-

25 An epistemological version of this exhibitionistic disdain for interiority is the "never a doubt" campaign that expressed itself in the gym. I had noticed several police officers from different municipalities working out in t-shirts with "Never a Doubt" written on the front and "Teaneck Police Dept" on the back. B., a sergeant in the Edison police force, explained to me that these shirts showed solidarity with the Teaneck officer whose actions were investigated after he shot and killed an African-American youth in Teaneck several years ago. On another occasion this same sergeant told me, as we were doing legs together, that he works out not because he is insecure, but because he is "already confident." I had not asked him why he worked out.

26 From a song by Annihilator, "Show Me Your Gun," *Battlegrounds*, 1995.

assertion, raw impersonal sensuality, and romantic apocalyptic existential fantasy. Denizens of metal sub-cultures share these performative styles and values with that other heavy metal sub-culture known as bodybuilding. Unlike bodybuilding, however, most heavy metal, death metal, and hard-core music reveals and explores, rather than represses and denies, its own anguish and misery, its fear of and for others, its self-loathing, its dark side and its inside.

Its "inside" is relevant here. The lyrics of several albums released in the last few years narrate and dramatize the experience of boys abused, neglected, or raped by their fathers. The music carrying these lyrics, not surprisingly, ranges and rages from the mournful to the brutal. It is by turns majestic, dreamy, bitter. Heavy metal, like most genres of hard rock, has always been "about" resisting and contesting various authority figures and structures, including the parental, the governmental, and the environmental. The last two seem on occasion like mediated representations of the parental, targets of a symbolic yet displaced rage. Recently, however, bands such as Pantera, Life of Agony, and Korn have ripped the veils off these highly mediated representations of patriarchal power in order to accuse publicly certain perpetrators of intimate same-sex crimes.

Most heart-rending is the recent self-titled album by Korn, which narrates the experience of a son anally raped from childhood on by his father, with the implied knowledge and consent of the mother.[27] The album does not contain printed lyrics and, due to the rapidity and chaotic, strangled emotion with which some of them are delivered, it is hard to make out all of what is being said. The singer cries, sobs, screams, talks, sings, plays bagpipes. A lot of what he says is nevertheless unmistakable. He is "just a pretty boy"; a "pussy"; a "faget" [a song-title, and spelled thus]; he "rightfully" belongs to the father; his father plans to "eat" him; he hurts; he wants to die; he hates his father; he loves his father; his mother is watching; God is not. Two vocalizations are particularly relevant here. In one song the singer screams repeatedly, "I'm just a faget! I'm just a faget!" In another, ambiguously ventriloquizing the father or perhaps imaginatively identifying with the father, he screams, "You'll suck my dick and fucking like it!"

I can't overemphasize the shocking and shattering emotional power of this album. Listening to it by oneself is a frightening experience. Recently, however, Korn performed this music in New York City at a small club before an audience that was mostly white, male, teenage, high on various substances, and manifestly heterosexual. They appeared to be the usual Beavis and Butthead types often known as "dirtbags," and I have no doubt that they were. Yet many in the audience were familiar with the album and, when the singer uttered the words quoted above, they screamed along with him. A room full of teenage boys—a male space?—earnestly screamed: "I'm just a faget! I'm just a faget!" and, "You'll suck my dick and fucking like it!" This could not have happened ten years ago, and probably not even five years ago. It would seem that some kind of healthy psychological evolution, some kind of consciousness

27 Korn, *Korn*, Immortal Records (a division of Sony), 1994. The performance I cite took place at Irving Plaza, New York, in July 1995

raising and emotional bonding, is occurring in a community all too commonly dismissed by those outside it as stupid white trash.

Korn and its audience were avowing the existence of a male interiority so secret it had to be ripped open to be shared. Vulnerability, victimization, sadness, longing, confusion, and a kind of humbled survivalist triumph emerged along with murderous bitterness. The singer's involuntary feminization provoked and proved the existence of the very fears and feelings the world of male bodybuilding is designed to deny, a denial seemingly emblazoned on every single artifact produced by gym culture. For example, the Apollon recently began selling a plastic drinking cup (the kind with the protruding straw) decorated with the figure of a male bodybuilder drawn from the waist up. He appears to have the torso, arms, and shoulders of Arnold, topped by the head of Sylvester Stallone. He is wearing wrap-around sunglasses. Above his head, emblazoned in the heavens as it were, looms the word "APOLLON" in bold balloon caps, while across his nether region the word "GYM" is inscribed. On the back of the cup, in tall black capital letters that take up the whole white surface from top to bottom, appear the words, "WHERE ONLY THE STRONG SURVIVE!"

Hey, somebody might think as he exits the gym, I survived another workout. These words would seem to imply that inside the Apollon Gym evolution is in progress; to enter is to leap into a Darwinian struggle from which only the fittest will emerge. The weak, the flaccid, the passive, and the feminine will presumably not survive.

Or rather, that would seem to be the fantasy of the bodybuilder who enters the gym in order to kill off that part of himself. As the typically un-self-aware Tom Platz put it in *Ironman*, "The discipline oozing out of every serious gym in the country would make the toughest New York S & M club look like a brownie meeting."[28]

28 *Ironman* (October 1995), p. 181.

Definitions Fitness Center #2, New York 1993

THANHAUSER AND ESTERSON

Thanhauser and Esterson's design for the Definitions Fitness Center, a 4,000-square foot health spa occupying a loft in New York City, challenges conventional standards of visual privacy and propriety. A series of unisex shower and changing "cabanas" clad in burnished aluminum punctuate a large curving wall sheathed in copper. Each cubicle consists of backlit, translucent glass walls that create the illusion of privacy when seen from within (since reflected light makes the surface of the walls appear opaque) while projecting the anonymous silhouette of its occupant when viewed from outside. These shadow nudes discretely but emphatically engage the play of voyeurism and desire already at work within the space of the gym.

*View of
Changing
Rooms*

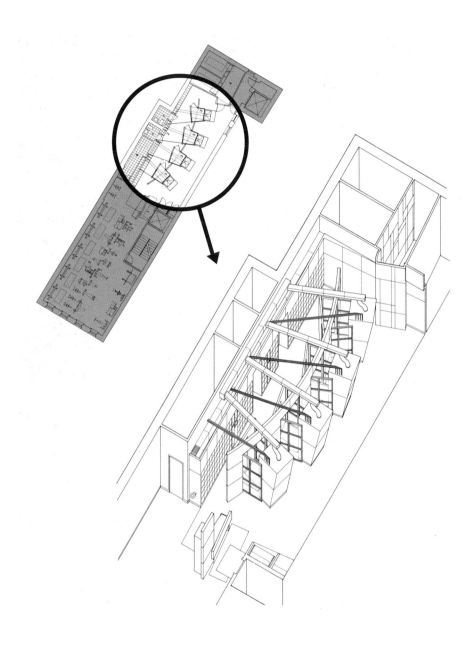

*Floorplan and
Axonometric of
Changing "Cabanas"*

*View
of Changing
Room Doors*

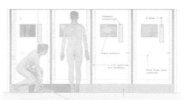

Badlands Health Club,
NYC

MATTHEW BANNISTER

Badlands Health Club, located in the shell of the former Badlands bar at the intersection of Christopher and West Streets and now occupied by a gay peep show, takes as it point of departure an analysis of the architecture of gay and straight video stalls. In straight booths, isolated subjects, protected from the intrusive gaze of neighbors by enclosing partitions, look "straight" ahead at video monitors. Unlike heterosexual peep shows, gay video stalls permit lateral scopic interaction between consenting occupants. The partitions that separate adjacent stalls possess glass windows covered by operable screens activated by red and green buttons. When both parties consent to lower the respective screens that divide them, they see their own reflected image superimposed on the glass window that frames the body of their neighbor: self and other fuse to become an object of desire trapped in the thin space shared by adjoining stalls.

Inspired both by the uni-directional gaze permitted by straight video partitions and the reciprocal gazes facilitated by those found at gay booths, the Badlands Health Club consists of a giant rock-climbing wall intersected by scuba diving tanks pierced by multiple apertures ranging in scale from "glory holes" to "picture windows." These openings permit various kinds of scopic and tactile interactions between recreating bodies as rock climbers ascending the wall come face to face with either scuba divers swimming inside the wall, or other rock climbers straddling its opposite surface. In addition, the wall contains several rest stops—meeting places isolated from the club but visible from the exterior. Seen from the vantage point of the street and Pier 14, the health club appears to spectators below as an animated billboard of rock.

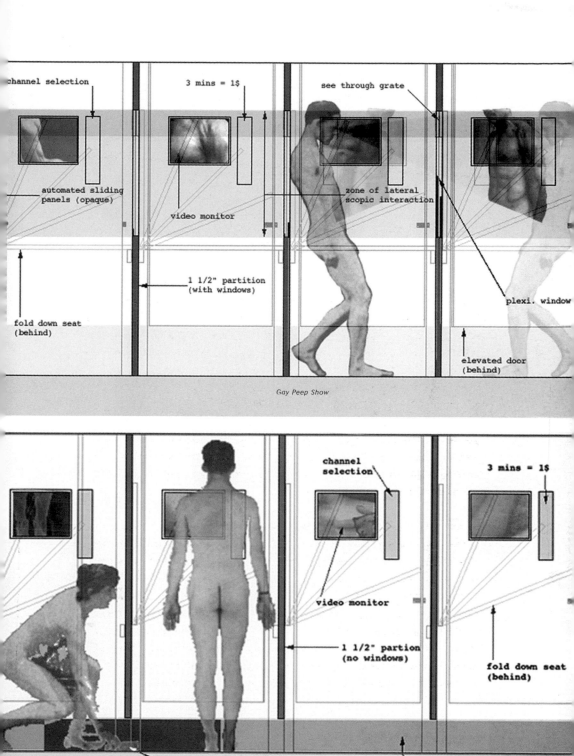

channel selection

3 mins = 1$

see through grate

automated sliding
panels (opaque)

zone of lateral
scopic interaction

video monitor

1 1/2" partition
(with windows)

plexi. window

fold down seat
(behind)

elevated door
(behind)

Gay Peep Show

channel
selection

3 mins = 1$

video monitor

1 1/2" partion
(no windows)

fold down seat
(behind)

the note "pass"

zone of lateral interaction

Straight Peep Show

Facade Detail

View From West Street

east rock wall

scuba pool

*Sectional Detail through
Locker Room, Climbing Wall,
and Scuba Diving Tank*

Building Cross Section

end

OTTOshaft
Documenta IX, Kassel, Germany
1992

MATTHEW BARNEY

REFERENCE
INTRO. PAGE 21

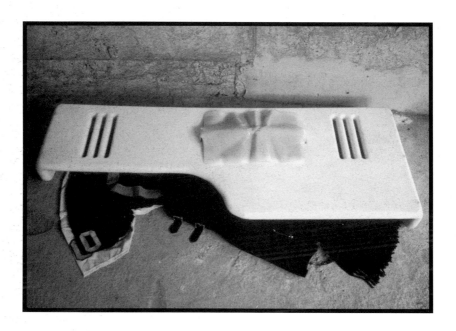

OTTOshaft: The Al Davis Suite
[1992]
Detail of Installation
Documenta IX, Kassel, Germany

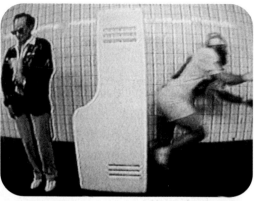

OTTOshaft
[1992]
Detail from OTTOdrone
Video Still

OTTOshaft: The Al Davis Suite
[1992]
Detail of Installation
Documenta IX, Kassel, Germany

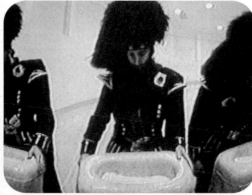

OTTOshaft
[1992]
Detail from OTTOdrone
Video Still

OTTOshaft FASCIA: The Jayne Mansfield Suite
[1992]
Detail of Installation
Documenta IX, Kassel, Germany

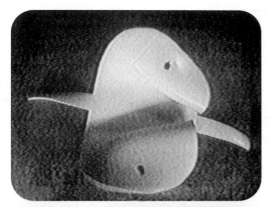

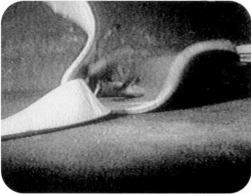

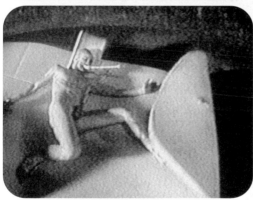

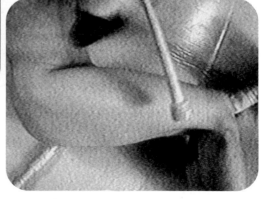

OTTOshaft
[1992]
Detail from AUTOdrone
Video Still

ESSAYS BY

GEORGE CHAUNCEY

D.A. MILLER

WORKS BY

TOM BURR

STEPHEN BARKER

MARK ROBBINS and BILL HORRIGAN

FELIX GONZALEZ-TORRES

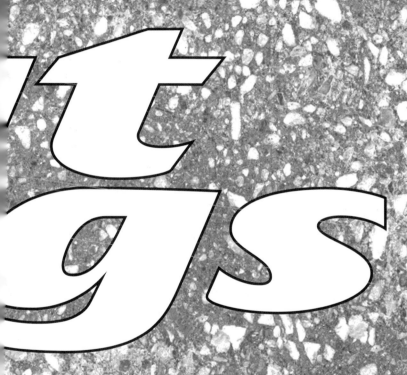

'Privacy Could Only Be Had in Public': Gay Uses of the Streets
GEORGE CHAUNCEY

There is no queer space; there are only spaces used by queers or put to queer use. Space has no natural character, no inherent meaning, no intrinsic status as public or private. As Michel de Certeau has argued, it is always invested with meaning by its users as well as its creators, and even when its creators have the power to define its official and dominant meaning, its users are usually able to develop tactics that allow them to use the space in alternative, even oppositional ways that confound the designs of its creators.[1]

Nothing illustrates this general principle more clearly than the tactics developed by generations of gay men and lesbians to put the spaces of the dominant culture to queer purposes. Struggles over the control of space have been central to gay culture and politics throughout the twentieth century. In the 1930s, after the upheavals and urban cultural experimentation sparked by Prohibition (1920-33) had allowed gay life to become remarkably integrated into the broader cultural life of New York (and other cities) and visible in its "public" spaces, a series of measures were enacted to exclude homosexuality from the public sphere—the city's cafés, bars, streets, and theaters—where authorities feared it threatened to disrupt public order and the reproduction of normative gender and sexual arrangements. For the next thirty years, many of the most important sites of public sociability, including bars, restaurants, and cabarets, were threatened with closure if they allowed lesbians or gay men to gather openly on their premises; and men and women risked arrest if they carried themselves openly as homosexuals on the streets of the city or even at gay parties held in "private" apartments. Even before formal anti-gay regulations were enacted in the 1920s and 1930s, the social marginalization of homosexuals had given the police and popular vigilantes even broader informal authority to harass them. The formal and informal prohibition of gay visibility in the spaces of the city had a fundamental influence on the development of gay cultural practices.[2]

This essay examines the tactics used by gay men in early twentieth-century New York City to claim space for themselves in the face of the battery of laws and informal practices designed to exclude them from urban space altogether. One of my purposes is to challenge the myths that govern most thinking about gay life before Stonewall, particularly the myths that gay people before the 1960s inevitably remained isolated from one another, invisible to straight people and to other gay people alike, or confined to the most marginalized and hidden of urban spaces. But analyzing the queer uses of urban space also highlights the degree to which struggles over the production and control of space played a central role in shaping gay cultural practices more generally—and the degree to which the struggles over queer uses of the city were shaped by and influenced broader class, gender, and racial/ethnic struggles over urban space. Analyzing the role of the production and contestation of queer space in the everyday life of gay men with a high degree of historical specificity also has implications

1 Michel de Certeau, *The Practice of Everyday Life*, trans. Steven F. Rendall (Berkeley: University of California Press, 1984), esp. pp. xviii-xx, pp. 29-42.

2 For a more fully developed analysis of the changing regulation of gay life in the early twentieth century, see my *Gay New York: Gender, Urban Culture, and the Making of the Gay Male World, 1890-1940* (New York: Basic Books, 1994), from which this essay is drawn.

for the theorization of urban space in general. Most importantly, it demonstrates the degree to which the boundaries between spaces defined as "public" and "private" are socially constructed, contingent, and contested; and it illuminates the range of forces—informal as well as official, oppositional as well as dominant—seeking to exert definitional and regulatory power over the production of urban space.

To many New Yorkers in the early twentieth century, gay men seemed to be an almost ubiquitious presence in the streets, parks, and beaches of the city. In 1904, the bodybuilding publisher Bernarr Macfadden denounced "the shoals of painted, perfumed, Kohl-eyed, lisping, mincing youths that at night swarm on Broadway in the Tenderloin section, or haunt the parks and 5th avenue, ogling every man that passes and—it is pleasant to relate—occasionally getting a sound thrashing or an emphatic kicking." In the following decade another New Yorker declared that "Our streets and beaches are overrun by . . . fairies," and in the 1920s and 1930s one of the city's tabloids regularly published cartoons that caricatured the supposed efforts of fairies to accost sailors and other men on Riverside Drive.[3]

As the comments of observers attest, gay men claimed their right to a place in the city's public spaces. It was in such open spaces, less easily regulated than a residential or commercial venue, that much of the gay world took shape. The city's streets and parks served as vital meeting grounds for men who lived with their families or in cramped quarters with few amenities, and the vitality

3 Bernarr Macfadden, *Superb Virility of Manhood: Giving the Causes and Simple Home Methods of Curing the Weaknesses of Men* (New York: Physical Culture Publishing Co., 1904), pp. 175-176; E. S. Shepherd, "Contribution to the Study of Intermediacy," *American Journal of Urology and Sexology* 14 (1918), p. 242.

and diversity of the gay street scene attracted many other men as well. Streets and parks were where many men—"queer" and "normal" alike—went to find sexual partners, where many gay men went to socialize, and where many men went for sex and ended up being socialized into the gay world.

Part of the gay world taking shape in the streets was highly visible to outsiders, but even more of it was invisible. As Macfadden's comment makes clear, gay men had to contend with the threat of vigilante anti-gay violence as well as with the police. In response to this challenge, gay men devised a variety of tactics that allowed them to move freely about the city, to appropriate for themselves spaces that were not marked as gay, and to construct a gay city in the midst of, yet invisible to, the dominant city. They were aided in this effort, as always, by the disinclination of most people to believe that any "normal"-looking man could be anything other than "normal," and by their access, as men, to public space.

Although gay street culture was in certain respects an unusual and distinctive phenomenon, it was also part of and shaped by a larger street culture that was primarily working-class in character and origin. Given the crowded conditions in which most working people lived, much of their social life took place in streets and parks. The gay presence in the streets was thus masked, in part, by the bustle of street life in working-class neighborhoods. Gay uses of the streets, like other working-

class uses, also came under attack, however, because they challenged bourgeois conceptions of public order, the proper boundaries between public
and private space, and the social practices appropriate to each.

CRUISING THE CITY'S PARKS

The city's parks
were among the most popular—and
secure—of New York's gay meeting
places, where men gathered regularly to
meet their friends and to search (or
"cruise," as they called it by the 1920s)
for sexual partners.[4] One of the ostensible purposes of parks, after all, was to
offer citizens respite from the tumult of
city life, a place where citizens could
wander aimlessly and enjoy nature. This
provided a useful cover for men wandering in search of others.[5] Few gay
men stood out among the other couples, families, and groups of friends
and neighbors who thronged the parks,
socializing, playing sports, and eating
their picnic suppers.

Cruising parks and
streets provided many young men and
newcomers to the city with a point of entry into the rest of the gay world, which
was sometimes hidden from men looking for it by the same codes and sub-
terfuges that protected it from hostile straight intrusions. "It was quite a handi-
cap to be a young guy in the 1920s," remembered one man, who had moved to
New York from Michigan. "It took an awfully long time to learn of a gay
speakeasy."[6] The parks and streets were perhaps the most common place for
newcomers to meet men more familiar with that world, and these men became
their guides to it. A German Jew who immigrated to New York in 1927, for
instance, recalled that within two or three weeks of his arrival, "I found my way
to Riverside Drive and the Soldiers and Sailors Monument." He still knew almost
no one in the city, but his cruising quickly remedied that. "It was 1927, about two
or three days before the big reception parade for Lindbergh after he came back
from his flight to Paris, and the bleachers were already up there. I met a man
there and we started talking. He was a Harvard man and taught ethical culture.
And that was the best contact I made, he and I had a wonderful affair." The affair
lasted two years, the friendship many more, and his Riverside Park pickup
became his most important guide to the new world.[7] [see FIGURE 1]

The German immigrant was not the only
man to begin a relationship with someone he met while cruising. Many relationships began through such contacts, and many friendships as well. "E. is a very
sentimental lad," Parker Tyler wrote to Charles Ford in the summer of 1929. "The

4 In a 1929 letter that also confirms Fifth Avenue's significance as a cruising area, Parker Tyler wrote: "Took a walk on
Fifth Ave. last Sunday night, just to see what it was like after
over a year of absence....Some 'cruisers' but all pretty stiff
except undesirables." (Tyler to Charles Henri Ford, 9 July
1929; see also his letter of 4 July 1929)

5 On the middle-class ideology of parks and the class
conflict generated over their use, see the masterful study
by Roy Rosenzweig and Elizabeth Blackmar, The Park and
the People: A History of Central Park (Ithaca: Cornell
University Press, 1992); Daniel Bluestone, Constructing
Chicago (New Haven: Yale University Press, 1991), pp. 7-
61; and Roy Rosenzweig, "Middle-Class Parks and
Working-Class Play: The Struggle over Recreational Space
in Worcester, Massachusetts, 1870-1910," Radical History
Review 21 (1979), pp. 31-48.

6 Leo, interview by author.

7 Jeffrey Gottfried, interview by author. Rene Hubert, also
an immigrant German Jew, had a similar experience ten
years later, when he arrived in New York with no job and
knowing no one. While sitting in Central Park, he was
approached by a man who subsequently invited him to a
series of parties where he met other gay men. Within a year
he had developed an extensive network of friends, and
learned of a number of other places where gay men met
(Rene Hubert, interview by author).

darling faun almost wept to me because tonight is the anniversary of our first meeting: 42nd St. and 5th Ave. = Fate."[8] The novelist Glenway Wescott recorded in his diary the story of N., who, upon hearing of the Central Park cruising strip for the first time, "hastened to it the next night, and there encountered his great love."[9]

The streets and parks were social centers for groups as well as individuals. Many groups of youths who could afford no other recreation gathered in the parks, and young men just coming out could easily find other gay men in them. Sebastian Risicato, an eighteen-year-old Italian-American living with his parents in the Bronx in 1938, for instance, heard about Bronx Park from the gay crowd he spent time with outside an older gay man's beauty salon on Gladstone Square. He went to the park and quickly became part of the gang of young "painted queens" who gathered near the 180th Street bridge. It was a "big social scene" as well as a cruising ground, he recalled. "We met and we dished [gossiped]. . . I would meet [my best friend], and the other sisters, and we'd go for a soda, then we'd come back, and cruise down and see if a number came by." At the park he learned about other places where gay men gathered and also met several people who became life-long friends.[10]

8 Parker Tyler to Charles Henri Ford, July 1929.

9 Glenway Wescott, *Continual Lessons: The Journal of Glenway Wescott, 1937-1955*, ed. Robert Phelps with Jerry Roscoe (New York: Farrar Straus & Giroux, 1990), p. 81 (diary entry for 13 April 1941).

10 Sebastian Risicato, interview by author.

11 Henry Isaacs, interview by author. Isaacs was a regular at Prospect Park in the 1940s and 1950s; for a brief account of gay friends meeting in the park in the 1920s, see Samuel Kahn, *Mentality and Homosexuality* (Boston: Meador, 1937), pp. 216-217. For more on Battery Park, see Chapter 3 of my *Gay New York*; for Riverside Park, see Jeffry Gottfried's story (note 7) above.

Because of its central location, Bryant Park, a small park adjoining the Public Library on 42nd Street near Times Square, became well known to straight and gay men alike as a meeting place for young "fairies" in the 1920s and 1930s. Brooklyn's Prospect Park, although less well known to the general public, served the same social role for somewhat older and more conventional-looking gay men. One high school teacher recalled that although he went to Prospect Park primarily to cruise, he became friendly with several of the other "regulars" who frequented the park and often took breaks from cruising with them, sharing information and casual conversation. Battery Park, on the southwest tip of Manhattan, was a popular rendezvous for seafaring men. Riverside Park, stretching along the western shore of Manhattan, where ships of all sorts were moored, was also a major cruising area and social center, especially for seamen and their admirers. Two landmarks in the park, Grant's Tomb at 122nd Street and the Soldiers and Sailors Monument at 89th Street, were especially renowned as meeting places in the gay world.[11]

Not surprisingly, Central Park, because of its location, vast stretches of unsupervised, wooded land, and heavy patronage, was especially renowned within the gay world both as a social center and as a cruising ground. At the turn of the century, men met each other next to the Belvedere Castle, on the west lawn near 63rd Street, and in other "secluded spots," according to trial records, and by the 1910s the benches at the

[FIGURE 1]
Soldiers and Sailors
Monument
Riverside Drive

[FIGURE 2]
The Ramble
Central Park

southwest corner of the park at Columbus Circle—across the street from Mother Childs—had become a major pickup site.[12] In the 1920s so many men met on the open lawn at the north end of the Ramble that they nicknamed it the Fruited Plain.[see FIGURE 2] In the 1920s and 1930s, hundreds of gay men gathered every temperate evening in the park south of 72nd Street, on the benches at Columbus Circle, along the walk leading into the park from the Circle, and at the fountain and plaza by the lake. The greatest concentration of men could be found (packed "practically solidly," according to one account) on the unbroken row of benches that lined the quarter-mile-long walk from the southeastern corner of the park to the mall, a stretch nicknamed Vaseline Alley by some and Bitches' Walk by others. "You'd walk down and there'd be a lot of real obvious queens, and some closet queens, and sometimes guys would come down on their bikes," one man remembered; there was always lots of "socializing."

12 *People v. Matthews* (CGS 1896); *People v. Koster*, DAP 21,728 (CGS 1898); *People v. Carlson*, DAP 20,546 (CGS 1898); *People v. Frerer*, DAP 20,950 (CGS 1898); *People v. Meyer and Ward*, DAP 43,369 (CGS 1903); *People v. Franc and Hurley*, DAP 154,475 (CGS 1924); *People v. Hartwich*, DAP 156,909 (CGS 1924); *People v. Coree*, DAP 160,472 (CGS 1925); all cases from NYMA. For gay men's own stories of picking up men in Central Park in the late 1920s and early 1930s, see accounts in George W. Henry, *Sex Variants* (New York: Paul B. Hoeber, 1941), by Thomas B., p. 105, Eric D., p. 153, and Daniel O'L., p. 432.

13 "N.Y.'s Central Park Greatest Circus Without Canvas Anywhere in U.S.," *Variety* (23 October 1929), p. 61. The article also noted, "Many arrests are made among the nance element."

14 Thomas Painter, "The Prostitute" (typescript, 1941, KIL), pp. 32-35; see also Wescott, *Continual Lessons*, p. 81 (diary entry for 13 April 1941); Rosenzweig and Blackmar, *The Park and the People*, pp. 479, 405; interviews with Dick Addison; Sebastian Risicato; Donald Vining; and Jeffrey Gottfried, who also commented that when he moved to New York in 1927, "I went to Central Park and certainly at that time the Goldman Band Festivals were the ideal meeting spots." The popularity of the southeastern corner of the park by the end of World War I is indicated by the large number of arrests made by the two officers assigned to the nearby Central Park zoo cages in the first half of 1921: Frederick H. Whitin, "Sexual Perversion Cases in New York City Courts, 1916-1921," bulletin 1480, 12 November 1921, box 88, COF. "Vaseline Alley," a nickname assigned to several streets and alleys where men had sex, alluded to the use of Vaseline petroleum jelly as a lubricant.

"The nance element holds regular conventions in Paddies Lane," *Variety* reported in the fall of 1929. "Tis their rendezvous!"[13]

In the late 1930s, particularly after Mayor Fiorello La Guardia had closed most of the city's gay bars in a pre-World's Fair crackdown, hundreds of gay men gathered at the band concerts offered at the Central Park Mall on summer nights, meeting friends, socializing, and cruising. "They are so thick in the crowd," declared one gay man at the time, "that if one were to walk through with a strikingly handsome male friend, one would be conscious of creating something of a sensation—there would be whisperings, nods, suddenly turned heads, staring eyes."[14] Most nongay observers noticed only the most obvious "nance element" in the crowd and along the walks, but gay men themselves were fully aware of their numbers on such evenings and exulted in transforming Central Park into a gay park.

The enormous presence of gay men in the parks prompted a sharp response from the police. They regularly sent plainclothesmen to cruising areas to entrap men; in the grounds around the Central Park zoo in the first half of 1921 alone, they made thirty-three arrests. They periodically conducted sweeps and mass arrests of suspected homosexuals in the parks, either to increase their arrest statistics, to get some publicity, or to force men to remain more covert in their cruising. In 1943, the police arrested Donald Vining and several other men sitting on the benches by an entrance to Central Park simply because they were in a cruising area; a judge dismissed the charges, but only after the men had spent a night in jail. Four years later seventeen-year-old Harvey Milk was arrested in a similar sweep in a Central Park cruising area: the police arrested the shirtless men they found there whom they suspected were gay, charging them with indecent exposure. They ignored the family men standing nearby, with their shirts off but their children in tow. [15]

The parks endured as a locus of sexual and social activity for homosexual and heterosexual couples alike, despite police harassment, in part because the police found them challenging to regulate. They were physically more difficult to raid than an enclosed space, offered more hiding spaces than a street, and although LaGuardia began closing Bryant Park at night in 1944 in order to "prevent undesirables from gathering," the larger parks, at least, were impossible to seal off.

Gay men also gathered on the city's beaches, which were enormously popular in the decades before air conditioning. More than a million people might crowd onto the Coney Island beach on a hot summer afternoon; photos of the scene portray a huge mass of bathers indiscriminately covering virtually every grain of sand, but the beach, too, had a more carefully delineated social geography. Different ethnic groups, sports groups, and other groups colonized sections of the beach and organized their use of its space in distinctive ways. While some gay men joined their ethnic compatriots, either individually or in groups, either blending in or making their gayness clear, other gay men claimed a certain section of the beach as their own and sometimes attracted notice for doing so. They sometimes put on for other beachgoers a "show" that outpaced even the shows at the Life and Mother Childs, turning their towels into dresses and fancy hats, swishing down the beach, kicking up their heels. Groups of friends from a neighborhood, bar, or cafeteria sometimes congregated in a subsection of the gay section of the beach. A large group of deaf gay men, for instance, regularly gathered on one of the city's beaches in the 1940s, according to several hearing men who saw them. Other, less obvious men, found the beaches a good place to mingle with the crowd in search of sexual partners, and the muscle beach section was often a prime target. In the years after World War II the police sometimes arrested men at Riis Beach, in particular, but gay men seem to have faced little opposition earlier in the century. [16] [see FIGURE 3]

The confidence that men gained from their numbers and campiness on the beach—and from the absence of a strong reaction to their openness—led them to become remarkably bold on occasion.

15 Donald Vining, *A Gay Diary* 4 vols. (New York: Pepys Press, 1979-1983), 1, pp. 284-285 (entry for 31 August 1943); Vining suspected, probably correctly, that the police were simply seeking to meet their arrest quotas. Milk would later be elected as an openly gay candidate to the San Francisco Board of Supervisors; see Randy Shilts, *The Mayor of Castro Street: The Life and Times of Harvey Milk* (New York: St. Martin's Press, 1982), pp. 3-4.

16 Interviews with Mike Romano, Mitch Hearst, and Joel Honig. For examples of men cruising at Coney Island and meeting men there, see Antonio L., quoted in Henry, *Sex Variants*, p. 422; Victor R., ibid., p. 443. Unfortunately, I have been unable to learn more about the group of deaf gay men or to interview anyone who was a member of it. It seems likely that it existed, though, since it was recalled independently by three different men in separate interviews. On the development of a gay beach community near New York City, see Esther Newton, *Cherry Grove, Fire Island: Sixty Years in America's First Gay and Lesbian Town* (Boston: Beacon, 1993).

[FIGURE 3]
Riis Beach

A male beauty contest held at Coney Island's Washington Baths in the summer of 1929, for instance, took an unexpected turn. To the surprise of a *Variety* reporter who served as one of the judges, most of the people who gathered to watch the contest were men. And to her further surprise, most of the men participating in the contest wore paint and powder. "[One] pretty guy pranced before the camera and threw kisses to the audience," she wrote. "One man came in dressed as a woman." Others had mascara on their eyelashes. "The problem," as she put it tongue-in-cheek, "became that of picking a male beaut who wasn't a floosie no matter how he looked." The judges settled on a contestant they knew to be married (which *Variety* reported just in case any of its readers had not yet realized who the other "floosies" were). On a packed beach on a hot summer afternoon, gay men had taken over a male beauty contest, becoming its audience, its contestants, its stars. [17]

THE SOCIAL ORGANIZATION OF THE STREETS

Along with the parks and beaches, the streets themselves served as a social center, cruising area, and assignation spot. Gay men interacted on streets throughout the city, but just as various immigrant groups predominated in certain neighborhoods and on certain streets, so, too, gay men had their own streets and corners, often where gay-oriented saloons and restaurants could be found and along which men strolled, looking for other men to pick up.

The streets could be dangerous, though, for men faced there the threat of arrest or harassment from the police and from anti-gay vigilantes. The police regularly dispatched plainclothes officers to the most popular cruising areas, and the results of their surveillance could be devastating. An arrest made in 1910 illustrates both the police's familiarity with gay haunts and the hazards the police could pose. At midnight on December 15 a forty-four-year-old clerk from Long Island had gone to Union Square, one of the city's best known cruising areas at the time, and met a seventeen-year-old German baker who had walked over from his Park Row lodging house. They agreed to spend the night together and walked to a hotel on East 22nd Street at Third Avenue where they could rent a room. Both men had evidently known that the Square was a place where they could meet other men. So, too, had the police. Two detectives, apparently on the look-out for such things, saw them meet, followed them to the hotel, spied on them from the adjoining room through a transom, and arrested them after watching them have sex. The older man was convicted of sodomy and sentenced to a year in prison. [19]

The police action at Union Square was not an isolated event. Around 1910 the police department added the surveillance of homosexuals (whom they often labeled "male prostitutes") to the

17 "Floozies Forgotten in Male Beauty Contest," *Variety* (14 August 1929), p. 47. As striking as the existence of the male beauty contest is the humorous, tongue-in-check tone with which *Variety* reported it. It gently ridicules the contestants, but it ridicules even more the "Coney Island dowagers" serving on the jury who hadn't a clue about what the sophisticated reporter saw transpiring, and seems to take glee in the exasperation of the chief judge, who did know what was going on.

18 *People v. Williams*, DAP 80,706 (CGS 1910). The fate of the younger man is uncertain.

responsibilities of the vice squad, which already handled the investigations of female prostitutes.[19] Around 1915, the squad assigned one of its plainclothes officers, Terence Harvey, to "specialize in perversion cases." He patrolled the parks, theaters, and subway restrooms known as centers of homosexual and heterosexual rendezvous alike; he arrested some men after seeing them meet in gay cruising areas and following them home, and he entrapped others. He appears to have been quite effective, for he won the praise of the anti-vice societies and was responsible for almost a third of the arrests of men charged with homosexual activity in the first half of 1921.[20]

Most of the men he and the other members of the vice squad arrested were charged not with sodomy, a felony, but with disorderly conduct, a misdemeanor that was much easier to prove and did not require a trial by jury.[21] By the early 1910s the police had begun to specify in their own records which of the men arrested for disorderly conduct had been arrested for "degeneracy."[22] The state legislature formalized this categorization in 1923 as part of its general revision of the disorderly conduct statute. The statute, like the use of the vice squad to pursue homosexual cases, reflected the manner in which the authorities associated homosexual behavior with female prostitution, for it used wording strikingly similar to that used to prosecute female prostitutes in its definition of the crime as the "frequent[ing] or loiter[ing] about any public place soliciting men for the purpose of committing a crime against nature or other lewdness."[23] As a practical matter, the authorities generally interpreted this statute to apply only to the "degenerates" who solicited "normal men" for sex and not to the men who responded to such solicitations, just as prostitutes were charged while their customers' behavior remained uncensured. In most cases this was because the "normal" man was a plainclothes policeman (who, presumably,

19 The evidence concerning the organization of the vice squad's anti-homosexual activities before the 1940s is limited, but it is clear that the squad continued to assign officers to homosexual cases. In the 1930s, for instance, another plainclothes officer in the vice squad explained that "at one time my job was to arrest degenerates," and that he had arrested "degenerates from the parks known as bushwackers . . . [and] degenerates from the park for annoying children . . . . [and] a number of degenerates in toilets and subways" (Gloria Bar & Grill, Inc., v. Bruckman, et al., 259 A.D. 706 [1st Dep't 1940], testimony of Frederick Schmitt, contained in Record on Review, pp. 243-50). The squad also periodically shifted its primary focus from prostitution to homosexuality, and back again (see, for example, the report that the squad, after stepping up its efforts to arrest homosexuals immediately following World War I, had decided to redirect its primary attention to prostitutes [bulletin 1504, 24 March 1922, box 88, COF]). On the organization of the policing of homosexuality in later years, see, for example, William Wolfson, "Factors Associated with the Adjustment on Probation of One Hundred Sex Deviates" (M.S.E. thesis, City College of New York, 1948).

20 In the fall of 1919, he followed a Swedish longshoreman and Italian printer he had seen meet at Union Square to the home of the printer on East 21st Street, where he arrested them (Society for the Suppression of Vice record books, vol. 4, pp. 386-87, cases 108-9, 6 October 1919, SSV). See also the description of the elaborate ruses he used in a case in which he became involved concerning a dentist who had approached a Committee of Fourteen investigator at the Childs Cafeteria at Columbus Circle: bulletin 1484, "A Perversion Case," 28 November 1921, box 88, COF; H. Kahan reports, 11 June and 19 July 1921, box 34, COF. Officer Harvey arrested 88 (30 percent) of the 293 men convicted of degeneracy in the first half of 1921; given his specialized skills, his arrests resulted in an exceptionally high conviction rate (Whitin, "Sexual Perversion Cases").

21 Although some 89 percent of the men charged with degenerate disorderly conduct were convicted, less than half of the indictments for sodomy (and in some years less than a quarter) resulted in conviction. This calculation is based on the figures provided for sodomy prosecutions, 1900-1920, in the memorandum, "Extract from Annual Reports of the Chief Clerk of the District Attorney's Office," COF

22 This observation is based on my review of the manuscript docket books of the magistrates' courts in Manhattan in the 1910s. By 1915, the annual report of the magistrates' court confirmed that such records were kept when it specified the number of men arrested for degeneracy, even though no such offense had yet been specified by the legislature (Annual Report, City Magistrates' Courts [First Division] [Manhattan and the Bronx], 1915, p. 106).

23 Penal Law, Chap. 41, Article 70, Section 721, sub-section 8, as cited in Cahill's Consolidated Laws of New York: Being the Consolidated Laws of 1909, as amended to July 1, 1923, ed. James C. Cahill (Chicago: Callaghan, 1923), p. 1416

had responded only to the degree necessary to confirm the "degenerate's" intentions), but it also applied to some cases in which the police had observed "fairies" solicit men they regarded as "normal."[24] In other cases, the police labeled and arrested both of the men involved as "degenerates."

Although the law was used primarily to prosecute men for trying to pick up another man (cruising), the police and sympathetic judges sometimes interpreted it loosely enough to encompass the prosecution of men who simply behaved in a campy, openly gay way, as in the case of men arrested when the police raided a cafeteria or bar homosexuals frequented. An exceptionally high percentage of the arrests on such charges resulted in convictions—roughly 89 percent in one 1921 study. Although different judges were likely to impose different sentences, the same study found that in general they were unusually harsh in such cases. Less than a quarter of the men convicted had their sentences suspended, while more than a third of them were sentenced for a period of days or even months to the workhouse, and a similar number were fined. An average of 650 men were convicted for degeneracy each year in Manhattan in the 1920s and 1930s.[25]

The police and the social purity groups were not the only forces to threaten gay men's use of the streets. A variety of other groups also sought to ensure the maintenance of moral order in the city's streets on a more informal—but nonetheless more pervasive, and, often, more effective—basis. The men who gathered at the corner saloon or poolroom often kept an eye on the street and discussed the events unfolding there, shopkeepers took an interest in the activities outside their stores, and mothers watched the movements of their children and neighbors from their stoops and windows. On most blocks in the tenement neighborhoods, gangs of youths kept "their" street under near-constant surveillance from their street corner outposts. Although the first concern of such gangs was to protect their territory from the incursions of rival gangs, they also kept a close watch over other strangers who threatened the moral order of the block. These groups often disagreed among themselves about what that moral order properly was, but gay men had to contend with the threat of the popular sanctions any of them might impose against "inverts" and homosexuals, from gossip to catcalls to violence.

Gay men responded to the threat of both formal and informal sanctions by developing a variety of strategies for negotiating their presence on the streets. Perhaps nowhere were more men willing to venture out in public in drag than in Harlem. Drag queens regularly appeared in the neighborhood's streets and clubs, where they tended to be more casually tolerated than in most of the city's other neighborhoods.[26]

24 See Whitin's description in his memorandum, "Sexual Perversion Cases." It should also be noted that although prostitution and homosexual solicitation were criminalized in different sections of the Code of Criminal Procedure, the police grouped them together as "crimes against chastity" in their annual reports.

25 The figure given for the average number of men convicted of degenerate disorderly conduct is based on the statistics published in the annual reports of the New York Police Department and of the City of New York Magistrate's Court, 1920-1940; the 1921 study was prepared by the Frederick Whitin of the Committee of Fourteen, and reported in his memorandum, "Sexual Perversion Cases."

26 For more on the relative tolerance of gay men in Harlem, see my *Gay New York*, pp. 244-267.

Still, it took considerable courage for men to appear in drag even in Harlem, since they risked harassment by other youths and arrest by the Irish police-men who patrolled their neighborhood. Over the course of two weeks in February 1928 the police arrested thirty men for wearing drag at a single club, Lulu Belle at 341 Lenox Avenue near 127th Street. Five men dressed in "silk stockings, sleeveless evening gowns of soft-tinted crepe de chine and light fur wraps" were arrested on a single night.[27]

Some drag queens refused to cower before the police and defied them all the way to the courthouse. Two "eagle-eyed" detectives patrolling Seventh Avenue early one Sunday morning in 1928 enjoyed watching the amusing antics of four young women who "seemed well lit up and out for a glorious morning promenade" until they realized the "girls" were "pansies on parade." They quickly arrested the quartet and marched them to the 123rd Street police station; the next morning the men were sentenced to sixty days in the workhouse. Still defiant, the drag queens, aged eighteen to twenty-one, mocked the officers by shouting "Goodbye dearie, thanks for the trip as we'll have the time of our lives" as they were led out of the courtroom.[28]

Not all drag queens were so defiant. After a policeman casually looked at a twenty-one-year-old "woman" as they passed each other on 117th Street late one night in 1928, the "woman," fearful that the policeman had realized he was a female imperson-ator, began to run. Keen to learn what the "woman" had to hide, the patrolman chased "her" down the street, up some stairs, and across the rooftops until cornering her. Although later commenting that "'she' could run faster than any 'woman' he had ever chased," the policeman realized he had arrested a drag queen only when they got to the station. The queen had good reason to fear arrest. He had already been arrested twice, once for degenerate disorderly conduct and once for masquerading as a woman, and had served three months in the workhouse on the latter charge.[29]

Other men who had no interest in wearing drag nonetheless announced their sexual interests equally boldly and created a visible gay presence by speaking, carrying themselves, and dressing in other styles that the dominant culture associated with fairies, even though this, too, could result in harassment from onlookers. In 1918 an agent witnessed the response of passersby to several "fairies" near Herald Square: they "mocked them and called in effeminate fashion after some of them and threw kisses at them." Agents witnessed groups of youths heckling fairies in Harlem as well, and Ralph Werther was attacked by several gangs near the Bowery, even though he was taken under the protection of others. In the 1920s groups of family men who lived near Riverside Drive sometimes accosted men they thought to be gay and threatened them with violence if they did not leave the neighborhood. In 1930 Parker Tyler and a gay friend

27 *Amsterdam News* (15 February 1928), p. 1.

28 "Two Eagle-Eyed Detectives Spot 'Pansies on Parade,'" *Inter-State Tattler* (10 March 1932), p. 2.

29 "'She' Turns Out to Be a 'He' in Court: Fur-Coated 'Woman' Gives Cop Liveliest Chase of His Life," *Amsterdam News*, (8 February 1928), p. 16.

30 J.A.S., Report on street conditions, n.d. [c. 12 September 1918], box 31, COF; Gene Harwood, interview by author; Parker Tyler to Charles Henri Ford, [August] 1930. Tyler's account of his encounter with the sailors formed the basis of a scene in the novel the coauthored with Ford, *The Young and Evil* (Paris: Obelisk, 1933), pp. 181-191. Ironically, a social worker who began working with men arrested on homosexual charges in the 1930s commented that it was usually not the fairy who was arrested, but the average look-ing man, because fairies had learned how to avoid the police (Alfred A. Gross, "The Troublesome Homosexual," *Focus* 32 [January 1953], p. 16). Although Gross did not explain his finding, he implied that it was because fairies were likely to be more deeply involved in the gay world and attuned to the political dynamics of the streets. "It is the unwitting, employed, middle-class individual," he added, "who usually gets picked up [by the police]."

31 T. Griswold Comstock, Ph.D., M.D., "Alice Mitchell of Memphis," *New York Medical Times* 20 (1892), p.172. He added: "Instances have been authenticated to me where such perverts when meeting another of the same sex, have at once recognized each other, and mutually become acquainted and have left in company with each other to prac-tice together their unnatural vices." See also, for example, William Lee Howard, "Sexual Perversion in America," *American Journal of Dermatology and Genito-Urinary Diseases* 8 (1904), p.11 ("by some subtle psychic influence these perverts recognize each other the moment they come in social contact"); James Kiernan, "Insanity: Sexual Perversion," *Detroit Lancet* 7 (1884), p. 482 ("these patients claim to be able to recognize each other"); G. Adler Blumer, "A Case of Perverted Sexual Instinct (Contraere Sexualempfindung)," *American Journal of Insanity* 39 (1882), p. 25. Krafft-Ebing made a similar observation of German "inverts" in "Perversions of the Sexual Instinct: Report of Cases," *Alienist and Neurologist* 9 (1888), p. 570.

were chased by "quite a lot of sailors and civilians in their shirt sleeves" on Riverside Drive and were "saved" only by the sudden appearance of some policemen. When the police took one of the sailors and the two gay men to the station, Tyler felt he was in as much trouble as his assailant; as soon as he had a moment alone in the patrol car he spit on his handkerchief to wash off his tell-tale mascara. (The judge eventually dismissed the charges against all of them.)[30] Often fairies did not encounter such hostile reactions, but their willingness to risk them should be regarded as a form of defiance and resistance to a hetero-sexist cultural system. The intensity of the reaction their openness sometimes provoked indicates that many "normal" people regarded it as such.

Given the risks in-volved in asserting a visible pres-ence in the streets, most gay people chose not to challenge the conven-tions of heterosexual society so directly. But they resisted and under-mined them nonetheless by developing tactics that allowed them to identify and communicate with each other without alerting hostile out-siders to what they were doing. Such tactics kept them hidden from the dominant culture, but not from one another. Whereas fairies used codes that were intelligible to straights as well as to gays, such as flashy dress and an effeminate demeanor, other gay men (the "queers") developed codes that were intelligible only to other men familiar with the subcul-ture, which allowed them to recognize one another without drawing the attention of the uninitiated, whether they were on the street, in a the-ater, or at a predominantly straight cocktail party or bar. They were so effective that medical researchers at the turn of the century repeatedly expressed their astonishment at gay men's ability to identify each other, attributing it to something akin to a sixth sense: "Sexual perverts read-ily recognize each other, although they may never have met before," wrote one doctor with some alarm in 1892, "and there exists a mysteri-ous bond of psychological sympathy between them."[31]

The "mysterious bond" between gay men resulted in large part from their participation in the gay subculture and consequent knowledge of its codes and tactics, both almost wholly unfamiliar to the doctors. It resulted as well from their simple attentiveness to the signals that might identify like-minded men; most other city residents were preoccupied with other matters or remained deliberately oblivious to the surfeit of stimuli on the streets. Involvement in the gay world familiarized men with the styles of clothing and grooming, mannerisms, and conventions of speech that had become fashionable among men in that world but were not stereotypically associated with fairies. Those fashions served as signs, "neither masculine nor feminine, but specifically and peculiarly homosexual," observed the writer and gay activist Donald Webster Cory in the early 1950s; these were "difficult for [outsiders] to pinpoint," but enabled men to recognize one another even as they concealed their identities from others.[32]

Gay men also made tactical use of the gender conventions governing men's public interactions. They took full advantage of the cultural injunction against men looking at other men in the same sexually assertive way they gazed at women; a "normal" man almost automatically averted his eyes if they happened to lock with those of a stranger, whereas a gay man interested in the man gazing at him returned his look. "The eyes, the eyes, they're a dead giveaway," recalled one man who was introduced to the gay world during World War II when he stumbled upon a major cruising area in London, Leicester Square. "If someone looks at you with a lingering look, and looks away, and then looks at you again. If you looked at a straight man he wouldn't stare back, he'd look immediately away."[33] In order to confirm the interest indicated by eye contact, or as a way of initiating contact, men made use of a number of utterly conventional gestures. Perhaps the most common simply involved asking a man for a match or for the time of day. Thomas Painter joked in 1941 that asking for a match in New York had become the equivalent of accosting, and the gay novelists of the thirties delighted in parodying the interaction. The technique was so well known within the gay world (and to the police) that Max Ewing, a young writer who moved in both the gay and high society circles centered around Carl Van Vechten, could satirize it (along with police entrapment and gay actors and chorus boys), in his 1933 novel, *Going Somewhere*. In one scene an actor who needed to get to the theater by eight "went up to a man who was standing in front of a clothing shop window and asked him if he knew what time it was. This man was a plain-clothes detective, so the boy was arrested, and sent to Welfare Island for seven weeks. Nothing could be done about it. The cast of the show regretted the episode, for the boy was `an awfully nice kid.'"[34] The man who made such a request could rest assured that a man unaware of its coded significance would simply respond to it straightforwardly, since men often asked

32 The various gay magazines published in the 1950s periodically published articles with titles such as "Can Homosexuals Be Recognized?" One particularly insightful such article by that title, although written by Donald Webster Cory twenty-five years after the period under discussion here, noted several of the same signs used by gay men a generation earlier, and it was wryly, but appropriately, illustrated with pictures of men staring into each other's eyes, men walking in peculiar ways, and articles of clothing and adornment fashionable among gay men: certain kinds of shoes and sandals, large rings, scarves, and the like. "Can Homosexuals Be Recognized?" *ONE Magazine* 1 (September 1953), pp. 7-11. For an extended discussion of the semiotics of inversion, see my *Gay New York*, Chapter 2.

33 Wystan Winters, interview by author.

34 Thomas Painter, "The Homosexual," (typescript, 1941, KIL), p. 25; Ewing, *Going Somewhere* (New York: Knopf, 1933), p. 182.

other men for such things, while a man interested in responding to its hidden meaning would start a conversation.

Gay men used such subcultural codes to make contact and communicate with each other throughout the city, but they also made tactical decisions about the safest places to meet. Like other marginalized groups seeking a public presence, gay men had to hone their sense of the social dynamics governing various neighborhoods and the possibilities each presented.[35] In constructing a gay map of the city, they had to consider the maps devised by other, sometimes hostile, groups, so a tactical logic governed the location of gay cruising areas. They tended to be clustered in theater and retail shopping districts, where many gay men worked and where heavy pedestrian traffic offered cover, such as Union Square, Herald Square, and Harlem's Seventh Avenue and 135th Street; along the socially less desirable avenues darkened by elevated trains thundering overhead, particularly Third and Sixth Avenues, where few powerful interests would notice them; close to the parks where men gathered, such as Fifth Avenue in the twenty blocks south of Central Park (and, in later years, Central Park West in the Seventies); along Riverside Drive and other parts of the waterfront, where many seamen and other unmarried or transient workers were to be found; and, in general, in the same "vice" areas where other forms of disreputable sexual behavior, particularly prostitution, were tacitly allowed to flourish, or that for one reason or another provided a measure of privacy and "cover" to gay men seeking to meet. [see FIGURE 4]

As the historian Susan Porter Benson has observed, the elaborate display windows that department stores began installing in the late nineteenth century had quickly become the locus of one of the few acceptable street cultures for middle-class women, who could stroll down the street looking at them and conversing with other browsers, "their loitering in public space," as Benson notes, "legitimized by its association with consumption." As men, gay men had less need to justify their presence on the streets, but they took advantage of the same legitimizing conventions. One man who had indicated his interest in meeting another might stop before a window and gaze at the display; the second could then join him at the window without attracting undue attention and strike up a conversation in which they could determine whether they wanted to spend more time together.[36] "Fairies hang out in the saloon opposite Bloomingdales," a Macy's saleswoman claimed in 1913, and, she added, the blocks of Third Avenue in the East Fifties, a marginal retail strip under the El, were "their favorite beat."[37] A study of arrests for homosexual activ-

35 James Duncan, "Men Without Property: The Tramp's Classification and Uses of Public Space," *Antipode* 10 (March 1978), pp. 24-34.

36 Susan Porter Benson, *Counter Cultures: Saleswomen, Managers, and Customers in American Department Stores, 1890-1940* (Urbana: University of Illinois Press, 1986), p. 18. Note that the incident described in Ewing's novel, *Going Somewhere*, took place at a shop window.

37 Natalie D. Sonnichsen report, 27 November 1913, box 39, COF. Sonnichsen heard this story from a saleswoman she had befriended while secretly investigating allegations of immorality among department store workers on behalf of the Committee of Fourteen. Third Avenue in the East Fifties would become one of the city's premier gay bar strips and cruising areas in the years following World War II.

ity in 1921 provides further evidence of the extent to which cruising was concentrated in retail shopping districts, for it revealed that the subway stations at Lexington and 59th Street (where Bloomingdale's stood), Union Square (the site of numerous cheap retail outlets), and Herald Square (where Macy's, Gimbel's, and Saks-34th Street were located) each accounted for more arrests than any other station, and together accounted for three-quarters of the arrests reported in all subway stations.[38]

The evolution of East 14th Street from Third Avenue to Union Square as one of the preeminent centers of working-class gay life and of homosexual street activity in the city from the 1890s into the 1920s illustrates the factors which encouraged the development of a cruising area. Known as the Rialto, 14th Street once had been the center of a fashionable entertainment and residential district. But by the 1890s it had become an inexpensive retail district and a center of ribald entertainment for working-class men, where "theatres, museums for men only, drinking palaces, gambling joints, and worse abounded."[39] Its legitimate theaters had turned into vaudeville and burlesque houses, and its elegant restaurants had given way to working men's saloons. It was also a center of female street prostitution and, before the crackdowns of the early 1910s, of brothels. It was in this context that 14th Street had become the "chief stamping-ground in the New York metropolitan district" of fairies and other gay men in the 1890s.[40] Ralph Werther spent many a night there, attracting the attention of young men as he promenaded up and down the street in the flashy clothes that proclaimed his identity as a fairy. Twenty years later, in 1914, the German homosexual emancipationist Magnus Hirschfeld (presumably on the word of his American informants) still described Union Square as a center of homosexual activity in New York.[41] Arrest records, novels, and diaries confirm that 14th Street remained an

38 Whitin, "Sexual Perversion Cases." There were thirty-three arrests at both the Union Square and Bloomingdale's stations, sixteen at Herald Square, ten at Times Square, and twenty at other subway stations, including a number at Grand Central. The subway arrests accounted for 38 percent of all arrests studied. The figures do not cover all arrests for homosexual solicitation made during the first six months of 1921, but only those heard before four of the eight relevant magistrates' courts in Manhattan. Those four courts, however, accounted for 86 percent of all such arraignments. The subway station at Bloomingdale's was also, at least occasionally, a place where men could go to meet female prostitutes; in 1927 a newsboy who sold his papers in the station served as a go-between for prostitutes working out of a nearby cafeteria, and arranged for an investigator to meet one there at 2:15 one morning (Report on Barney, newsdealer, underneath Bloomingdale's, 22 December 1927, box 36, COF). Whitin had discovered in one of his earliest studies of the geography of prostitution in New York that such vice was not confined to a single neighborhood, but tended to be found in the vicinity of the city's several retail shopping districts. (Frederick Whitin to the Rev. Calvin McLeod Smith, Buffalo Federation of Churches, 22 October 1920, box 59, COF.)

39 Ralph Werther, The Female-Impersonators (New York: Medico-Legal Journal, 1918), pp. 104-106, quote at p. 106; Timothy J. Gilfoyle, City of Eros: New York City, Prostitution, and the Commercialization of Sex, 1790-1920 (New York: Norton, 1992), pp. 210-212; Lloyd Morris, Incredible New York: High Life and Low Life of the Last Hundred Years (New York: Random House, 1951), pp. 181-193.

40 Werther, The Female-Impersonators, p. 98.

41 Magnus Hirschfeld, Die Homosexualitaet des Mannes und des Weibes (Berlin: Louis Marcus, 1914), p. 547. As noted above, in the first half of 1921 thirty-three men were arrested for homosexual solicitation at the Union Square subway station, more than at all but one other site (Whitin, "Sexual Perversion Cases"). On the Rialto as a center of female prostitution, see Gilfoyle, City of Eros, pp. 210-212; as a center of male prostitution, see Painter, "The Prostitute," pp. 20-21. Painter's comments on Union Square are less reliable than most of his information, since they are based on his reading rather than his own experience (which dated from the mid-1930s) or interviews with older gay men. Court cases suggesting the well-established role of Union Square as a center of gay male cruising, as well as of both casual and professional male prostitution, include People v. Casteels, DAP 76,910 (CGS 1910), in which a silversmith hired a room at the Union Square Hotel, then went out and returned with a youth, whom he presumably had met in the neighborhood; People v. Oreste, DAP 79,786 (CGS 1910), in which a watchman followed two men who walked from Union Square to a building on East 17th Street, where they hid themselves under the stoop to have sex before the watchman seized them; People v. DeMatti, DAP 126,271 (CGS 1919); People v. Wilson, DAP 129,057 (CGS 1920); People v. Ismail Solomon, DAP 178,147, (CGS 1929).

[FIGURE 4]
Central Park West

[FIGURE 5]
Bryant Park

important cruising area, especially for male prostitutes and for less obvious gay men, until the 1930s, when it was eclipsed by Times Square.[42]

The relationship between a neighborhood's changing social dynamics and its gay street scene can be seen even more clearly in Times Square, Union Square's successor. The shifting spatial and social organization of just one aspect of the Times Square's gay street culture—that of male prostitution—highlights the extent to which the apparent chaos of the most active street scenes masked a highly organized street culture, whose boundaries and conventions were well known to the initiated.

Times Square, already a busy center of female prostitution, became one of the city's most significant centers of male prostitution in the 1920s. Initially, two distinct groups of male prostitutes, whose interactions with customers were construed in entirely different ways, worked the Times Square area. Well-dressed, "mannered," and gay-identified hustlers serving a middle-class gay-identified clientele generally met their customers as the latter left the theater and walked home on the west side of Fifth Avenue from 42nd to 59th Streets. This was also a stretch where men who were not hustlers often met each other, and where hustlers could meet men walking to Central Park, another major cruising area (but not one where sexual contacts usually involved monetary exchange). Although a regular part of the Times Square scene, neither the hustlers nor their customers attracted much attention, since neither conformed to the era's dominant stereotypes of inverts. During the 1920s, a second group of prostitutes came to dominate 42nd Street itself between Fifth and Eighth Avenues: the effeminate (but not transvestite) "fairy prostitutes" who sold sexual services to other gay men and to men who identified themselves as "normal," including Italians and Greeks living to the west of the Square in Hell's Kitchen, as well as tourists from afar. The self-presentation of the prostitutes operating on the two streets differed markedly, as did the self-conception of their customers.[43] The proximity of the two groups points up the degree to which the Square's streets, like those in other parts of the city, were the site of multiple sexual systems, each with its own cultural dynamics, semiotic codes, and territories.

The transformation of 42nd Street during the 1920s and early 1930s had enormous repercussions for the street's gay scene. 42nd street was the site of the oldest theaters in the Times Square district, and the city's elite had regarded it as a distinguished address early in the century. By 1931, however, it had effectively become a working-class male domain. The conversion of two prominent 42nd Street theaters, the Republic [later Victory] and Eltinge [later Empire], into burlesque houses in 1931 had both signified and contributed to the masculinization of the

42 Charles Henri Ford and Parker Tyler's *roman à clef, The Young and Evil*, described 14th Street as "a most vulgar street, invariably alive with the sex-starved," and included a scene in which a gay character makes eye contact with someone in a 14th Street cafeteria and then follows him into Union Square in a taxi, ordering the cab to stop by the man so that he can pick him up (pp. 133-140).

43 Dorr Legg, interviewed; *St. EOM in the Land of Pasaquan: The Life and Times and Art of Eddie Owens Martin*, ed. Tom Patterson (East Haven, CT: Jargon Society, 1987), p. 146 (Martin hustled on 42nd Street before shifting to Fifth Avenue, where he could make more money); Daniel O'L. (an Irish fairy who hustled Greeks on Eighth Avenue), quoted in Henry, *Sex Variants*, pp. 431-432; and Painter, "The Prostitute."

Street. Not only the strippers inside but the large quasi-pornographic billboards and barkers announcing the shows outside intensified the image of the street as a male domain, threatening to women.[44] The masculinization of the street was confirmed by the conversion of the remaining theaters to a "grind" policy of showing male-oriented action films on a continuous basis and the opening of several men's bars and restaurants that catered to the increasing numbers of sailors, servicemen, and unemployed and transient men who frequented the street.

As the gender and class character of 42nd Street changed, it became a major locus of a new kind of "rough" hustler and of interactions between straight-identified servicemen and homosexuals.[45] The deepening Depression of the 1930s led growing numbers of young men—many of them migrants from the economically devastated cities of Pennsylvania, Massachusetts, New York, and the industrial South—to support themselves or supplement their income by hustling.[46] Not gay-identified themselves, many became prostitutes for the same reason some women did: the work was available and supplied a needed income. "In the Depression the Square swarmed with boys," recalled one man who became a customer in 1933. "Poverty put them there."[47] According to another account, 1932 was a critical year, when growing numbers of "transient boys . . . . went to Times Square to `play the queers.'"[48] They were joined by many soldiers and sailors, long attracted to the Square, who began hustling as well. These new hustlers, aggressively masculine in their self-presentation and usually called "rough trade" by gay men, took over 42nd Street between Seventh and Eighth Avenues, forcing the fairy prostitutes to move east of Sixth Avenue, to Bryant Park.[49] [see FIGURE 5]

The precise locus of the hustlers' and other gay men's activity on 42nd Street shifted several times over the course of the 1930s. The details of the moves are unimportant in themselves, but they reveal something of the social organization of the streets in general, for they resulted largely from the shifting geography of the gay bars and other commercial sites where men met. The corner of Broadway and 42nd near the Times Building was popular in the late 1920s, when the building's basement arcade and the Liggett's

44 Margaret Mary Knapp, "A Historical Study of the Legitimate Playhouses on West Forty-Second Street Between Seventh and Eighth Avenues in New York City" (Ph.D. diss., City University of New York, 1982), pp. 389-390.

45 Tennessee Williams recalled cruising Times Square with Donald Windham in the early 1940s, where he made "very abrupt and candid overtures [to groups of sailors or GIs, phrased so bluntly that it's a wonder they didn't slaughter me on the spot . . . . They would stare at me for a moment in astonishment, burst into laughter, huddle for a brief conference, and, as often as not, would accept the solicitation, going to my partner's Village pad or to my room at the `Y'." Tennessee Williams, *Memoirs* (New York: Bantam, 1976), p. 66; see also pp. 123, 172. Some verification of their activity in Times Square is offered by a letter Williams wrote Windham on 11 October 1940, while he was visiting his family in Missouri: "Have to play jam [straight] here and I'm getting horny as a jack-rabbit, so line up some of that Forty-second Street trade for me when I get back. Even Blondie would do!" (*Tennessee Williams' Letters to Donald Windham, 1940-1965*, ed. Donald Windham [New York: Holt, Rinehart, Winston, 1977], p. 17); see also Donald Windham, *Lost Friendships: A Memoir of Truman Capote, Tennessee Williams, and Others* (New York: William, Morrow, 1987), p. 114. *Broadway Brevities*, 2 November 1931, referred to gay men and servicemen making the block bounded by Broadway, Seventh Avenue, and Forty-second and Forty-first Streets "their special hangout."

46 The social and regional backgrounds of Depression-era hustlers are impossible to determine with certainty—no census-taker made note of them—but the ones cited here were reported by the normally reliable Painter on the basis of his interviews with a sample of 67 of them in the mid- and late 1930s: "The Prostitute," pp. 125-127.

47 Will Finch, notes on peg-houses (male brothels), dated 24 April 1962, KIL.

48 Painter, "The Prostitute," pp. 110, 115, recounting the histories of two hustlers.

49 This mapping and that of the following paragraph is based primarily on Painter, "The Prostitute," pp. 22-23, 30; Finch, "Homosexual Resorts in New York, as of May 1939," Finch papers, KIL, and *Broadway Brevities* (4 July 1932), p. 12; 2 November 1931.

drugstore upstairs functioned as meeting places.[50] Men gathered in the middle of the northern side of the block between Seventh and Eighth Avenues in the mid-1930s, when it was the site of the Barrel House, the most famous sailor-prostitute-homosexual bar of the era. It was "wholly uninhibited . . . as to `accosting,'" recalled one patron. "You could count a dozen [hustlers] lined up on the curb outside the Barrel House, in addition to the number inside who had the price of a beer to get in."[51] They moved to the south side of the street after the police closed the Barrel House and the Marine Bar & Grill took its place. During the war they settled near Sixth Avenue, where several cheap luncheonettes and sailor and hustler bars, such as the Pink Elephant, stood under the Elevated.[52]

The hustler scene followed the bars so closely in part because the bars attracted customers and offered shelter from the elements, but also because the streets and bars functioned as extensions of each other. Each site had particular advantages and posed particular dangers in men's constant territorial struggles with policing agents, as the men subject to that policing well knew. The purchase of a beer at a bar legitimized behavior involved in cruising that might have appeared more suspicious on the streets, including a man's simply standing about aimlessly or striking up conversations with strangers. But while the police periodically tried to clean up the streets by chasing hustlers and other undesirable loiterers away, they could not permanently close the streets in the way they could close a bar. In a heavily trafficked, non-residential area such as 42nd Street, no one had the same interest in controlling pedestrians' behavior on behalf of the police that a bar owner threatened with the loss of his license had in controlling his customers. While the police might harass men on the street simply for standing about with no apparent purpose, bars might evict them simply for touching, and plainclothesmen might arrest them for trying to pick up a man in either locale. The relative dangers of either site varied and depended on the momentary concerns of the police, and much of the talk on the streets was necessarily devoted to their shifting tactics. On more than one occasion in the 1930s and 40s a man noted in his diary that all of the street's hustlers had suddenly disappeared, apparently aware of some danger their customers did not perceive.[53]

Although bars were the major gathering place for men after the repeal of Prohibition in 1933, the numerous cheap cafeterias, Automats, and lunchrooms that crowded the Times Square area had a similar symbiotic relationship with the "public" life of the street throughout the 1920s and 1930s. Thompson's Lunch Room on Sixth Avenue between 42nd and 43rd Streets was reputed to be a gay rendezvous in 1920, as was "a place on W 46 St [in 1921] where fairies [are] supposed to hang out and meet men."[54]

50 Report on Fairies' hangout in basement, Times Square Bldg., 42nd Street and Broadway, 2 March 1927, box 36, COF.

51 See Will Finch, autobiographical notes, 1935, Finch papers.

52 John Nichols, "The Way It Was: Gay Life in World War II America," *QQ Magazine* 7 (August 1975), p. 54.

53 Finch diary, for example, 29 October 1947, KIL.

54 I say "reputed" to be such rendezvous because the Committee of Fourteen investigator H. Kahan visited both places "looking for fairies and pimps" in 1920, which suggests he had heard they would be there, but he was unable to "make any connections with any of them," possibly because both places were almost empty at the time of his visit: report, 28 April 1920, box 34, COF. See also the investigator's report, 27 April 1921, box 34, COF.

Men also moved back and forth between the streets and the large cafeterias located in the Square, and according to one 1931 account, during the winter the Automat across 42nd Street from Bryant Park became a favorite haunt of the men who gathered in the park during the summer.[55]

Numerous movie and burlesque theaters, especially those in gay cruising areas, also became a part of the gay circuit. The small, dark, and unsupervised nickelodeons that began to appear in working-class neighborhoods in the 1890s had immediately aroused the concern of social purists, who feared they would become the site of illicit mingling of the sexes. The theaters also developed an unsavory reputation in middle-class society at large, which the nascent movie industry overcame only by building huge, elegant theaters (appropriately known as movie palaces) in the 1910s and 1920s.[56] Even some of the palaces became known as trysting spots for heterosexual couples, however, and a few, particularly in less reputable areas, became places where gay men (as well as straight men simply interested in a homosexual encounter) could meet one another. Although men pursued other men in all sections of the theaters, the standing room area and the balconies were particularly suitable as meeting areas. Ushers, some of whom were gay themselves (and some of whom supplemented their income by introducing male patrons to female prostitutes working in the theaters), seem generally to have avoided the balconies (where heterosexual couples also often met) and left them free from surveillance.[57]

In the first six months of 1921 at least sixty-seven men were arrested for homosexual solicitation in movie theaters in Manhattan, including an astonishing forty-five men at a single theater at 683 Sixth Avenue, near 22nd Street. A City Magistrate who had heard the cases of many of the men arrested there claimed that the theater had been "the resort of male degenerates" for the previous two or three years "to such an extent that from one to two policemen are detailed to sit in the audience almost constantly." The judge thought it had acquired a reputation among gay men "as a place where men of a certain class [that is, homosexual] will meet congenial spirits." He claimed to have tried the case of a tourist who had learned of the theater before visiting New York and gone there "within two hours of his arrival in the city."[58]

Since moviegoing was a perfectly legitimate way to spend the afternoon, theaters were places where young men could go to search out other gay men and begin to learn about the gay world. "I thought I was [the] only one like this until I reached High School," recalled one

55 *Broadway Brevities* (2 November 1931), p. 2. In his interview, Frank Thompson reported this was still the case in the 1940s.

56 Peiss, *Cheap Amusements: Working Women and Leisure in Turn-of-the-Century New York* (Philadelphia: Temple University Press, 1986), pp. 145-153, esp. p. 151; Robert Sklar, *Movie-Made America* (New York: Random House, 1975), Chapter 2.

57 For reports of ushers acting as go-betweens between male patrons and female prostitutes, see H. Kahan's reports on the Olympic Theater, East 14th Street, 18 March 1919, and on B.F. Kahn's Union Square Theater, 56 East 14th Street, 23 June 1919, box 33, COF.

58 Magistrate J.E. Corrigan to Mayor John F. Hylan, 14 December 1920, "Dept. of Licenses, 1920" folder, box 218, Mayor Hylan Papers, NYMA. Corrigan urged the mayor to permanently revoke the license of the theater (which had already lost its license temporarily several times in the previous two years), and the mayor ordered his license commissioner to do so (Secretary to the Mayor to Commissioner John G. Gilchrist, 15 December 1920, same folder), but the theater was still open the following year, when the forty-five men were arrested there (Whitin, "Sexual Perversion Cases"). The name of the theater is not given.

thirty-four-year-old black man in 1922. After learning a bit about the gay world from the other homosexuals he met in school, though, "I used to go to matinees, meet people like myself, get into conversation and [I] learned that this is a quite common thing. They put me wise."[59] Another man who frequented the 42nd Street theaters during World War II met several men there who became friends. He and his friends shared stories of their adventures there, suggesting that such venues were not just sites for anonymous, furtive encounters but could also serve valued social (and socializing) functions.[60] The theaters, like other locales, were subject to periodic crackdowns, and gay men depended on the grapevine to protect themselves. On one occasion in 1945 the man mentioned above stopped going to the 42nd Street theaters for several weeks because gay friends had warned him that they were infested with plainclothesmen.[61]

FINDING PRIVACY IN PUBLIC: THE MULTIPLE MEANINGS OF "PUBLIC SEX"

Men used public spaces to meet their friends and to find potential sexual partners. But they also used them for sex. Poorer men, especially, had few alternatives. Unable to bring male partners home to crowded tenement quarters, unable to afford even an hour's stay at a Raines Law hotel or flophouse, they were forced to find secluded spots in the city's streets and parks where they could, for a moment, be alone with their partners. But they were joined there by other men as well, including middle-class men with access to more private quarters who found "public sex" exciting, and a variety of men who were not gay-identified but nonetheless used such sites for various purposes. The encounters in such "public" spaces thus had different meanings for different men—and suggest the complexity of the city's sexual topographies.

Sodomy trial depositions from the 1890s and early 1900s record the range of spaces used by workingmen for sexual encounters: an Irish laborer and a schoolboy discovered by a suspicious patrolman in a covered wagon standing on a lower Manhattan street one night in 1889; two laborers caught in an ice wagon in an Italian immigrant neighborhood in 1896; a German deli worker and an Irish waiter seen on a loading platform on a deserted industrial street at 3 A.M. one night the same year; an Irish porter and an Italian laborer discovered in a recessed doorway another night; and, throughout the period, couples apprehended in vacant lots and in the nooks and crannies of the tenements—the outhouse in the backyard, the roof, the cellar, the darkened stairway.[62] The absence of private quarters forced men constantly to improvise, in

59 Kahn, *Mentality and Homosexuality*, pp. 197-198. This man was recounting his experiences as a youth in London, where he began visiting theaters around 1905, but men had similar experiences in New York: for example, Martin Goodkin, interviewed. An NYU doctoral student, though more hostile, reported the same phenomenon in the burlesque theaters on 14th, 42nd, and 125th Streets: David Dressler, "Burlesque as a Cultural Phenomenon" (Ph.D. diss., New York University, 1937), pp. 161, 204, 210.

60 See, for example, Vining, *Diary*, 1, p. 260 (entry for 8 March 1943); p. 263 (4 April 1943: he accompanied someone home from the Selwyn and "we talked a blue streak of theatre, ballet, music, personalities, etc. and I'd have enjoyed the conversation alone" [that is, without sex]; p. 270 (27 May 1943); p. 271 (6 June 1943: "another dull fruitless night" at the New Amsterdam); p. 276 (7 July 1943).

61 See, for example, Vining, *Diary*, 1, p. 371 (10 January 1945: "[Friends] warned me against theater cruising because of the plainclothesmen"); p. 374 (26 January 1945: "There was a policeman by the Selwyn box office so I wasn't surprised to find no standees row.") A civilian, he also complained that the danger posed by plainclothesmen made servicemen, always a desirable catch, "rely more on [other] service men since they're sure they're not detectives."

other words, to seize whatever relatively hidden space they could find, whenever they found a sexual partner.

But they also developed a more finely calibrated sexual map of the city: certain streets, sections of parks, and public washrooms where men regularly went for sex and knew they were likely to find other men. They shared many of those sites with young heterosexual men and women, who sought privacy in them for the same reasons many gay men did. Both groups, for instance, found the city's parks particularly useful. They were dark at night, and the larger ones offered numerous secluded spots in the midst of bushes and trees where couples could find privacy in even so public a space. Police and anti-vice investigators regularly noted the troubling appearance of unsupervised heterosexual couples spooning on secluded benches and disappearing into the bushes in the city's numerous parks. "We didn't see anything else but couples laying on grass, or sitting on benches, kissing and hugging each other . . . especially [in] the dark sections which are poor lighted," an agent reported of Central Park in 1920.[63] Agents surveying the problem at Van Cortlandt Park in the Bronx late in the summer of 1917 observed a similar scene: soldiers met prostitutes and other women at the nearby subway station and walked into the park, where they hid in the bushes and near the boat house. They also discovered that men interested in meeting other men took similar advantage of the park's hidden spaces, for they noticed "many soldiers in the dark spots on [the] way in [the] Park to the Inn, walking arm and arm hugging and kissing."[64] Police records suggest how common a practice it was for men to use the parks for sexual encounters. In the last five years of the nineteenth century, park police arrested men found having sex in the recesses of Central, Riverside, Mount Morris, City Hall, Tompkins Square, and Battery Parks, and by early in the twentieth century they had arrested men in Washington Square Park as well.[65]

Of all the spaces to which men had recourse for sexual encounters, none were more specific to gay men—or more highly contested, both within the gay world and without—than the city's public comfort stations and subway washrooms. The city had begun building the stations in the late nineteenth century in parks and at major intersections, partly in an effort to offer working men an alternative to the saloons, which until then had afforded virtually the only publicly accessible toilets in the city. By 1925, there

62 People v. Duggan and Malloy (CGS 1889) (covered wagon); People v. Jerome (CGS 1896) (ice wagon); People v. Nicols (CGS 1896) (doorway); People v. Dressing and Doyle (CGS 1896) (loading platform); People v. Schimacuoli, DAP 22,087 (CGS 1898) (vacant lot); People v. Vincent, DAP 16,430 (CGS 1897) (outhouse); People v. Ranson, DAP 21,292 (CGS 1898) (several youths in the basement of a building); People v. Viggiano, DAP 46,835 (CGS 1904) (two Italian youths on the roof of their building in Italian East Harlem); and People v. Heartstein, DAP 125,604 (CGS 1919) (a thirty-nine-year-old Hungarian laborer and a Jewish teenager, in the common toilet-room of a rooming house and a few nights later on the roof of a tenement).

63 Report by H. Kahan, 27 August 1920, box 34, COF "Many girls were here with sailors and later on the girls were seen walk out from park alone . . . A few white girls were also seen going in Park escorted by Japanese or Chinese." he added.

64 Reports on Van Courtlandt Park, 22 August; 19, 20 September 1917, box 25, COF.

65 For cases of men caught in City Hall Park, see People v. Clark and Mills, DAP 10,481 (CGS 1896); People v. Johnson and Weismuller (CGS 1896); for Tompkins Park, see People v. Stanley (CGS 1896); for Battery Park, see People v. Adams and Dawson, DAP 11,476 (CGS 1896); People v. Lang and Meyer, DAP 32,264 (CGS 1900); for Mount Morris Park, see People v. Burke and Ginn, DAP 20,366 (CGS 1898); People v. Abbey, DAP 162,316 (CGS 1925); for Riverside Park, see People v. Mohr, DAP 11,497 (CGS 1896); People v. Morton, DAP 11,498 (CGS 1896); People v. Pendergrass and Serpi, DAP 110,748 (CGS 1916); for Washington Square Park, see People v. Carrington and Rowe (CGS 1910). Other sources corroborate the trial evidence; one imprisoned hustler told a doctor in 1922, for instance, that he had had his first homosexual experience in Central Park, apparently in the 1910s, and had "been earning a livelihood in the parks and hotels through homosexual acts, etc." (Kahn, Mentality and Homosexuality, p. 67; see also pp. 77, 171, 216-217).

were eighteen comfort stations in Manhattan.[66] A wave of arrests in 1896, shortly after the first stations opened, indicates that several of them, including the ones at Battery Park, City Hall Park, and Chatham Square, all near concentrations of cheap transient lodging houses, had quickly become regular homosexual rendezvous. The public comfort station at City Hall Park appears to have developed a particularly widespread reputation as a meeting ground, drawing men from throughout the city. A twenty-eight-year-old salesman from West 34th Street met a twenty-four-year-old clerk from Brooklyn there one night in March 1896, for instance; later that year a porter living in a Bowery rooming house met a cook there who was visiting the city from Westport, Connecticut.[67]

As the city's subway system expanded in the early years of the century, its washrooms also became major sexual centers. Men who had met on the subway could retire to them easily, and men who wanted a quick sexual release on the way home from work learned that there were men at certain subway washrooms who would readily accommodate them. Encounters could take place at almost any station, but certain washrooms developed reputations for such activity. By the 1930s the men's washroom in the Times Square subway station and the comfort station at Times Square were used so frequently for sexual encounters that they became widely known among gay men as the "Sunken Gardens" (possibly an allusion to the song by Beatrice Lillie about the fairies at the bottom of *her* garden), a name subsequently sometimes applied to other underground washrooms. Gay men dubbed all the restrooms (often called "t-rooms," short for "toilet-rooms," in early twentieth-century slang) "tearooms," which allowed them to discuss their adventures surreptitiously in mixed company, and may also have been an arch comment on the rooms' significance as social centers. If "tearoom" normally referred to a gracious cafe where respectable ladies could meet without risk of encountering inebriated males, it could ironically name the less elegant locale where so many gay men met.[68]

Bourgeois ideology—and certainly the ideology that guided state regulation—regarded comfort stations as public spaces (of the most sordid sort, in fact, since they were associated with bodily functions even more stigmatized than sex), but the men who used them for sex succeeded in making them functionally quite private. As the sociologist Laud Humphreys' research in the 1960s revealed, public washrooms became a locus of homosexual encounters throughout the country not only because of

66 Stanley H. Howe, *History, Condition and Needs of Public Baths in Manhattan* (New York: New York Association for the Improvement of the Condition of the Poor, publication no. 71, n.d. [1911]), p. 10; *R.L. Polk & Company's General Directory of New York City*, vol. 134 (1925), p. 39.

67 *People v. Johnson and Weismuller; People v. Clark and Mills*, DAP 10,481 (CGS 1896). The men in the first case were discharged; in the second case, the cook was discharged and the porter sentenced to two years in the state penitentiary. For Battery Park, see, for example, *People v. Adams and Dawson*, concerning a fifty-year-old cook from East 109th Street found with a twenty-seven-year-old laborer; and *People v. Lang and Meyer*, concerning two Germans, one a ship's steward, the other a porter who lived on Canal Street.

68 Although the term was still in use in the 1970s and 1980s, its origins had long since been forgotten; not even the sociologist Laud Humphreys, author of the well-known study of homosexual encounters in such locales, could explain its etymology: *Tearoom Trade: Impersonal Sex in Public Places* (Chicago: Aldine, 1970), 2n. For examples of the casual use of the term "toilet room," see *People v. Vincent*, DAP 16,430 (CGS 1897), and *People v. George Weikley* (CGS 1912). A 1929 glossary of homosexual slang defined "tea house" as "a public lavatory frequented by homosexuals": Aaron J. Rosanoff, "Human Sexuality, Normal and Abnormal, From a Psychiatric Standpoint," *Urologic and Cutaneous Review* 33 (1929), p. 528. On the comfort station at Longacre [Times] Square becoming known as the "Sunken Gardens," see Louis E., quoted in Henry, *Sex Variants*, p. 196. On Beatrice Lillie's song, see my *Gay New York*, Chapter 10.

their accessibility to men of little means, but also because it was easy to orchestrate sexual activity at even the most active of tearooms so that no one uninvolved in it would see it, thus providing the participants, as Humphreys put it, "privacy in public."[69]

The vice squad and other policing agents were well aware of men's ability to conceal their encounters from intruders. By the 1910s they had developed ways to circumvent the men's tactics and keep the tearooms under surveillance. Most commonly, the vice squad hid policemen behind the grill facing the urinals so that they could observe and arrest men having sex there or in the stalls. In 1912, agents of the Pennsylvania Railroad even cut holes in the ceiling of the men's room at their Cortlandt Street ferry house in order to spy on men using the facilities. The observers' need to hide was significant; as even the police admitted, the men they observed would have stopped having sex as soon as they heard someone beginning to open the outer door. The police also periodically sent plainclothesmen into the public comfort stations and subway washrooms to entrap men. In the earliest recorded incident, in 1914, a plainclothesman stationed at the Chatham Square comfort station got into a conversation with another man there, agreed to go with him and a third man to a secluded part of Battery Park, and then arrested both of them.[70] A 1921 study confirmed the risks these police tactics posed to the men who met in such locales: fully 38 percent of the arrests of men for homosexual activity that year were made in subway washrooms.[71] Nonetheless, enforcement efforts were only sporadic. The police could hardly monitor every subway station's washroom every day, and tearooms continued to be widely used for decades.

Arrests could have catastrophic consequences. Conviction often resulted in a sentence of thirty to sixty days in the workhouse, but the extralegal sanctions could be worse. An arrest could result in a man's homosexuality being revealed to family members, employer, and landlord, either because the police called to "confirm" a man's identity, employment, or residence or because the man himself had to explain his incarceration. Augustus Granville Dill, an activist in the National Association for the

69 One man often served informally as a sentry who could warn the others about the approach of strangers, and, given the possible consequences of approaching the wrong man, even two strangers alone in an isolated tearoom usually sought to confirm their mutual interest in an encounter through a series of nonverbal signs before overtly approaching each other. The most popular tearooms had elaborate and noisy entrances, which alerted men to the approach of another and gave them time to stop whatever they were doing. To reach one tearoom famous among gay men in the 1940s, located on the eighth floor of the RCA Building at Rockefeller Center, for instance, those arriving had to pass through several doors in a long corridor, thus providing the men in the room ample warning of their approach. See Humphreys, *Tearoom Trade*, pp. 1-15; and Edward William Delph, *The Silent Community: Public Homosexual Encounters* (Beverly Hills, Calif.: Sage Publications, 1978), based on the author's field work in New York in the 1970s. I am also indebted to the analysis of the social dynamics of tearoom encounters provided by two men on the basis of their own experiences in them in the 1940s and 1950s: Grant McGree, interviewed; and Martin Goodkin, interview by author.

70 *People v. Martin*, DAP 13,577 (CGS 1914). Most men apprehended in subway tearooms were charged with disorderly conduct, but a few were prosecuted for sodomy, and the more extensive records of their cases provide details about police methods unavailable in the records of the magistrates' courts. See, for example, *People v. Bruce and Clark*, DAP 118,852 (CGS 1918), which indicates two officers were stationed in the closet of the subway tearoom at the 135th Street and Lenox Avenue station of the IRT in Harlem; *People v. Chapman and Tamusule*, DAP 156,845 (CGS 1924), two officers stationed at the Stone Street entrance to the BMT line; and *People v. Murphy and Tarrence*, DAP 156,956 (CGS 1924), police at the 125th and Lenox Avenue station of the IRT. For the Pennsylvania Railroad case, see *People v. George Weikley (aka Wallis)* (CGS 1912). The agents cut the hole in the ceiling after discovering that men had drilled holes in the partitions between booths in order to facilitate sexual encounters. Also see James D., quoted in Henry, *Sex Variants*, p. 264.

71 Frederick H. Whitin, "Sexual Perversion Cases." For other evidence from the 1920s and early 1930s of men having encounters in subway washrooms, see the accounts in Henry, *Sex Variants*, by Michael D., pp. 135, 137, and Eric D., p. 154. Such encounters in later years were described by Martin Goodkin and Willy W. in their interviews.

Advancement of Colored People and the business manager of its magazine, *The Crisis*, was widely known and admired in Harlem circles. He had a reputation as a dandy, who always wore a bright chrysanthemum in his buttonhole and was known to engage in flamboyant behavior in public. In 1928, he was arrested in a subway washroom. W.E.B. DuBois, the editor of *The Crisis*, promptly fired him.[72]

The men who used subway tearooms tended to be relatively poor and to have relatively little access to other kinds of private space, either because of their poverty or because their own homes were unavailable to them for homosexual trysts. Among other sources, two surveys in 1938 and 1940 of homosexual inmates at the city jail, many of whom would have been apprehended in the tearooms, suggest this. Almost half the inmates surveyed were laborers (another 13 percent had no job at all) and a third lived in tenement houses with families. Only 3 percent to 5 percent were professionals or lived in "superior" housing.[73] "Subways were *the* meeting place for everyone," recalled one black man of his days as a poor youth in Harlem in the 1920s and 1930s. "Every station had a restroom then and you could always meet people there. People who didn't have a place to stay could take the train up to the Bronx and always find someone who'd give them a place to stay and some money."[74]

It would be wrong, though, to suppose that *only* poor men frequented the tearooms, for many other men visited them as well. Indeed, the constant sexual activity in the city's public restrooms involved thousands of men for whom the encounters had widely varying meanings. Even among gay men, views about the propriety of such visits varied enormously. Some men, particularly those who were professionally successful in jobs that required them to pass as straight, found it astonishing that anyone in their circles would *risk* going to a tearoom, given the threat of arrest and the availability of alternatives to men highly integrated into gay society. Others were as likely as the anti-vice societies to regard such encounters as shameful, for they expected the same level of romanticism, monogamy, and commitment to be involved in gay relationships that bourgeois ideology expected of marriage. (The painter Russell Cheney sought to forswear his visits to comfort stations after falling in love with the literary critic F.O. Matthiessen in 1925, for instance; such escapades, previously so important to him, seemed inconsistent with the life his newfound

72 Augustus Granville Dill entry in Bruce Kellner, ed., *The Harlem Renaissance: A Historical Dictionary for the Era*, ed. Bruce Kellner (Westport, CT: Greenwood, 1984), pp. 100-101.

73 George W. Henry and Alfred A. Gross, "The Homosexual Delinquent," *Mental Hygiene* 25 (July 1941), p. 426; idem., "Social Factors in the Case Histories of One Hundred Underprivileged Homosexuals," *Mental Hygiene* 22 (1938), p. 597. It should be noted, though, that wealthier men were less likely to be imprisoned (and thus less likely to appear in the survey) because they were more likely to be able to pay a fine (or pay off the arresting officer). Indeed, it was widely believed in the gay world that men caught be the police in tearooms were subject to police extortion: a man arrested by the Pennsylvania Railroad's agents at the Cortlandt Street ferry station in 1912 charged that company detectives had tried unsuccessfully to blackmail him before turning him over to the police (*People v. George Weikley [aka Wallis]* (CGS 1912), although his accusation, while plausible, cannot, of course, be taken at face value, since he may have fabricated it simply to undermine the testimony of the detectives against him. A generation later, at the height of the postwar anti-gay crackdown in 1948, Will Finch reported that "three first hand sources" had informed him that "the police are now in the midst of a 'drive' to clean out doings in public toilets, and spy on them through holes specially made, or gratings for ventilators, then rush in and nab them when they get going...The police try to shake them down themselves. Only if they haven't enough money on them to pay off the police do [the police] take them into the court" (Finch diary, 7 March 1948).

74 Howard Raymond, interview by author.

love made him wish to lead.)[75] As a result, even many of the men who visited the tearooms were ashamed of the practice and never revealed them to their friends.

A different and perhaps more dominant strain of gay male culture valued sexual adventurism, experimentation, and variety. Men who shared this perspective were likely to regard tearooms more positively because of the unparalleled access they provided to a large and varied group of men. Some men found the very anonymity, unpredictability, and danger of encounters in public places to be sexually exciting. They took such encounters as a matter of course and many regaled their friends with stories of their tearoom exploits. Some men involved in long-term nonmonogamous relationships even took their lovers to see the particularly active sites they had discovered.[76]

Tearoom encounters' very lack of romanticism and emotional involvement made them particularly attractive to another group of men. If some men used tearooms because police harassment and poverty left them nowhere else to go, others used them because anti-homosexual social attitudes left them unable, emotionally, to go elsewhere. Pervasive anti-homosexual social attitudes kept many men who were interested in other men from fully acknowledging that interest to themselves, and many of them sought sexual encounters in spaces, such as public washrooms, that seemed to minimize the implications of the experiences by making them easy to isolate from the rest of their lives and identities. The same association of tearooms with the most primal of bodily functions reinforced men's sense that the sexual experiences they had there were simply another form of release, a bodily function that implied nothing more about a man's character than those normally associated with the setting.

The same lack of commitment also made the tearooms attractive to straight men interested in a quick sexual release and to yet another group of men who acknowledged their homosexual interests to themselves, but dared not visit a bar or restaurant with a gay reputation because of their other public roles and identities. A brief stop at a subway tearoom did not seem to involve the risk of suffering the loss in status that identifying themselves as gay to their everyday associates would. Anonymous encounters with strangers were the only way some men conscious of distinctively homosexual desires felt safe satisfying them. The existence of places like the tearooms made it easier for men to move in and out of the gay world, and many who had sexual encounters there participated no further in that world. Indeed, some of them regularly returned from those encounters to their conventional lives as respected family men. A quarter of the men arrested for homosexual activity in 1920-21, for instance, were married and many of them had children—although for those family men, the illusion of security offered by the tearooms had been shattered.[77]

75 See the letters reprinted in *Rat and the Devil: Journal Letters of F.O. Matthiessen and Russell Cheney*, ed. Louis Hyde (Hamden, Conn: Archon Books, 1978), for example, Cheney to Matthiessen, 2 February 1925, p. 76.

76 Martin Goodkin, interview by author; Martin Leonard; Roger Smith (who worked at a nearby department store) remembered finding the overtness of the sexual scene at the Herald Square tearoom so astonishing that he took his lover, Wystan Winters, to see it; Smith, interview by author.

77 Whitin, "Sexual Perversion Cases." This figure is derived not from Whitin's study of the cases heard in magistrates court in the first six months of 1921, but from his study of the two hundred arrests in which the Society for the Suppression of Vice was involved from January 1920 to October 1921, which accounted for some 15 percent of the total number of arrests made during this period. Fifty of the two hundred men arrested with the Society's participation were married, as were a large (but unspecified) number of the men convicted in the first half of 1921. It should be noted, of course, that some married men participated quite fully in gay life, but many more kept their distance from it.

Men went to the tearooms for a variety of reasons, and their encounters could have radically different meanings for each participant. But the encounters often affected how even men little involved in other aspects of the gay world regarded that world. They reinforced the negative impressions of many men, for they seemed to offer vivid confirmation of the cultural association of homosexuality with degeneracy by putting homosexuality and homosexuals almost literally in the gutter. Even the men most attracted to the tearooms as sexual meeting grounds had to be influenced by a culture that regarded such locales and such practices with disgust.

But the tearooms also offered more positive insights into the character of the gay world. Even anonymous participation in the sexual underground could provide men with an enticing sense of the scope of the gay world and of its counterstereotypical diversity, which led some of them to decide to explore that world further. The sheer numbers of men they witnessed participating in tearoom sex reassured many who felt isolated and uncertain of their own "normality," especially since most of the participants were not "flaming queens" but "normal"-looking men of diverse backgrounds.[78] When a physician at the New York City jail in the early 1920s asked gay prisoners, many of whom had been arrested for cruising tearooms and streets, to estimate the number of homosexuals in New York, some guessed there must be half a million, or at least a hundred thousand; even the more conservative put the figure at fifty thousand to a hundred thousand.[79] While such figures hardly constitute reliable estimates of the size of the city's gay population, they provide vivid evidence that men who frequented the streets and tearooms perceived themselves to be involved in an underworld of enormous dimensions. Such an impression could be particularly important to men just beginning to explore the gay world. "From the `gay side' of the Astor Hotel bar to the bushes behind the 42nd Street library [in Bryant Park]," recalled Martin Goodkin of his early forays into New York's gay underworld, "to the public tearoom right outside of Fordham University (where I was once arrested by entrapment. . .) to the eighth floor restroom in the RCA Building to the restroom across the street in the parking garage . . . and on and on and on, New York seemed to be one big cruising ground, especially to this teenager." It was an electrifying realization, he recalled, and a reassuring one, for it persuaded him that he had discovered and become part of a vast secret world, with its own territories and codes, whose existence would ensure he never felt isolated again.[80] [see FIGURE 6]

THE CONTESTED BOUNDARIES BETWEEN PUBLIC AND PRIVATE SPACE

The streets and parks had particular significance for gay men as meeting places for gay men because of the special constraints they faced as homosexuals, but they were hardly the only people to use

78 Even the probation officers who investigated the backgrounds of some of the men arrested for homosexual solicitation in 1921 commented that "perhaps half did not impress [them] as [being] of the homo-sexual type," by which they presumably meant the men did not conform to the stereotypical image of the "pansy." See Whitin, "Sexual Perversion Cases."

79 Kahn, *Mentality and Homosexuality*, pp. 135-136.

80 Martin Goodkin to author, 16 May 1987; Goodkin, interview by author. For a set of thoughtful reflections of the function and meaning of this sort of process of identification, see Samuel R. Delaney, *The Motion of Light in Water: Sex and Science Fiction Writing in the East Village, 1957-65* (New York), p. 173, and Joan Scott, "The Evidence of Experience," *Critical Inquiry* 17 (1991), pp. 773-797.

these venues for socializing and even for sexual encounters in the early twenti-eth century. Indeed, gay street culture was in many respects simply part of a much larger working-class youth street culture and was policed as part of the policing of that larger culture. Many of the same forces drawing working-class gay men into the streets drew other young working-class men and women as well. The pull of social ties was impor-tant to both groups, who were keen to create a communal life in the streets and other public spaces. There women bar-gained with peddlers or socialized with their neighbors on the stoop, men met in nearby saloons, children played and searched for rags and other useful items. But there were material reasons for street life as well. The most impor-tant, as noted previously, was that most working-class men and women, gay and straight alike, lived in crowded tene-ments, boardinghouses, and lodging houses, which offered them few ameni-ties and virtually no privacy. Young peo-ple in search of sex and romance dis-covered that "privacy could only be had in public," in the evocative phrase of Samuel Chotzinoff. As a result, recalled Chotzinoff, who was raised in a Jewish immigrant family on the Lower East Side, the streets of his neighborhood in the evening "were thick with promenading couples, and the benches around the fountain and in Jackson Street Park, and the empty trucks lined up at the river front, were filled with lovers who had no other place to meet." [81] Men interested in homosexual encounters were not the only people to make use of such so-called public spaces.

81 Samuel Chotzinoff, *A Lost Paradise* (New York: Knopf, 1955), pp. 81-82. The same point about the lack of privacy in the tene-ments was made by Elsa Herzfeld in her study of families in Hell's Kitchen, *Family Monographs: The History of Twenty-Four Families Living in the Middle West Side of New York City* (New York: Kempster, 1905), pp. 33-35. On the efforts of men living in room-ing houses to spend time outside them, see Perry R. Duis, *The Saloon: Public Drinking in Chicago and Boston, 1880-1920* (Urbana: University of Illinois Press, 1983), pp. 86-87 (although he does not deal with sexual matters or with gay life, I have found Duis's discussion of the class differences in the organization and use of urban space quite helpful, especially Chapter 3), and Roy Rosenzweig, *Eight Hours for What We Will: Workers and Leisure in an Industrial City, 1870-1920* (New York: Cambridge University Press, 1983), pp. 56-57.

82 Russell Sage Foundation, *West Side Studies, vol. I: Boyhood and Lawlessness* (New York: Survey Associates, 1914), pp. 21, 155. The study also emphasized the lack of privacy available in the tenements, given their thin walls and the usual absence of closed doors between rooms, pp. 57-58. See also recollections of men and women who grew up in the pre-World War II middle west side about the widespread use of movie theater balconies and tenement hallways for sexual encounters, recorded in Jeff Kisseloff, *You Must Remember This: An Oral History of Manhattan from the 1890s to World War II* (New York: Harcourt Brace Jovanovich, 1989), pp. 564-565.

Nor were the tenement-roof rendezvous the exclusive domain of gay men. A 1914 study of the working-class Irish and German youth of the Hell's Kitchen district west of Times Square found conditions there no different from those described by Chotzinoff. "The youth of the district and his girl" found "uses" for the "dark, narrow passages" of the tenement hall-ways, the report observed, and "certain roofs of the neighborhood [had] a name as a rendezvous for children and young couples for immoral practices." [82] Moreover, as noted previously, undercover agents surveying the sexual uses of the city's parks noted the presence of both same-sex and mixed-sex couples. Denied the privacy the home was ideally supposed to provide, in other words, young men and women throughout the tenement districts tried to construct some measure of privacy for themselves in spaces middle-class ideology regarded as "public."

The men who sought homosexual encounters in the streets, then, were participating in and expanding a street cul-ture already developed by working-class youths seeking freedom from their fam-

[FIGURE 6]
Rockefeller Center

ilies' supervision. That culture sustained a set of sexual values and a way of conceptualizing the boundaries between public and private space that paralleled those governing many aspects of gay men's behavior—and that middle-class ideology found almost as shocking in the case of heterosexual couples as in homosexual. The purposes and tactics of gay men out cruising resembled those of young men and women out looking for a date in many respects. The casual pickups men made on the streets were hardly unique to male couples in this era, for many young women depended on being picked up by men to finance their excursions to music halls and amusement parks, as the historians Kathy Peiss and Joanne Meyerowitz have shown. It was common on the streets for men to approach women with whom they were unacquainted to make a date. This distressed middle-class moral reformers, who considered casual pickups almost as undesirable as professional prostitution, if they distinguished the two at all.[83] The fact that these couples met in unsupervised public places and even had sex there was even more shocking to middle-class reformers, in part because it challenged the careful delineation between public and private space that was so central to bourgeois conceptions of public order.

The use of public spaces for sexual purposes was only one aspect of a more general pattern of class differentiation in the uses of the streets and in the norms of public sociability, a difference that deeply troubled middle-class reformers. Struggles over the proper sexual and social order were central to the process of class differentiation, constitution, and conflict in the Progressive Era. Those struggles were fueled by middle-class fears about the apparently pernicious social effects of urbanization, which were graphically represented by the disorderly, unregulated, and alien character of working-class street life. The 1914 Russell Sage Foundation study of the conditions of young people in Hell's Kitchen indicted the unruly culture of the streets as the source of the "lawlessness" of neighborhood boys, even as it painted a portrait of working-class life starkly different from that of its readers. "Streets, roofs, docks, hallways,—these, then, are the West Side boy's playground, and will be for many years to come," observed the report, which warned that the boys' parents, "so long accustomed to the dangers of the streets, to the open flaunting of vice, drunkenness, and gambling on all sides, . . . do not take into account the impression which these conditions are making upon young minds."[84] Although the dangers *these* conditions posed to the character of the young were not limited to the sexual, this was certainly a concern of the reformers. Appalled by the overt sexualization of public space and the public character of sexual interactions in working-class neighborhoods, the report observed that "children of both sexes indulge freely in conversation which is only carried on secretly by adults in other walks of life [middle-class adults]." And although it did not stress the point, it

83 Kathy Peiss, *Cheap Amusements*, pp. 54-55, 106; idem., "'Charity Girls' and City Pleasures: Historical Notes on Working-Class Sexuality, 1880-1920," in *Passion and Power: Sexuality in History*, ed. Kathy Peiss and Christina Simmons (Philadelphia: Temple University Press, 1989), pp. 57-69; Joanne J. Meyerowitz, *Women Adrift: Independent Wage Earners in Chicago, 1880-1930* (Chicago: University of Chicago Press, 1988), pp. 101-106.

84 Russell Sage Foundation, *Boyhood and Lawlessness*, pp. 21, 76. See also Cary Goodman, *Choosing Sides: Playground and Street Life on the Lower East Side* (New York: Schocken Books, 1979), and David Nasaw, *Children of the City: At Work and at Play* (Garden City, NY: Anchor Press/Doubleday, 1985).

warned that the boys' unrestricted involvement in the life of the streets resulted in their becoming familiar with the "many sexual perverts" to be found in the neighborhood, whom they might otherwise have avoided, which led to "experimentation among the boys, and to the many forms of perversion which in the end make the degenerate . . . Self-abuse is considered a common joke," it added, "and boys as young as seven or eight actually practice sodomy."[85]

The Progressive movement to construct parks, playgrounds, and after-school programs of organized recreation and education, which would "Americanize" immigrant children, reflected middle-class reformers' concerns about the corrupting influences of the street on working-class youth. So, too, did the escalation of campaigns by the forces of social purity against working-class street culture and sexual culture, which resulted in an expansion of the vice squad and in the campaigns against the Raines Law hotels, saloons, cabarets, and other commercial amusements, which had a powerful effect on gay life.

The efforts of the police to control gay men's use of "public" space, then, were part of a much broader effort by the state to (quite literally) police the boundaries between public and private space, and, in particular, to impose a bourgeois definition of such distinctions on working-class communities. Gay men's strategies for using urban space came under attack not just because they challenged the heteronormativity that normally governed men and women's use of public space, but also because they were part of a more general challenge to dominant cultural conceptions of those boundaries and of the social practices appropriate to each sphere. The inability of the police and reformers to stop such activity reflects their failure to impose a single, hegemonic map of the city's public and private spaces on its diverse communities.

85 Russell Sage Foundation, *Boyhood and Lawlessness*, p. 155

Gay men developed a gay map of the city and named its landmarks: the Fruited Plain, Vaseline Alley, Bitches' Walk. Even outsiders were familiar with sections of that map, for the "shoals of painted, perfumed, . . . mincing youths that at night swarm on Broadway in the Tenderloin section, . . . the parks and 5th avenue" made the gay territorialization of the city inescapable to Bernarr Macfadden and many others. But even more of that map was unknown to the dominant culture. Gay men met throughout the city, their meetings invisible to all but the initiated and carefully orchestrated to remain so. Certain subway stations and public comfort stations, as well as more open locales such as parks and streets, were the sites of almost constant social and even sexual interactions between men, but most men carefully structured their interactions so that no outsiders would recognize them as such.

The boundaries of the gay world were thus highly permeable, and different men participated in it to different degrees and in different ways. Some passed in and out of it quickly, making no more than occasional stops at a subway tearoom for a quick sexual encounter that had little significance for their self-identity or the other parts of their life. Even those men who were most isolated from the organized gay world got a glimpse of its size and diversity through their anonymous encounters in washrooms and recessed doorways, however, and those encounters provided other men with an entree into a world much larger and more highly organized than they could have imagined. The streets and parks served them as social centers as well as sites of sexual rendezvous, places where they could meet others like themselves and find collective support for their rejection of the sexual and gender roles prescribed them. The "mysterious bond" between gay men that allowed them to locate and communicate with one another even in the settings potentially most hostile to them attests to the resiliency of their world and to the resources their subculture had made available to them.

While the gay geography of New York has changed over the course of the twentieth century, certain significant sites have endured for decades.

The photographs accompanying this text, shot by an unknown photographer in the 1940s and 1950s, show that several spaces prominent during the 1910s and 1920s continued to be important. Discovered in a photo album anonymously given to the Out of the Closet Thrift Shop in Manhattan, they are now part to the Gay Beach Collection at the National Museum and Archive of Lesbian and Gay History, New York City.

The appearance of anyone in these photographs should not be taken as an indication of his sexual orientation.

Rambles
Central Park

Postscript

These photographs document gay life at the bars and piers lining West Street on Manhattan's waterfront during the 1970s. Taken by the late Leonard Fink, these images were donated by his estate to the National Museum and Archive of Lesbian Gay History, New York City.

Keller Bar
[1976]

West Street
[1977]

Badlands
[1979]

Pier 52

end

The Piano Bar
D.A. MILLER

AND NO ONE CARES HOW LATE IT GETS.

No place better realizes his juvenile dream of grown-up space than this piano bar: where he produces so many signs of adultness that one would almost think he is suffering from a delusion that (despite his frequent patronage or his manifest majority) there may even now arise some difficulty about his right to be here, which he is prepared to assert by exercising it in every way possible. As he inhales the intoxicating bitterness of adult life through the tobacco, or imbibes it in the alcohol, whose prodigal consumption starting from the moment he gets past the door only the eagerness of his intemperance per-suades us is not a formal condition of admission, like the removal of one's shoes in a Japanese foyer, he is celebrating not so much how far he has journeyed from a place—his mythically straightlaced home or home town—as his distance from a time, that of his childhood, when he couldn't abide either of these acrid tastes. And if it were not enough that the law had already designated both substances for adults only, he must further subject them to protocols connoting adult ways of consuming them. Well versed in the manual of sophisticated smoking, for instance, he pinches the cigarette tensely between thumb and forefinger, as though held with any less rigidi-ty it would be in danger of slipping from his grasp, or even of disintegrat-ing, while his remaining fingers, left to fend for themselves by the mental or motor exertions this vise requires, fly ungovernably into the air. So he means to signify the adult theme of Work, having understood from his father, who even off the job never had time for him, that smoking, only apparently allied with the conditions of leisure, relaxation, pleasure, was really of a piece with all those worrisome, demanding obligations of adult life that, unlike a child who "didn't have to" perform them, but had only to hear how indispensable the driven performance of them was to putting clothes on his back and a roof over his head, couldn't be neglected. Or, adopting the pose shown on a different page, he sets the cigarette stiffly at arm's length behind him or to his side: by which gesture he burns incense to adult Self-determination, the triumph of his will to smoke—or not—as he pleases, when—but only when—he wants. If "the habit" now makes that vic-tory wholly imaginary, he is at any rate free of the asthmatic manifestations that formerly would have greeted the faintest wisp of one of those great clouds amid which, comfortable as a rococo divinity reclining on them, he now sits perched atop his stool. Or again, having turned another page, he waves his cigarette in so generous an arc that he might be a conjurer and it his wand. From the ashes that he scatters no less grandiosely than if they had come from the cinerary urn of a loved one, what is reborn is himself, a big boy now: this gesture of Largesse having literally secured his enlarge-ment by the simple expedient of doubling the amount of space that others must allow him. The ingestion of alcohol (as distinct from its application, in the form of cologne, where mere proof of use is required) has similarly to bear the supplementary mark of sophistication, here inscribed by the fan-ciful nomenclature of *the cocktail,* that once mystifying set of names which he can never now pronounce without taking secret pride in the worldly initiation that has entailed their correct usage, or—what is the same thing—without feeling deep relief, whenever he orders a "screwdriver," a "grasshopper," a "greyhound," a "Manhattan," that the bartender does not scowl, or smirk, or give any other sign of being asked to bring forth from his shaker a tool, an insect, an animal, the whole metropolis.

SOMEWHERE BETWEEN FORTY AND DEATH.

Having long ago passed out of its heroic age (if it ever knew one), his body now presents a gruesome phantasmagoria of the middle-aged male body in hell—being resistlessly tortured under demon architects who add hideous new wings onto the graceful old structures of belly and waist; demon engineers with pulleys that drop first the ass, then the jaw; demon artists adept at doodling lines across the face and distressing the canvas of the skin; demon hairdressers so cruel that they dye hair gray, or thin it out, give it a tonsure, even remove it altogether, while feigning to make amends for such depredations by inserting tiny thick toupees in ears and nose. And in their midst, a vengeful she-devil, smarting from gender oppression, is busy resculpting this body into a female one, rendering it mammiferous and broad—so her victim cries out—*where a broad should be broad*, and daring to recess, by this new disposition of mass, the cock itself! Yet he is not particularly dejected—not here, at any rate—by the fact that he is out of shape. On the contrary, the garment *de rigueur* on his upper body—a luxurious sweater (variously cashmere, alpaca, handwoven, brightly colored, "designed") whose full falling drapery, only pretending to wrap the trunk in a veil of mystery, shall faithfully imitate the thickening, slackening, and pleating of the flesh beneath, or whose snug fit, causing it to "ride" up the back or at the sides, shall directly expose these processes to view—flaunts pots and handles with as little modesty as the plain white t-shirt, more binding than a hair shirt but likewise bespeaking a discipline of iron rods and fasting, displays the gym rat's cuts and ripples. For just like a cardigan (or a blazer, or a foulard), his body too is an element of the dress code required by the celebration of adulthood here in progress. Hence he is disposed to wear it in the condition of Maturity, as the body of a parent. Only having "let himself go," evidently, is he entitled to assume the equally manifest condition of being free, light, airy: the body of a child.

I TALK TO THEM ALL IN VAIN.

With the same unshrinking determination that another kind of man might evince in scarifying a too delicate pair of hands, he has sacrificed the natural beauty of his face to its vivacity of expression. Instead of having a face, he makes them; and though his features are good, they never repose long enough for their owner to be held good-looking. On the contrary, they are always busy rolling, darting, tilting, arching, narrowing, puffing, flaring, puckering, biting, and otherwise assisting a discourse that, on the part of a man to whom language comes fast and fluently, seems curiously unsure of its ability to be understood. Not enough, in ordinary conversation, to entrust his point to overstatement, repetition, an emphasis of inflection; in addition, it must be captioned by a grimace that would make it literally as plain as the nose and other parts of his face. What would be his despair if he knew that his inter-locutors accept his communication (provided they do) only after they have voided the whole violent drama of its performance—when, with every improbability corrected, every excess reproportioned, all that is left them to consider is some platitudinous "grain of truth" whose sheer familiarity condemns such unnecessary fanfare still further? Yet of course it is precisely out of such knowledge that there descends over his face, even to the point of somewhat muffling his speech, that spirit of self-negation that (perhaps mindful of the lifted eyebrow that is its sym-bol, or of the tension that it breathes into the other features as well) every beholder calls *archness*. For, as if these features were not suffi-ciently busy realizing the hyperexpressive intention confided to them, they simultaneously take on the extra burden of ironizing it, embedding within all its signs other signs that make it impossible to take straight, and so solicit the marginalization that it will be accorded in any case. Small wonder that so lively a face often looks "tired," exhausted by the exorbitant muscular expenditures to which the intuition of their futility has only added; or that so theatrical a face sometimes acquires an inscrutable air, having chosen to withhold what it can't give away.

DIS-DONC DONC DONC DONC DONC.

Yet almost as, on that other man, the hand gnarled in a long course of sores and injuries appears ugly until we see it exercising the craft responsible for its deformation (when, patently war-ranted by the work whose demands have shaped just this tool, it assumes such nobility that we are seized with an almost religious desire to kiss it, as if it were bearing stigmata) so, no sooner does this man join the choristers at the piano, and sing with them the Broadway songs that are the only music played here, than his absurd face, with all the contradictory agitations that were making it illegible, achieves point and poignancy in the same long breaths. Like old bits of rubbish transfigured by the significance they acquire from having been the implements of an ancient rite, the looks and tones before without rhyme or reason are now necessitated as the requisite medi-ations—or simply the inevitable consequences—of a practice that is as cen-tral to the piano bar as any rite can have been to an antique cult. And this is: that of putting the words of songs into a kind of vocal italics whose meta-morphic force is so radical that, whether being putatively sung in the middle ages or the South Pacific, by a courting cowboy or a cloistered nun, every lyric now becomes a figure for present-day metropolitan homosexuality, which no lyric has ever cared, or dared, literally to mention.

'STEAD OF TREATED WE GET TRICKS.

Thanks to this cataclysmic reformat-ting, Lancelot claiming "Had I been made the partner of Eve/We'd be in Eden still" no longer amazes Camelot with his chastity, nor does Eliza wishing "I could have spread my wings/And done a thousand things" remain angelic or even female. And when in the den of her fellow thieves, Nancy mentions "pockets left undone on many a behind," the "fine life" being celebrated no more concerns picking pockets than the "trouble" worked up by Harold Hill in River City—or for that matter the "Boys' Band" supposed to stave it off—bears on playing pool. "Adelaide's Lament" (since not just single words or lines, but whole songs may be set in these italics) is revamped for the role of a heartbroken queen, and "I'm Still Here" for that of an old one. The heterosexual griping loses its grip on "Dames," as does the heterosexual gratitude on "Thank Heaven for Little Girls," where without them what little boys would do is now a question with an answer. And so, effortlessly, on. In the ease and immediacy of gaying up the repertory there isn't spared even the notion of a song that could not release, thus rubbed, a gay genie who had always been lying cramped inside it, but now wafts vaporously, to more or less mischievous effect, over every line.

SOMEONE MAY BE LAUGHING.

No matter that their few obsessive points and strategies of attack, which may be grasped in a minute, are rehearsed for hours at a stretch, the genie's antics never lose their power of being, to everyone present, hysterically funny. Strangely, though, even as these are in full swing, they disclose a melancholy whose ubiquity in the atmosphere, if always sensed, has until now remained as indistinct, as discreet, as that of the dust on the velvet drapes, or the grease-strains on the old club furniture. Just as what Mame coaxes "right out of the horn," revivifying us in the process, is only the blues, so the practice that is channeling the patrons' high spirits into fits of hilarity would bespeak less a desire to *clear* the brooding air—for which such places, especially over the faces of their patrons, are of course well known—than the thrill of drawing from it a certain illumination, of (in the root sense) *elucidating* it. At moments—say, when the genie plays such havoc with a Rodgers and Hammerstein medley that the stranger you see across a crowded room is only that evening's trick, and Ado Annie's irresistible "Romeo in a sombrero and chaps," having left the range behind with his silly hat, looks as if he were ready for the Black Party, perhaps to meet, during another song, someone from Austria older and wiser, telling him what to do—at such moments, the melancholy seems lit up as the irony of a practice that can only know itself as derivative and deviant. For unlike the aboriginal dandy who incorporates Western coins into his dress with supreme indifference to how they are used, or how his own use of them is viewed, in the civilization of their source, the allegorist of the piano bar, having been raised on the Broadway musical, is too thoroughly cognizant of the intended meanings of a lyric not to be equally so of the absurdity that would be charged against his double entendres, not to mention the contempt that would rain on them, if they ever left the shadows of what he also bears in mind therefore is no more than a subculture prevailed over by the culture at large. So deeply operative in him are the effects of that imagined wider circulation that they have been shaping

Michael Perelman
Boxed Set [1995]
Oil on Panel
TOP: *Stormy Weather*
BOTTOM: *Bill*

TOP: *At the Palace*
BOTTOM: *Go Lose That Long Face*

all along a practice that makes up for the insolence of producing gay meaning by the courtesy of producing it *as nonsense*, in defiance of not just established interpretations, but even established principles of interpretation. He may not shrink before spoiling the loveliest song with his preposterous readings, but in doing so neither does he omit to call attention to their factitiousness and hence his powerlessness to offer them *for real*. It is as though he could not conceive of truth, beauty, reason, meaning, value, except as the exclusive properties of the mainstream cultural order that he thus lets condemn him—that he thus lets us know condemns him willy-nilly—to a trivial aberrance.

PEPPERED WITH ACTUAL SHEPHERD.

Yet at other moments, say, when the genie transforms Madame Rose into a momma's boy's momma, and West Side delinquents into Village deviants (but lets Bosom Buddies remain sisters); when he lends an outsider's animus to the satire on "the little things that make marriage a joy" in *Company*, or stands idly by, as though to say "it's all right with me," while a lyric (like the one to the song of that title) does his job for him—now, his work of appropriation doesn't seem all that inappropriate. Now, indeed, it becomes work of an altogether different kind: an archeological excavation that unearths a joint between these gay meanings and the received ones that, contrary to previous impression, oddly appear to be based on them, like a medieval church laid on the foundation of a razed pagan temple, or an archaic palace erected over a still older place of sacrifice of which the people had grown ashamed. It is not that gay men are denied access to the sphere of cultural origination, but that as the price of admission they must surrender all right to being *recognized* in this identity, which now seems responsible for the melancholy of the place, for the irony of a practice that is bearing witness to an intimate, fundamental, and even spectacular truth about the Broadway musical that may nonetheless not be told on the legitimate stage—may not be told anywhere, for that matter, but here, in this shabby-pretentious ghetto bar, where it must be as overstated as everything else about the man to whom its revelation is entrusted.

ANYONE CAN WHISTLE, THAT'S WHAT THEY SAY.

For like a third-rate magician who, thinking to take advantage of his inferior talent for illusionism, devises a novelty act in which he gives away the familiar tricks of his betters (disappointing all the same the general public that feels deprived of former delight along with former deception), this man is out to betray the habitual prestidigitation of the whole enormous population of gay composers, lyricists, librettists, choreographers, and others who, dexterously striking the sexual specificities of their experience with the wand of worldly ambition, cause these to evaporate into a cloud of nuance so diffuse and elusive that only the additional sleight-of-hand of a feigned tokenism can ever recondense it into representation. Indispensable to his treachery, therefore, is his complete somatic compliance with the stereotype of himself. It is thanks to this abandon that the homosexuality visible on stage only in the wake of its perpetual displacement acquires a legible, an undeniable body, one whose variously hysterical palpitations, keeping time to the music that sets them going and that they echo and amplify with brazen fidelity, manifest a link that theatrical production is—well it might be!—tireless in glossing over. With all the unanswerable impertinence of a poor relation or a spurned friend, he thus solicits recognition from a genre whose *arriviste* pretense of not knowing him, or whoever else might be shirking the heterosexual obligation romanticized in its old-fashioned weddings and pajama games, the spectacle of his unmatched familiarity with even its minor specimens shall unmask, and whose frequent winks of apology for this slight his overready comprehension shall deprive of all tact, so as to demonstrate beyond a doubt that the most distinctive historical mission of the musical theatre that everyone hummed was to give expression to those who, like him, couldn't whistle.

SMOKE ON YOUR PIPE AND PUT THAT IN.

But this proposition, which his whole practice is dedicated to affirming, has no social standing, or support, outside it. For what could be particularly gay about any representation at a time when, on penalty of demonization, nothing particularly gay was allowed to enter it? And, even now, what kind of evidence could establish this particular gayness in a culture where, homosexuality remaining a quasi-criminal charge to be "proven," doubt will hasten to fortify any room, however infinitesimal, that is left for it to occupy? Just think: the golden-age musical that best persuaded the general public of the artistic "seriousness" of the form—and did so, naturally enough, on the basis of a virility so sure of itself, or at any rate, so truculently put forward, that it could even get away with the *jetées* of classical ballet, without anybody daring to say, though anybody might have seen, from their first cigarette, that the Jets were leaping straight out of the pages of Genet—this was entirely the conception of four gay men who must have been, in a strict sense of the phrase, nothing if not brilliant. By contrast to the opera, or Bette Davis movies, or any other general cultural phenomenon that enjoys, as we say, a gay *following*—in other words, that gay subjectivity comes to invest only after a creation at which it wasn't presumably present—the Broadway musical, with "disproportionate numbers" of gay men among its major architects, is determined from the inside out by an Open Secret whose fierce cultural keeping not all the irony on a show queen's face can ever quite measure, nor all his flamboyance of carriage undo.

I HEAR SINGING AND THERE'S NO ONE THERE.

Hence, from the labors of so improbable, so unprovable an argument, he will sometimes need to repose in the experience of self-evidence. Haunting all the adult practices in the place, there has always been a specter of regression for which, even as their sophistication would strive to exorcise it, their self-destructiveness or their silliness was serving as medium. And more than elsewhere such regression abides in the choral singing that, while essential to the very notion of the Piano Bar, is totally devoid of the grown-up quality suggested by smoking a Dunhill, drinking a Black Russian, or wearing a Corgi, and without these coefficients, would frankly recall the Sunday boys' choir, the bus to summer camp, or the high school spring musical. Sometimes, then, as soon as he joins the chorus in "Oh, What a Beautiful Mornin'!" or "Tonight," his countenance not only sloughs the strain of the years, so thoroughly in fact that his full mustache, his graying temples, the crow's feet at his eyes, and the deeper lines around his mouth (all of which of course remain) appear as foreign to his true expression as if they had been the result of an accident, or a concession to the surrounding masquerade, but also throws off the grip of youth itself, in the form of that habitual muscular concentration with which, as a child, he learned to belie the perturbation of his features, and so established the (smiling or serious or just blank) mien of *rigor mortis* that he still assumes against being looked at. The activity of singing—in this, reinforced by the anonymity of membership in a chorus—retracts him deep into a womb where what may be called his social physiognomy disappears along with every trace of his usual busy campaign to promote this or that of its aspects, and whence he seems as ageless as we do in the self-portraits we draw while asleep. Even when, small or strident, untrained or outright ruined, his song is not sweet to hear, the sight of how intimately he is given over to it—so much so that we can hardly avoid thinking he is pouring his soul, or singing his heart out—retains the potential to be ravishing in the extreme. (Lacking the better bodies, the Piano Bar will never be short on dreamy faces.)

SOMEHOW, SOMEDAY, SOMEWHERE.

During the course of singing, for no reason he would ever be capable of giving, sudden tears drop from his abstracted eyes, or he catches his breath in the middle of a line just as though he were heaving a sob, or practically gasping for life. Like a half-witted docent who is sufficiently informed to gather us before the most significant paintings in the gallery, but too ignorant to tell us why we are pausing *here*, his voice is escorting him through the master-episodes of youthful suffering, seldom recalled with much precision or in any detail, and often lost to narrative reconstruction altogether, but nonetheless known "by heart," thanks to the music that long ago combined with them as closely—and now evokes them as inevitably—as if they had been so many verses. Yet the voice that is thus always poised on the verge of breaking down never actually does so, or only does so for a moment, when in any case its spasms are covered over by lost boys (and Wendys among them) singing on different schedules of remembrance. All the faltering only seems to renew its determination to *sing out*—one might suppose in response to La Merm's inarguable command—and as it quavers and pants its way through what accordingly becomes a kind of race against its own threatened extinction, so exalted is it by the nearness of victory (to claim which it merely needs to keep singing) that, albeit dependent on the same old lungs and larynx, it all of a sudden miraculously outreaches itself, to achieve a volume, sustain a note, scale an octave, undertake a counterpoint or harmony, forbidden to its powers but a minute before. In the process of this prodigious enhancement (whether having a real basis in his at last relaxed vocal cords, or being only a subjective or group fantasy that a recording could easily contradict), the suffering he revisits is raised to ecstasy, as though while recalling them, his voice could also at last proclaim the shadow-truth of those former moments of misery, which lay simply and even stupidly in his demand for, as it was called, the *happiness* in the tune. For, compared to when he would sing and dance to cast albums in the seclusion of the family basement, hearing in them a more particular address than the general one that elsewhere drowned it out, but never guessing that his secret audition was (wherever the Broadway musical flourished) so utterly normative that every urban gay community had institutionalized it in a bar like this one—compared to then, such utopianism, without exactly being gratified, has become so far less abstract that once whispered solos are booming forth in chorus.

Circa 1977,
Plazspitz
Park Installation
TOM BURR

Circa 1977
[1995]
Details of Installation

This landscape report was developed for a small triangulated plot of land called Platzspitz, which is situated at the confluence of the rivers Sihl and Limmat in the center of Zurich, Switzerland. Platzspitz has endured a long and diverse history as a public site, some of which is brought to the surface in what follows. More specifically, the landscape report focuses on the park's condition and character during the 1970s and, in particular, the late 1970s. Its ultimate goal is to picture the park as it may have looked in the 1970s—to imagine the condition of the park's landscape, its trees, bushes, soil and ground cover, its walkways, benches and lamp posts, its erosion and levels of maintenance, circa 1977.

UNSENSATIONAL

From the point of view of this particular landscape's management, which is to say from the point of view of the official Municipal Gardens, the 1970s was an unsensational period for Platzspitz. It was unsensational in retrospect, given the park's turbulent recent history as one of the largest and most visible "needle parks" in Europe, a condition that continued into the early 1990s, and received international media attention. Moreover, it was unsensational when compared to the park's transformation in the late 1700s into a "Baroque Pleasure Garden." Rows of linden trees lined the walkways, creating long, elegant riverside promenades that provided Zurich with one of its most vivid and vital social spectacles, where one went to be seen and to see others strolling the length of the Limmat and the Sihl. It is also deemed unsensational in light of the most recent phase in the history of Platzspitz: a massive SFr 1,200,000 renovation has restructured both the park and the park's use by its public. All traces of the 1970s have been obscured if not altogether destroyed; trees have been removed, shrubbery leveled, and the park's vistas and walkways extensively restructured. Platzspitz during the 1970s remains, for many, something of a non-period, a vacant temporal space that abuts other, more sensational periods. Many people seem to have partially forgotten or dismissed the period, due to a lack of prominent spectacle with which to anchor it. What does remain, in many people's minds, is an image of a place that was in need of repair or cleaning up, a place that had been left largely to its own devices.

and effecting a series of separations and divisions within the existing parkscape. In addition to the abundant evergreen clusters, large beech trees towered over everything, and beech saplings had seeded beneath their canopies and throughout the wooded edges of the area, creating dense thickets of a medium height that lent a form of cover to those who wandered along the pathways, and virtual camouflage to any who strayed off the designated paths and into the planted regions. Yet another area of dense foliage surrounded the public toilet, a small brick and stucco building that had been built on the bank of the Limmat in 1914. Various forms of understory, as well as additional dark clusters of *taxus*, partially obscured one side of the small structure, producing a contiguity between the dark spaces of the shrubbery and the secluded interior of the public toilet. At the third side of the triangulated

OVERGROWN
Mr. Studhalter, who became chief of the Municipal Gardens in the early 1970s, remembers Platzspitz as an excessively overgrown site. Heavy evergreen growth occurred throughout the park. Multiple large clusters of *taxus*, rhododendrons, and holly divided the relatively small space of the park into a series of outdoor passageways and rooms; the largest of these structures were located at the edges of the park above the banks of the two rivers, and throughout the elevated hillside area, which then, as now, was occupied by the playground. These labyrinthine spaces dominated the park in the 1970s, creating numerous hidden enclaves that remained out of view from the surrounding vicinity, offering shelter and seclusion to anyone who ventured into their midst,

Platzspitz stands the Landesmuseum, the Swiss National Museum, which was completed in 1898, and which separated the park from the railroad station and the busy center of Zurich beyond. Large chestnut trees towered over the romantically conceived fortress-like structure, their umbrage increasing the darkness of the park and contributing further to its generally overgrown character and appearance during the 1970s.

ISOLATED
Mr. Studhalter suggests that this overgrown environment was a negative development for Platzspitz. The overabundance of voluminous shrubbery and the vast seeding of saplings due to generally negligent maintenance created too many isolated spaces. In his opinion, the isolated spaces led to a widespread mistrust of Platzspitz by many, and to the

gradual decline in visitors to the park over several decades leading up to the 1970s. By the late 1970s, workers used the park during lunch time, and people brought their children to play for short periods during the middle of the day, but on the whole Platzspitz served as a passageway from one area of town to another; the bridges at the tip of the park offered quick and easy passage over the two rivers. The isolation created by the configuration of branches and foliage reinforced an existing sense of isolation, insofar as the inauguration of the train station in 1847 had effected the virtual separation of the park from the whole of the city. What was once a large, continuous tract of open land, spreading out from the junction of the two rivers into the heart of Zurich, was vastly reduced by the placement of the train station across the middle of the peninsula, which at the same time rendered it largely

pletion of the recent renovation. Had such a plan been implemented, she submits, the conditions would not have reached such extreme levels, and the park would have continued to attract a more general public.

WEEDY

A mixture of disturbed native woodland, abandoned ornamental planting, and much successional growth became rampant in Platzspitz in the late 1970s. The heavily overgrown conditions during this period had considerable repercussions for the various elements that constituted the existing landscape. Although serious, the vegetation conditions observed during the 1970s were not surprising in a landscape that had borne the stresses—both manmade and natural—of centuries of continued use. Some of the older trees, having reached or passed maturity, were dying out. Other stands, subject to ero-

disconnected from the hub of modern Zurich. Mr. Studhalter suspects that, against this backdrop, the isolation produced by the arboreal growth led to a further unattractive development: at night, the park became the domain of alcoholics, hustlers, and homosexuals, who thrived in the seclusion offered by the dim lighting, the maze-like network of pathways, and the dense flora. Had the park had the sufficient funds or foresight to curtail the overgrowth that occurred over the period of several decades, and that resulted in the unkempt and unsavory conditions reported by Mr. Studhalter, he feels that things might have gone differently. What the Municipal Gardens lacked during that period was a "*Master Plan*," according to the Municipal Garden's landscape architect, Judith Rohrer, who succeeded Mr. Studhalter and is responsible for the design and com-

sion on riverbed slopes and in the areas worn by heavy traffic, showed grave signs of declining health. Roots had become exposed and the ground layer disturbed; the soil became compacted and its capacity to retain water was thereby reduced. Because of the erosion, litter, widespread throughout the heavily trafficked areas, created soil conditions unfavorable to the germination of any but the most hardy of dominant canopy species, the germination of more "weedy" species was favored. After hundreds of years of human use as an urban park, much of the original shrub and herbaceous layers had died off, along with large portions of the understory, and very little new planting had been done to compensate for those losses. From time to time the shrub layers had been partially reduced, in a conscious effort to improve public safety in the wooded areas. The disturbed edge conditions along several of the pathways had also resulted in a dense undergrowth of shrubs and weedy species, while many of the ornamental shrubs along the pedestrian paths had also gone without maintenance for many years and had become unsightly or unhealthy, and in many instances dense and overgrown.

VULGAR

In 1979, a proposal was made to overhaul Platzspitz. "Zuri-Park," as Platzspitz in its new incarnation was to be called, would feature roller-coasters and monorails, a Western Saloon and a Ghost House, cafés and snack bars, and a Ferris wheel higher than the Hotel Zurich. "Zuri-Park" was the brainchild of Erich Gerber, director of tourism at the time, who proposed the mini-Disneyland nestled in Platzspitz as an antidote to the unpleasant associations the park had acquired throughout the 1970s and to its lack of

Gerber claimed many people did not even know about, adding that the park remained disturbing, particularly at night, and, in a very definite way, unsatisfying.

THE PLACE HAD STYLE

According to one man who frequented Platzspitz in the late 1970s, the site was very different from the way it is now. The place had style, he explains. People were running around in flowered shirts and white silk shawls, and the scene as a whole was very light and airy. 75 percent of the gay men who went to Platzspitz, he speculates, were simply curious to see who was there and what was going on. Sometimes they would meet, beneath the trees or along the park benches, and later go over to the nearby Old Mary's bar, which no longer exists. Another man explained that Platzspitz had been a contact point and cruising park for gay men at least since 1940. As he remembers it, you

general use. Gerber promoted his project by stating that Platzspitz would only be enhanced by such an upscale development, preferring to call his vision a "leisure park" or, better yet, a "family park," rather than by the more vulgar designation, "fairground." Gerber described his vision as running counter to the temporary fairs that travel from town to town each summer, presenting Zuri-Park instead as a permanent fixture in the cityscape, one that would be conceived, constructed, and maintained as an elegant place of the highest standards, and that would draw a disenchanted public back into Platzspitz. According to "Zuri-Park" thinking, the rebirth of Platzspitz would be guaranteed, thereby creating a cultural and geographical center for Zurich's public life. In all of these respects, "Zuri-Park" would stand in sharp contrast to the existing Platzspitz, a place

would walk along the river, sit on the benches, and wait for someone to talk to you, sometimes the conversations would move briskly and you would visit the toilets at the far end of the park, by the river. He went on to describe the park and the bushes, which were higher than the average man, densely planted, and offered excellent refuge, but concluded by saying that he ceased visiting the park often after the 1960s as too much crime occurred then. One woman recalled her experiences of Platzspitz in 1978, when she was seventeen years old and spent three evenings a week at the Schindlergut youth center. On each of these evenings between 10:30 PM and 11:30 PM, she would walk to the Main Station, from the Wasserwerkstrasse to the Drahtschmidli, and over the bridge to Platzspitz. As she remembers it, it was clear that Platzspitz "belonged" to gay men. The feeling one had walking from the Schindlergut to Platzspitz was of great danger, she explains, but as soon as she reached Platzspitz she felt safe (despite the lack of good lighting along the park's pathways), due to the presence of gay men. Another woman suggested that the park had to be cleaned up after a certain point, because of the proximity to the Landesmuseum and its many visitors, for whom this scene might have been unappealing. When asked about their recollections, two younger men from the HAZ, one of Zurich's gay organizations located directly across the river from Platzspitz, responded that they had no idea that the park had once been a cruising park, or that it had any significance for gay people at all. A third replied that perhaps he had heard that once, a friend of a friend had mentioned something that gave him the idea that this might have been the case.

existing parkscape in areas, usually deep within the shrubbery, and visible from the official pathways only by way of downward glimpses and sideways glances. Deposits of bottlecaps and cigarette butts; popsicle sticks and multi-colored foil wrappers; discarded jars, tubes, and cans; muddy tissues; and an occasional forgotten item of clothing were left beneath the branches and only partially revealed to users of the primary paved walkways. Today Platzspitz is enjoying a period of renewal. Trees have been thinned out drastically, and more than seventy removed in the last two years. The overgrown *taxus* and holly bushes, which were so emblematic of the previous decades, have been cut back drastically to allow for their new growth to emerge; and now their height is being carefully maintained, allowing for an open view of the landscape in all directions. The new Platzspitz is one

RENOVATED

During the 1970s the maintenance of Platzspitz was more concerned with the continual removal of rubbish and debris left by the various groups of people who used the park than with the careful and conscientious preening the park presently enjoys. Bottles and cans and other usual forms of recreational garbage would overflow beyond the bounds of the trash cans, and become scattered beneath and within the complex network of shrubbery, and pressed into the barren soil and mud. Many paths formed outside the original routes, and meandered in and between small trees, shrubs, and other forms of understory, and beyond the official domain of the standard maintenance. Therefore, a light to medium littering of trash would often punctuate the

of sweeping vistas and long shots, both from within the triangular patch of land, and from the Landesmuseum, which borders it. It remains open to the city streets that lie just beyond the two rivers, and can be taken in quickly from all sides, viewed at once in its totality. A new system of lighting has been introduced into the park as well, consisting of powerful halogen lamps that were designed specifically for the park and that radically increase the artificial lighting of the park, further allowing it to be easily viewed from a distance. These lamps are now referred to, and available on the commercial market, as "Platzspitz lights." Although Platzspitz has for the most part been closed during the year since its renovation, movements have already begun to reintroduce the park, slowly and carefully, into Zurich's urban life.

Nightswimming,
New York
Cities

STEPHEN BARKER

REFERENCE
INTRO. PAGE 24

*The appearance of anyone in
these photographs should not
be taken as an indication of
his sexual orientation.*

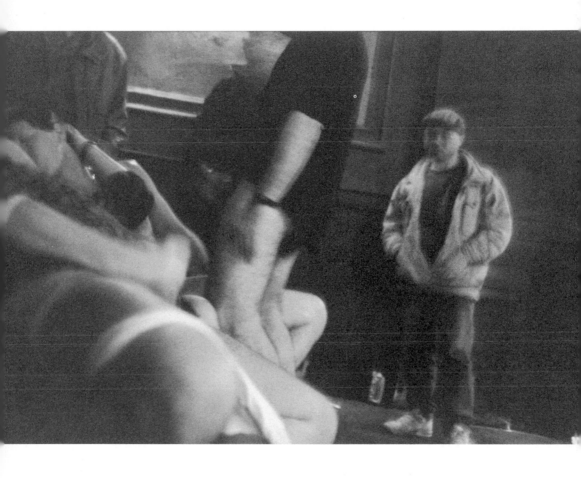

end

Fashion Plate

MARK ROBBINS
with text
by
BILL HORRIGAN

Every representation of a being entity is automatically an indiscretion. <small>HUGO VON HOFFMANSTAHL, *BOOK OF FRIENDS*</small>

THIRTY-SIX VIEWS OF THE GRID
<small>[REHEARSAL EXCERPT FROM A MUSICAL FOLLY]</small>

#1. This is being written ten feet away from a Peter Eisenman grid, hung parallel and perpendicular to my office window. Overture: I have stared at this grid for six years. Know nothing if not that.

#2. (Discuss retail clothes and marketing strategies; the poignancy and empowerment of purchase via mail order; a bachelor's lonely but perfectly groomed life on the Dakota prairie, thanks to catalogues; sidebar "human interest" profile of The Man Who Thought He Was David Belasco (he dressed in vestments).)

#3. Mark Robbins reports on a neighborhood bar in Columbus Ohio that appears to pride itself on providing a safe place for very young men to find out if they are, or to practice being, "gay." He says you can identify their pre-*débutant* status because they're draped exclusively in International Male™ (I.M.) couture—"harem" pants, "toreador" jackets, and so on, underneath which, presumably, a macramé posing strap or a "supportless" thong. The idea is that these kids, like some kids elsewhere, imagine the pre-pornographic universe of the I.M. catalogue to be a reliable barometer of what they will find once they become immersed in the heady, fabulous world of urban "gay culture."

#4. At this same bar, Mark Robbins reports, the young men in their cunning outfits repose and play tournament canasta with their wheezing elders, which will be another (#5) story. (See also #25a)

#5-10. (*Fashion Plate* by Mark Robbins: A Romance of/in the Grid. Black shoes are for big boys, or Italians, and also those pants are too tight for you. Daddy, look, that building has its zipper open. It's coming—in sections! Vitruvius Rules!)

#11. Catholic neither born nor bred, Mark Robbins is forever deprived of the experience of partaking of the sacrament of confession.

#12. The last time Jack went to confession (around the time of the waning of the Carter administration), he was home from Loyola, and from behind the blackened scrim window, the priest, a Franciscan, recognized his voice and addressed him by name; the priest was a friend of the family, and a high school boyfriend of his mother. From then on, confession, which had been Jack's favorite sacrament, became anathema; the hard-on thrills of anonymity and secrecy (a fiction in any case in a small parish such as his, but even so) had been deflated. He no longer anticipated the sound of his own voice saying: "I confess. " He needed to find out what people said when they partook of the sacrament of "reconciliation," which has erased confession as he knew it, as it was practiced in his boyhood. Confession is what had made him.

#13. "I am reconciled" lacks altogether the consoling tones of submission, the transcendent solace following from acknowledgment of frailty or wrong-doing or human imperfection, in light of divine solicitude and physical perfection. Jack is precisely not reconciled and so searches for a zone amenable to practices of subjection. He searches, that is, for a zone outside and apart from the world forged by Vatican II (roll, Jordan, roll); he wants to inhabit a "speaking position" there. For this, he reads Althusser (still), and Charles Péguy. Lord, make him an instrument of thy will.

#14. Mark Robbins imagines the *Fashion Plate* city to be zoned throughout for the convenience of confession. The plates aren't tectonic, or matching, and fashion is what is constantly passing. Proximity breeds transference. Space is automatically strange space. Focusing on your desire before all else, you take the size of space according to your desire. You see your desire; space obligingly conforms. Willing—is what space is. Space puts out, it goes all the way, and goes down. Does space repent? Never, never, never, never.

#15.   "One day he writes me: Description of a dream... More and more, my dreams find their setting in the department stores of Tokyo, the subterranean tunnels that extend from them and run parallel to the city. A face appears, disappears, a trace is found, is lost, all the folklore of dreams is so much in its place that the next day, when I'm awake, I realize that I continue to seek in the basement labyrinth the presence concealed the night before. I begin to wonder if those dreams are really mine, or if they are part of a totality, of a gigantic collective dream of which the entire city may be the projection." CHRIS MARKER, *Sunless*

#16a.   For Mark Robbins, the city is inevitably the example of Manhattan, as orally recounted and as worn and fitted, its muse the ramrodded figure of Gratteciella, she who forgets social niceties on occasion (the air is thin up among those setbacks) but remembers always, never forgets, "My Forgotten Man": at any moment, the forgotten man can be called upon the wicked stage, coaxed from the comfort of the heating grate or the cold-water walk-up to perform "a big number" on the *buena vista* of 42nd St.—on stage, on stage!! Then the unforgiving lights go down and everyone is left to mutter comic routines with Yiddish themes as the subway sends each forgotten man home (alone, too). It's a baggy pants kind of world.

#16b.   In Manhattan, Columbus, and New York, according to Mark Robbins (*Framing American Cities*, 1990-92), existence, far from being elsewhere, is right there, it's there, all right, but it's in sections; for his purposes, it's flesh-oriented and toned. Flesh welcomes—truly, it just lives for, so much so that from most distances it looks just like an actual, active, full-bodied surrender to—the assault of couture. As Daniel demonstrates in *The Roads to Freedom*, the flesh is always willing to reach out and admire the fine bias of any man's wares, then to hurry the day for the moment of confession.

#17-23.   (A Flashback to Manhattan's Menswear: Dan's tricking the hick into buying a sport jacket to wear to the Markham; Jack's turban; Scott's brown corduroy pants from Minnesota; Larry's *Solidarnosc* t-shirt in 1985; Dave's blue Future Farmers of America jacket worn as "formal" attire; Jason's Soviet-bloc suit, tractor-tailored.)

#24.   What unites, as our century declines, advanced trends in men's leisure-wear to our ongoing romance with the grid?

#25a.   Is it the fact that the piquant vocabulary of International Male's™ ready-to-wear collections has achieved global penetration among those aspiring to be active within whatever such "gay culture" they find their community hoping to emulate and establish? The Male Internationale emergent? Beyond the mountains and shores, beyond the flight of tyrants, of demons, the end of superstition? Could this be . . . ? But wait!

#25b.   "*Fashion: Madam Death, Madam Death!* *Death: Wait for your time, and I'll come without your calling me.* *Fashion: Madam Death.* *Death: Go to hell. I'll come when you don't want me . . . . Fashion: Come, in the name of your love for the seven deadly sins, stop a moment and look at me.* *Death: I'm looking.* *Fashion: Don't you recognize me? . . . I'm Fashion, your sister.* *Death: My sister? Fashion: Yes. Don't you remember that we are both Caducity's daughters?* **Death:** *What can I remember, I who am memory's greatest enemy?....* **Fashion:** *...I won't tell you about the headaches, the colds, the inflammations of all kinds, the quotidian, tertian, or quartan fevers that men catch to obey me, agreeing to shiver in the cold or to stifle in the heat according to my wishes, by protecting their shoulders with wool and their chests with cloth, and by doing everything my way, no matter how much it hurts them.* **Death:** *Then I believe that indeed you are my sister and, if you want me to, I'll hold it more certain than death itself....* LEOPARDI: *Dialogue Between Fashion and Death*

#26. December 1993: shirtless Slovakian boys dressed in backless spandex overalls, "voguing" to Morrissey in a supposed (*Spartacus*) "gay" disco in the mountains of Austria. Jack and his companion wondered if the boys were "gay." The night before they'd found another club where old men were playing cards with conspicuously outfitted young blond boys. Everyone was laughing.

#27-34. (Compare International Male™ and International Style (I.S.) in terms of stunning global domination in their respective (*but intimately related*) spheres. Penetrate psychosexual and/or biographical origins, vocabulary, underpinnings of I.S. The "flaunting" instincts of any "glass wall." I.S. as reaction-formation to Olmsteadian dialectic of profusion/seclusion (Mark Robbins telling story of Vaux eventually besmirching F.L.O. as "unmanly" with related conjecture as to what in God's name would ever constitute a sufficiently "manly" practice). According to a contemporary understanding, everything springs from Dan Graham's *Homes for America*, 1965-70.)

#35. Once the grid is sucked dry, spent, limp, you find it's a net. The city of nets is willing to be configured into a pouch, sling, or thong. Lord, make it an instrument of thy will.

#36a. *Oubliette* need not have been, although it was, the first French word Jack made a point, adolescently, of remembering; its presence in a Dumas comic book was conspicuous. Years later, a Dominican priest escorted Jack through a parish rectory, all doors open except the one leading to "the Monsignor's *oubliette*." He then fitted Jack in vestments, playfully at first, which rarely hung well.

#36b. In Mark Robbins' Manhattan, the palette of menswear rotates on liturgical schedules, in deference to the city's insistence on ritualized existence (cliff-dwelling, after all), democratic enough as such things go but tyrannical in its insistence on tight, svelte form before or apart from (bereft of, actually) function: who *needs* such muscles, as the citizens of Mark Robbins's Manhattan strive to display? This dream Manhattan (ditto Brooklyn) is unchanged from Whitman: its men labor.

They labor, side by side.

The poet, or the observer, seizes them in passing.

It's been a tolerable fantasy for the last hundred-plus years, this Manhattan, as have these men, agreeing to shiver in the cold or to stifle in the heat according to fashion's wishes, or to the wishes of their observers.

Voltaire: "What century are we living in?"

#36c. *Sleep tight, baby, milkman's on his way. Good night, baby, let's call it a day.*

[EXIT ALL.]

All that glitters is worth a second glance. The potent Gold Banded Thong glistens in nylon/Lurex®. Contoured front, thong back and elastic waist. [1]

Undress to thrill in the Tear-Away Bikini. A quick pull is all it takes. Lined in the front. Nylon and Lycra®. [2]

New colors, new waistband. There ain't anything quite so good that the guys who did it in the first place can't do it better yet. [3]

Styled for bodybuilding and men of action. [4]

Men who work out are more likely to have multiple, satisfying, even more intense orgasms. [5]

3 in 1: Posing, Training, Swimming Briefs. Excellent for all 3 purposes! Specially Low-Cut and Smartly Designed for Body-Builders. These 3 in 1 Briefs Cling to You and Give You a Complete freedom of motion. Made of Sparkling Lastex with knit pouch support. [6]

Torment is the third possible objective of genital bondage, caused by stretching and/or pulling genital components. [7]

Features handsome embroidered sporting designs of a mallard in flight, fly, leaping deer. Inside cuff grommets can be turned into gaiters with spare bootlaces or twine. Snap elasticized cuffs. Drop seat. [8]

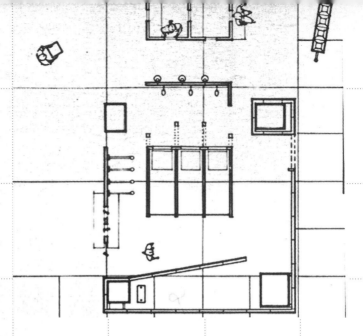

Siesta Pull-On Pant, Baggy Fit   "Classic Fit"   "Natural Fit"   "Relaxed Fit"

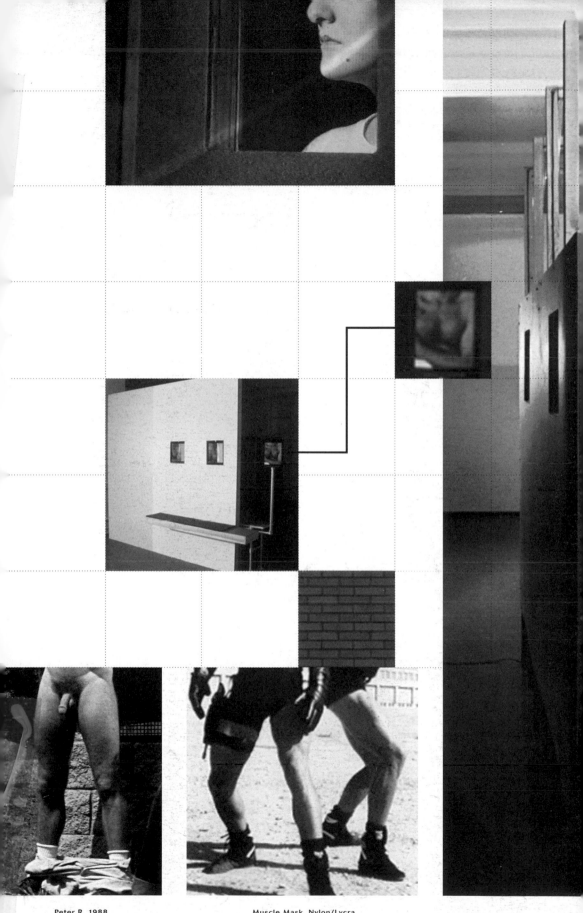

Peter R. 1988   Muscle Mask. Nylon/Lycra

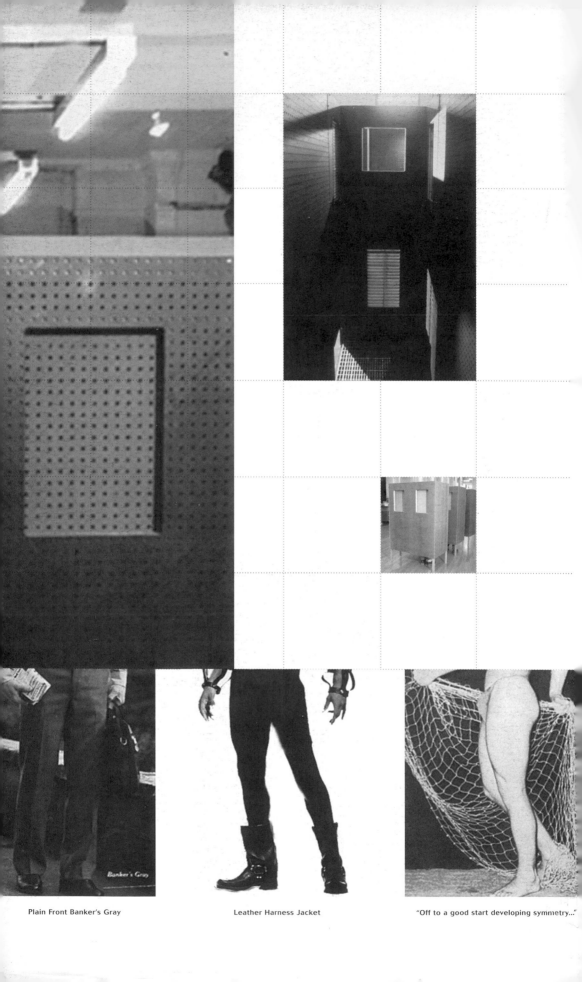

Plain Front Banker's Gray   Leather Harness Jacket   "Off to a good start developing symmetry..."

Leopard Safari Cut

BodyMaster 1

BodyMaster 2

Desert Issue Camouflage

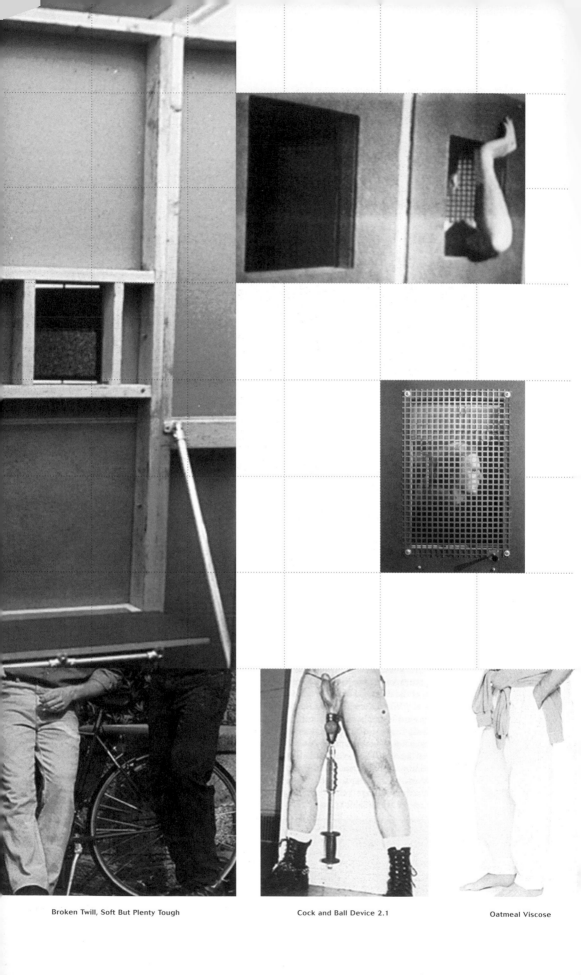

Broken Twill, Soft But Plenty Tough   Cock and Ball Device 2.1   Oatmeal Viscose

"With that big bat..."

Chino Shorts in all 9 Chino colors.

Indigo Cotton Denim Stretch Jean

at, sagging buns with *Super Shaper Briefs.*

xclusively Designed Men's added Briefs...Give You

EYE-CATCHING BUTTOCKS INSTANTLY!

T A GIRDLE!   100% UNDETECTABLE!

HE ONLY MEN'S UNDERGARMENT HAT CAN MAKE THESE CLAIMS!
- Fills out your rear end without fattening diets.
- Lifts, firms, and shapes your buttocks without exercises.
- Flattens your stomach without diet pills.

Fashion First!

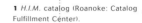

1 *H.I.M.* catalog (Roanoke: Catalog Fulfillment Center).

2 *International Male* catalog, ed. Donn B. Wilson (San Diego: IM Brawn of California, Inc., Fall 1993).

3 *J. Crew* catalog (Lynchburg: J. Crew International, Inc., Summer 1994).

4 *Shocking Gray* catalog (San Antonio: Shocking Gray Corp., Fall/Holiday 1993).

5 *Men's Workout*, ed. Michael Catarevas, volume 4, no. 5 (New York: Harris Publications, Inc., Sept. 1993).

6 *Tomorrow's Man*, ed. Paul Lange, vol IV no.1 (New York: Tomorrow's Man Publishing Co. Inc., December 1956).

7 *DungeonMaster*, ed. Anthony F. DeBlase, no.44 (San Francisco: Desmodus, Inc).

8 *L.L. Bean* catalog (Freeport: L.L. Bean, 1995).

"Spruce is a Standard, Comfort a Fetish"   Upright Rowing Exercise 1   Internet Download, 2400 baud

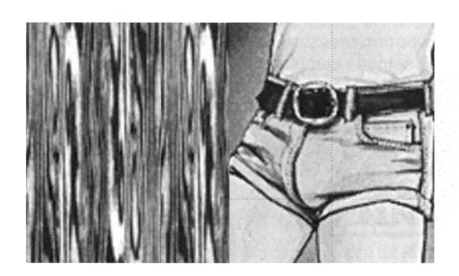

Untitled

*FELIX
GONZALEZ-TORRES*

REFERENCE
INTRO. PAGE 25

Untitled

[1991]
View of Billboard
30 DeKalb Avenue
at Flatbush Avenue,
Brooklyn

Untitled [1991]
View of Billboard
Second Avenue and
East 2nd Street

Untitled [1991]
View of Billboard
275 West
Street/Desbrosses Street

Untitled
[1991]
View of Billboard
31-11 21st Street
Long Island City

Untitled
[1991]
View of Billboard
144th Street/Grand
Concourse

CONTRIBUTORS

Vito Acconci
is an artist whose work has
been shown in solo exhibitions at the Museum of
Modern Art in New York, the
San Diego Museum of
Contemporary Art, La Jolla,
the Centre d'Art Contemporain
in Grenoble, and the Museum
of Applied Art in Vienna.
Recently, Acconci has focused
his attention on designs for
public spaces, including a
plaza at Queens College in
New York, a courtyard for an
elementary school in the
Bronx, a public garden at
MetroTech Center, Brooklyn,
and street furniture for
Tachikawa City, Japan.

Matthew Bannister
is an architect whose practice
is based in Princeton, New
Jersey.

Steve Barker
is a New York City artist whose
work has been exhibited in
Cologne, Berlin, Paris, and at
Regen Projects in Los Angeles.

Matthew Barney,
an artist who lives and works
in New York City, has exhibit-
ed his work at the Museum
Boymans-van Beuningen,
Rotterdam, The Tate Gallery,
London, Fondation Cartier,
Paris, San Francisco Museum
of Modern Art, Barbara
Gladstone Gallery, New York,
and Regen Projects, Los
Angeles.

Bureau,
founded in 1989 and located
in New York City, is a collaboration between artists Marlene
McCarty and Donald Moffett,
designers Claudia Brandenburg
and Mats Håkansson, and
studio staff Mary Day and
Lecia Dole. Transgressing
established boundaries
between artist, designer and
author, Bureau creates bodies
of work which both spring
from and intervene in the
social text of everyday life.

Tom Burr
is an artist who lives in New
York.

George Chauncey
is Associate Professor of
American history at the
University of Chicago. He is
the author of *Gay New York:
Gender, Urban Culture, and
the Making of the Gay Male
World, 1890-1940* (New York:
Basic Books, 1994) and coed-
itor of *Hidden from History:
Reclaiming the Gay and
Lesbian Past* (New York: New
American Library, 1989).

Steven Cohan,
Professor of English at
Syracuse University, is coau-
thor of *Telling Stories: A
Theoretical Analysis of
Narrative Fiction* (New York:
Routledge, 1988) and coedi-
tor of *Screening the Male:
Exploring Masculinities in
Hollywood Cinema* (New York:
Routledge, 1993). His writings
on film have appeared in
Camera Obscura, Screen and
The Masculine Masquerade
(Cambridge: MIT Press, 1995).

Lee Edelman
is Professor of English at Tufts
University. His books include
*Transmemberment of Song:
Hart Crane's Anatomies of
Rhetoric and Desire* (Stanford:
Stanford University Press, 1987)
and *Homographesis: Essays
in Gay Literary and Cultural
Theory* (New York and
London: Routledge, 1994).
He is currently working on
*The Invisible Spectacle:
Cinema, Psychoanalysis, and
Gay Male Sexuality*.

Diana Fuss
is Associate Professor of
English at Princeton
University. She is the author of
Essentially Speaking (New
York and London: Routledge,
1989) and *Identification
Papers* (New York and
London: Routledge, 1995).
She is also the editor of two
volumes: *Inside/Out* (New
York and London: Routledge,
1991) and *Human All Too
Human* (New York and
London: Routledge, 1995).

Robert Gober
is a sculptor based in New York
City. His work, widely exhibited
both in Europe and the United
States, has been shown at the
Paula Cooper Gallery, New
York, the Dia Center for the
Arts, New York, the Whitney
Museum, New York, the Venice
Biennale, and the Hirshorn
Museum and Sculpture Garden,
Washington, D.C. His recent
shows include the Carnegie
International Exhibition and a
one-person exhibit at the
Museum für Gegenswartskunst
in Basel, Switzerland.

Felix Gonzalez-Torres
[1957-1996]
was a New York City artist
whose work has been exhibited in a one-person survey at
the Solomon R. Guggenheim
Museum, New York as well as
at the Museum of Modern Art
in New York, The Museum of
Contemporary Art in Los
Angeles, the Hirshhorn
Museum and Sculpture
Garden in Washington, D.C.,
and The Renaissance Society
in Chicago.

Renée Greene
is an artist and writer who
lives in New York and Berlin.
Exhibited both in the USA
and Europe, she has shown
her work at the Pat Hearn
Gallery, New York, DAAD
Gallery, Berlin, Galerie
Metropol, Vienna, Worcester
Art Museum, MA, and the
Whitney Museum of American
of Art, New York. Her recent
books are *Camino Road*
(Madrid: Museo Reina
Sofia/Brooklyn: FAM, 1994) and
After the Ten Thousand Things
(The Hague: Stroom/Amsterdam:
Idea Books, 1994).

Bill Horrigan
is Media Curator for the
Wexner Center for the Arts at
the Ohio State University in
Columbus. His recent projects
include *Chris Marker: Silent
Movie* and *Bruce and Norman
Yonemoto: Three Installations*
for the Wexner Center, as well

as the American Center/Paris's inaugural film/video series, *This Body, This Soul, This Brick, These Tears: Disorder Today.*

Marcia Ian, an Associate Professor of Modern British and American Literature at Rutgers University, writes on body-building, psychoanalytic theory, heavy metal music, and Henry James. She is author of *Remembering the Phallic Mother: Psychoanalysis, Modernism, and the Fetish* (Ithaca: Cornell University Press, 1993).

Interim Office of Architecture (IOOA), a San Francisco-based collaboration between John Randolph and Bruce Tomb, produces a broad variety of interdisciplinary projects including designs for furnishings, interiors, sets, exhibitions, site-specific installations, and buildings.

Sheila Kennedy and Frano Violich dedicate their practice to exploring new possibilities for public architecture. Kennedy teaches at Harvard University Graduate School of Design, where she is an Associate Professor. Violich teaches as a Visiting Design Critic at schools of architecture in the United States and Mexico.

Rem Koolhaas is the founder of the Office for Metropolitan Architecture (O.M.A.) in Rotterdam. His international projects include Nexus Housing in Japan, the Netherlands Dance Theater in the Hague, the Kunsthal in Rotterdam, and the Congrexpo Building in Lille. He is also the author of *Delirious New York* (New York: Oxford University Press, 1978) and *S, M, L, XL* (New York: Monacelli, 1995). Solo exhibitions of his work have been mounted at the Museum of Modern Art, New York and the Wexner Center for the Arts, Columbus.

John Lindell is a visual artist based in New York whose wall drawings, sculptures, photographs, and video tapes have been exhibited at the Grey Art Gallery at NYU, Galerie Analix in Geneva, the Musée d'Art Modern de la Ville de Paris, the Centre George Pompidou and the Rotterdam International Film Festival.

Ellen Lupton is Curator of Contemporary Design at the Cooper-Hewitt National Design Museum and a founding partner in the studio Design/Writing/Research in New York. She has produced the exhibition/book projects *Mechanical Brides: Women and Machines from Home to Office* at the National Design Museum and *The Bathroom, the Kitchen, and the Aesthetics of Waste: A Process of Elimination* with J. Abbott Miller at MIT List Visual Arts Center.

D.A. Miller teaches English and Comparative Literature at Columbia University. His publications include *The Novel and the Police* (Berkeley: University of California Press, 1988) and *Bringing Out Roland Barthes* (Berkeley: University of California Press, 1992). His contribution to this volume is from his forthcoming book *Place for Us: Essay on the Broadway Musical* (Cambridge: Harvard University Press).

Michael Perelman is an artist who lives in New York.

Mark Robbins is Curator of Architecture at the Wexner Center for the Arts and Assistant Professor in the Knowlton School of Architecture at the Ohio State University. His installations have been published in a monograph, *Angles of Incidence* (New York: Princeton Architectural Press, 1992) and have been exhibited at The Museum of Modern

Art in Saitama, Japan, the Clocktower Gallery of the ICA in New York, and the Wexner Center for the Arts, in Columbus, Ohio.

Joel Sanders
is an architect practicing in New York and an Assistant Professor of Architecture at Princeton University. His design for *Artist's Live/Work Lofts*, Peekskill, NY and the *Kyle Residence*, Houston, received Progressive Architecture Design Citations in 1993 and 1994. His work has been exhibited at the Wexner Center for the Arts, Columbus, Artists Space, New York, and the Museum of Modern Art, New York.

Skidmore, Owings & Merrill (SOM)
has completed more than 6,000 architecture, interior architecture and planning projects around the world since its founding in 1936. Their reknowned designs include the Sears Tower and the John Hancock Tower in Chicago, the Lever House in New York, and the Bank of America World Headquarters in San Francisco.

Philippe Starck
is a designer of utilitarian objects, furniture, interiors and buildings who practices in France.

George Stoll
is an artist based in Los Angeles. His work has been displayed in solo exhibitions at the Paul Morris Gallery in New York, the Tri Gallery and the A/B Gallery in Los Angeles.

Thanhauser and Esterson Architects,
a partnership between Charles Thanhauser and Jack Esterson, is a Manhattan-based firm whose work has included building renovations for social service organizations and AIDS housing. They are currently designing a large renovation for Community Health Project, a health clinic in New York primarily serving the gay and lesbian community. Their project for the Definitions Fitness Center was included in "Light Contstruction" at the Museum of Modern Art (1995).

Andrea Zittel
is an artist based in New York. She has had one-person shows at the San Francisco Museum of Modern Art and the Carnegie Museum of Art. She has also exhibited at the Museum of Modern Art in New York, the Art Institute of Chicago, the Rooseum Center for Contemporary Art in Sweden, and Grazer Kunstverein in Austria.

end

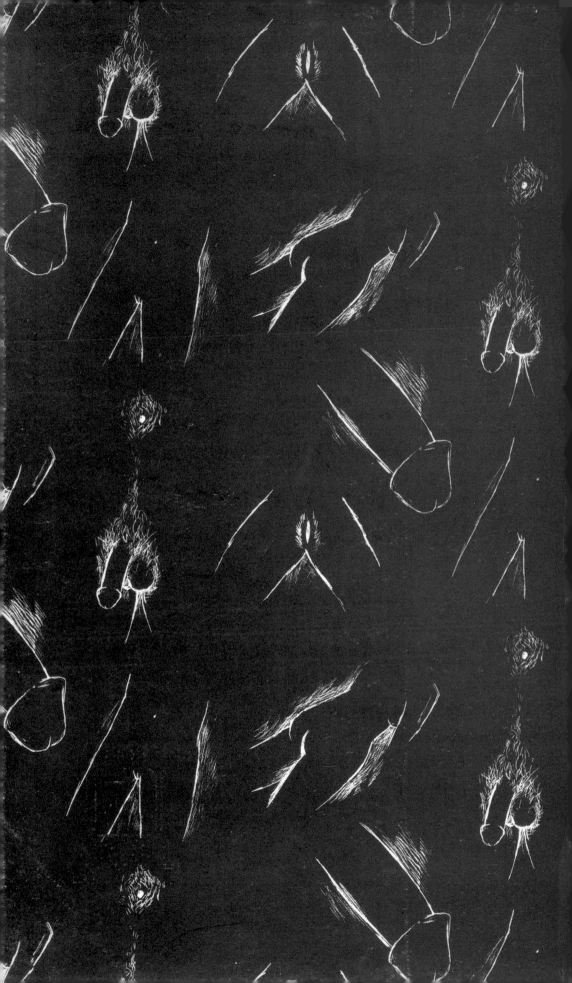